S0-AHD-515

THE WARMTH DIMENSION

Published in
cooperation with
National Council on
Family Relations

Series Editor: **Maximiliane Szinovacz**
Florida State University

Books appearing in New Perspectives on Family are either single- or multiple-authored volumes or concisely edited books of original articles on focused topics within the broad field of marriage and family. Books can be reports of significant research, innovations in methodology, treatises on family theory, or syntheses of current knowledge in a subfield of the discipline. Each volume meets the highest academic standards and makes a substantial contribution to our knowledge of marriage and family.

SINGLES: Myths and Realities, *Leonard Cargan and Matthew Melko*

THE CHILDBEARING DECISION: Fertility Attitudes and Behavior, *Greer Litton Fox, ed.*

AT HOME AND AT WORK: The Family's Allocation of Labor, *Michael Geerken and Walter R. Gove*

PREVENTION IN FAMILY SERVICES: Approaches to Family Wellness, *David R. Mace, ed.*

WORKING WIVES/WORKING HUSBANDS, *Joseph H. Pleck*

THE WARMTH DIMENSION: Foundations of Parental Acceptance-Rejection Theory, *Ronald P. Rohner*

Other volumes currently available from Sage and sponsored by NCFR:

ROLE STRUCTURE AND ANALYSIS OF THE FAMILY, *F. Ivan Nye*

CONFLICT AND POWER IN MARRIAGE: Expecting the First Child, *Ralph LaRossa*

THE AMERICAN FAMILY: A Demographic History, *Rudy Ray Seward*

THE SOCIAL WORLD OF OLD WOMEN: Management of Self-Identity, *Sarah H. Matthews*

ASSESSING MARRIAGE: New Behavioral Approaches, *Erik E. Filsinger and Robert A. Lewis, eds.*

SEX AND PREGNANCY IN ADOLESCENCE, *Melvin Zelnik, John F. Kantner, and Kathleen Ford*

THE WARMTH DIMENSION

Foundations of Parental Acceptance-Rejection Theory

Ronald P. Rohner

Published in cooperation with
the National Council on Family Relations

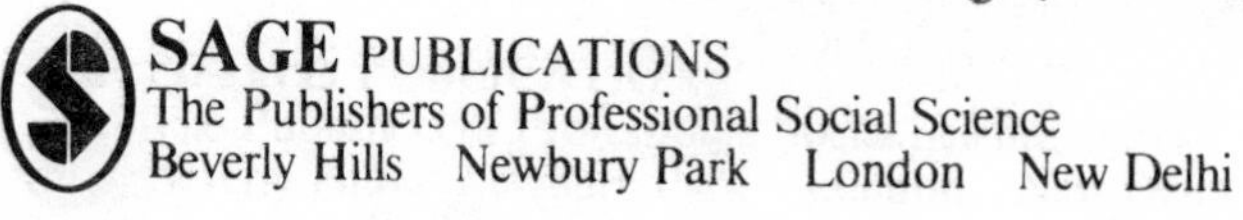

SAGE PUBLICATIONS
The Publishers of Professional Social Science
Beverly Hills Newbury Park London New Delhi

For information address:

SAGE Publications, Inc.
275 South Beverly Drive
Beverly Hills, California 90212

SAGE Publications Inc.
2111 West Hillcrest Drive
Newbury Park
California 91320

SAGE Publications Ltd.
28 Banner Street
London EC1Y 8QE
England

SAGE PUBLICATIONS India Pvt. Ltd.
M-32 Market
Greater Kailash I
New Delhi 110 048 India

Printed in the United States of America

Library of Congress Cataloging-in-Publication Data

Rohner, Ronald P.
The warmth dimension

(New perspectives on family)
Bibliography: p.
1. Parental rejection—Cross-cultural studies.
2. Parental acceptance—Cross-cultural studies.
3. Socialization—Cross-cultural studies. 4. Mental health—Cross-cultural studies. I. Title. II. Series.
BF723.P26R64 1986 155.9'24 85-19623
ISBN 0-8039-2353-8

FIRST PRINTING

Contents

To **Preston** and **Ashley**, my children—
whose lives have been touched
by parental acceptance-rejection theory,
and
who have helped me so much
to understand these matters

Series Editor's Foreword

Children have been neglected, rejected, and abused in the past and in many societies, yet it has been only during the last three decades that concerns about child maltreatment have come to the forefront of public attention and scientific inquiry. Research since the 1960s has provided answers to many questions on this issue, but—as is typical for relatively "new" avenues of inquiry—it left us with many unanswered questions as well. Most notable among the gaps and restrictions in the present literature on child maltreatment are its focus on selected forms of maltreatment such as physical or sexual abuse, its heavy reliance on data from the United States or at least from Western industrialized societies, and its emphasis on the conditions (more than the consequences) of abuse. The last item, of course, has long been addressed in research on socialization and parental discipline, but findings from this literature were only partially integrated into theories of child maltreatment and abuse.

Rohner's anthropological work, I believe, provides a contribution to the literature on child maltreatment because it overcomes some of these restrictions: It deals with the broad phenomenon of parental rejection of children, it uses data from various societies, and it addresses the consequences of rejection on children.

It was perhaps this last emphasis of the book that most attracted my attention. The cycle of violence—the enhanced use of violence by those exposed to it as children—is well documented in the family violence literature. But beyond general references to role modeling and similar abstract concepts, few concrete explanations of this phenomenon have been offered. The focal part of parental acceptance-rejection theory (PART), its personality theory, may very well lead toward more concrete explanations of the cycle of violence—or, more generally, toward more concrete explanations of the cycle of parental rejection. If it is true, as Rohner posits and research on parental discipline suggests, that rejected children develop personality characteristics furthering aggressive behaviors, then his theory may indeed help us better understand the dynamics of the cycles of violence and rejection. And coping theory, another component of PART, provides some insights into those conditions enabling individuals to break the cycle.

PART is grounded in years of empirical research; nonetheless, it is a new theory and one open to methodological and theoretical criticism. But if Rohner's book leads us only to ask new questions and to pursue new avenues of inquiry, it will have fulfilled its purpose and proved itself deserving of publication in this NCFR-Sage series.

—*Maximiliane Szinovacz*

Acknowledgments

Many people helped me during the years that parental acceptance-rejection theory was being developed and tested in the United States and cross-culturally. I cannot thank them all by name here, but I must extend my sincerest gratitude to the following scholars internationally for providing research results used in this book on parental acceptance-rejection, and children's and adults' personality dispositions.

Manjusri Chaki-Sircar collected data in West Bengal, India; Sandra Pettingill Park collected data in Korea; Byungchai C. Hahn collected data among Korean-Americans; Abdul Haque collected data in Nigeria among the Ibo, Hausa, and Yoruba; M. G. Tsell provided data on Tiv children of Nigeria; Zdenek Matějček provided data from two locations in Czechoslovakia; Robert C. Ness and Nancy Ness collected data in Newfoundland; Jai Prakash, M. K. Shrivastava, and Rekha Shrivastava provided data from Madhya Pradash, India; N. Y. Reddy provided data from Andra Pradesh, India; Michio Kitahara provided data from Sweden; Evelyn C. Rohner and others, working with me through the Center for the Study of Parental Acceptance and Rejection at the University of Connecticut, collected data among American schoolchildren, adolescents, and families; working through the Boys Town Center for the Study of Youth Development at the Catholic University of America, Emeline Otey, Sandra L. Starkey, José M. Saavedra, and I also collected data on American children and adults; Samuel Roll collected child and family data in Monterrey, Mexico; Ramzi Salamé provided data on French Canadians in Quebec; and José M. Saavadra collected data in Puerto Rico on adolescents there. To all these people and the many others who continue to help this program of research reach its objectives, I give my warmest personal thanks.

Maximiliane Szinovacz, Editor of the Sage Publications series New Perspectives on Families, helped strengthen the book immeasurably through her meticulous and thoughtful, line-by-line editing. Thank you, Maxi. And thank you too, Nancy, Ashley, and Preston—my family. My daughter, Ashley, and my son, Preston, scripted the manuscript on the computer, and my wife, Nancy, proofread their work and helped edit mine. It was fun to be able to turn the final production of this manuscript into a family affair. Finally, I want to thank the University of Connecticut Research Foundation, especially Nancy Organ, for typing a preliminary draft of this book.

Ronald P. Rohner

Introduction

Researchers in the United States and internationally have worked for more than 50 years on the antecedents, consequences, and correlates of parental acceptance and rejection—including over 25 years of my own research and writing in the field. This book represents a distillation and structuring of that work around a coherent theoretical framework known as parental acceptance-rejection theory, PAR theory, or simply PART. Unlike other books of its kind, which tend to draw from clinical and other disturbed populations, this work draws primarily from naturally occurring ranges of variation among presumably "normal," "healthy" families and children in the United States and cross-culturally.

The book is guided by a conceptual and methodological orientation aimed at establishing cross-culturally valid generalizations or "principles" about the worldwide antecedents, consequences, and correlates of parental acceptance and rejection—principles that can be shown empirically to hold true across social classes, racial groups, and ethnic groups in both the United States and internationally, as well as across time as nations change. This interest in creating empirically demonstrable cross-cultural generalizations about human behavior is the defining attribute of a slowly growing concern in the behavioral sciences, one I have elsewhere summarized under the label "anthroponomy" (Rohner, 1980, 1984).

In parental acceptance-rejection theory this search for cross-culturally valid principles is based on the assumption that with an understanding of the worldwide antecedents and consequences of acceptance-rejection—and of the mechanisms associated with the ability of some children to cope more effectively than others with perceived rejection—comes the possibility of formulating and implementing practicable policies affecting families and children throughout various social, ethnic, and other strata of society. It seems likely to me that social policies and programs of prevention, intervention, and treatment based on idiosyncratic beliefs at a particular point in time will eventually prove unworkable for some, and probably even exploitative for many minority populations. Policies and programs based on known "principles" of human behavior, however, stand a better chance of working as nations and people change.

The importance of this viewpoint is highlighted by Zigler (1978: 4), who charged that national policies in America regarding families and children are "determined by waves of fashion substantially unrelated to empirical research—even when the results carry the risk of significant damage to whole generations and subclasses of the population, and even when the surface rhetoric accompanying new programs implies that the policies being instituted represent the 'last word' in scientifically—and statistically—based knowledge." This viewpoint is echoed by Lumsden and Wilson (1983: 183), who assert that "society, through its laws and institutions,... regulates behavior. But it does so in virtual blind ignorance of the deep reaches of human nature."

Motivation for writing this book grew out of my own personally felt need to be able to refer researchers, students, educators, and health-care professionals to a single source describing PAR theory, its epistemological and methodological foundations, and its basis in empirical evidence. In an effort to appeal to the widest possible audience, I wrote the book in a more open-ended way than many technical research monographs. Although I remain faithful to research-based data, I also speculate frankly at times when I think responsible speculation and theorizing are warranted.

PARENTAL ACCEPTANCE-REJECTION THEORY

Parental acceptance-rejection theory, or PAR theory, as I shall refer to it throughout much of this book, is a theory of socialization that attempts to explain and predict major antecedents, correlates, and consequences of parental acceptance and rejection the world over.[1] At this time the theory focuses on four classes of issues. One class concerns the consequences of parental acceptance and rejection for behavioral, cognitive, and emotional development of children everywhere, as well as for the personality functioning of adults. Two principal questions are asked here: (1) Do children everywhere throughout our species—regardless of differences in culture, language, race, or other limiting conditions—respond in the same way to the perception of parental rejection? (2) To what extent do the effects of rejection in childhood extend into adulthood, and what personality dispositions are likely to be modified in the course of developing maturity? I find it convenient to call this portion of PAR theory "PART's personality theory."[2]

A second class of issue in PAR theory deals with the following question: Why are some children better able than others to cope with the effects of parental rejection and emotional abuse? That is, what gives some children the resilience to cope with the corrosive drizzle of day-to-day rejection without developing personality, social-cognitive, and emotional impairments to the same degree that most rejected children do? For ease of presentation, I call this portion of PAR theory "coping theory."

In addition to these issues about the consequences of parental acceptance-rejection, PAR theory attempts to predict major psychological, environmental, and maintenance systems antecedents of parental acceptance-rejection. That is, why are some parents warmer than others? Is it true, for instance, that parents are likely to accept or reject their children wherever specific social, economic, demographic, or other structural conditions arise? For example, are single-parent households universally at greater risk for various forms of rejection or emotional abuse than nuclear or extended families?

Finally, PAR theory is concerned with a class of issues about the sociocultural and expressive correlates of parental acceptance-rejection. For example, are the religious beliefs or other expressive behaviors of people related reliably and significantly to their childhood experiences of warmth or rejection? Why do some people choose one kind of occupation, profession, or task activity and other people choose a different one? Are such decisions related to these antecedent conditions of acceptance or rejection? I call these aspects of PAR theory (which are elucidated in the "sociocultural systems model" featured later in Figure 5) "sociocultural systems theory." I should note that some of these issues within PAR theory are not yet "theory" in the proper sense of "explanation." Nonetheless, I include under the rubric of PAR theory all matters discussed in this book pertaining to the antecedents, consequences, and correlates of parental acceptance and rejection.

At this time PAR theory focuses primarily on the warmth dimension of parenting. As author of the theory, I recognize, of course, that other dimensions of parental behavior—especially the control dimension (that is, parental permissiveness-strictness)—interact importantly with acceptance-rejection (that is, the warmth dimension) (see, for example, Rohner and Pettengill, 1985; Pettengill and Rohner, 1985; Saavedra, 1977, 1980). The significance of these interactions has not yet been developed sufficiently to be included in PAR theory or to report in this book, however. Thus it should be understood that PAR theory is still in a formative state even though it has reached a level of maturity sufficient to warrant book-length treatment.

It should also be understood that although some of the many hundreds of tests of relationship run in this program of research were guided by theoretical formulations, and tested several times in different sociocultural contexts—sometimes by the multimethod research strategy described in Chapter 2—other conclusions reported here derive from purely exploratory, often nontheoretically informed, monomethod tests. This latter category of conclusion must yet be replicated cross-culturally, following the dictates of the universalist approach described later. Accordingly, some research results described in this book are not as conclusive as may seem to be implied.

ORGANIZATION OF THE BOOK

The book amplifies on the four classes of conceptual issues discussed in the preceding section. It also describes the major methodologies and procedures used to assess the theory, and reports on recent cross-cultural and intracultural results of research bearing on the theory.

More specifically, Chapter 1 lays out PAR theory's epistemological assumptions and postulates, as well as its central concepts, including the concept of "anthroponomy," the "phylogenetic perspective," the "phylogenetic model," and the "universalist approach." Chapter 2 addresses the methodological question of *how* one might go about doing worldwide generalizing, anthroponomical research on parental acceptance-rejection. Chapter 3 enlarges the perspective of the first two chapters by placing PAR theory within the context of not only individual personality but also total sociocultural systems. Using the "sociocultural systems model" as a framework, empirical evidence is brought to bear in this chapter on some of the postulates and assumptions of PAR theory as they relate to environmental and maintenance systems antecedents of parental acceptance-rejection.

The remainder of the book follows the sequence of elements detailed in the sociocultural systems model. Chapter 4 deals with those elements in the model pertaining to the relationship between parental behavior (as defined by acceptance-rejection) and the personality development of children and adults. More specifically, the chapter highlights those personality dispositions that are an expected outcome of perceived rejection, as postulated in PART's personality theory. Much of Chapter 5 provides converging intracultural and cross-cultural evidence (drawn from a variety of methodologies, or *paradigms,* of research as well as *discrete* measurement procedures) bearing on the postulates of personality theory. Chapter 6 continues exploring the relationship between parental behavior and the personality development of children and adults by looking theoretically (and at times speculatively) at parental acceptance-rejection in life-span perspective. Two major questions are asked in this chapter: What effect does parental rejection seem to have when it is experienced for the first time at different stages in life? And, is there a period in human development when humans are especially vulnerable or susceptible to the effects of rejection?

Before moving to the final set of issues drawn in the sociocultural systems model, Chapter 7 pauses theoretically and empirically on a significant problem area relating to the fact that some children seem to cope more effectively than others with parental rejection. An emerging perspective called "coping theory" is developed in this chapter. In Chapter 8, I return squarely to the sociocultural systems model. It reviews cross-cultural and intracultural evidence bearing on institutionalized as well as personally "expressive" outcomes and correlates of parental acceptance and rejection, including individuals' religious beliefs, artistic preferences, and occupational choices. The final chapter, Chapter 9, summarizes PART's conceptual foundations, along with some of the most important conclusions drawn in formulating and testing the theory. In this concluding chapter I also discuss some of the remaining unanswered questions, and I point out major limitations in data and methods used.

In a book such as this it would seem odd if I did not mention the relationship between parental acceptance-rejection and the internationally recognized social problem, child abuse and neglect. Because child abuse and neglect is related problematically to acceptance-rejection (that is, some abused and neglected children do not perceive themselves to be rejected, and many rejected children are not legally reported as abused or neglected), I have elected to place discussion of this issue in Appendix A. Appendix B contains the child versions of the Parental Acceptance-Rejection Questionnaire and its complement, the Personality Assessment Questionnaire. Appendix B also contains the Background Data Schedule used for collecting social and demographic data on sample parents and children. All three of these instruments are used widely in national and international research on parental acceptance-rejection, and collectively they provide the bases for conclusions reported in parts of Chapter 5 and elsewhere in this book.

NOTES

1. I use the term "parent" throughout this book, but the term should be understood to mean the major caretaker(s) of the child, not necessarily the mother or father. In most of the world, mothers have the major responsibility for the care of young children, but, as shown by Rohner and Rohner (1982), grandparents, siblings, fathers, and others also exert substantial socializing influence.

2. In former writings (for example, Rohner, 1980, 1984) I referred to this portion of PART as "mainline PAR theory." Readers familiar with these earlier publications should understand that the meaning of the more descriptively precise phrase "personality theory" is identical to the earlier phrase, "mainline PAR theory."

1

Conceptual Foundations of Parental Acceptance-Rejection Theory

> Never knowing the consequences of a gesture, facial expression, or request. Sometimes a gift of flowers is received affectionately and sometimes it's dashed down with a shove and a tirade of abuse. Sometimes a request for a piece of gum is a "good idea" and sometimes it's "proof of your horrid greediness and irresponsible lack of concern for the cost of dental care." Sometimes looking sad is met with friendly concern, and sometimes you're berated and punished for being ungrateful. But you just never know [Cameronchild, 1978: 139].

PARENTAL ACCEPTANCE-REJECTION: THE WARMTH DIMENSION OF PARENTING

Individuals everywhere experience more or less warmth and affection at the hands of the people most important to them as they grow up (Rohner and Rohner, 1981). I call these people "parents," although they are not necessarily mother and father. The warmth and affection (or its withdrawal) each of us has experienced as a child can be placed on a continuum from a great deal to virtually none. I call this continuum the "warmth dimension" of parenting. One end of the warmth dimension is marked by parental acceptance and the other end is marked by rejection. As shown in Figure 1, parental acceptance, which refers to the warmth, affection, and love parents can give their children, has two principal expressions: physical and verbal. Physical

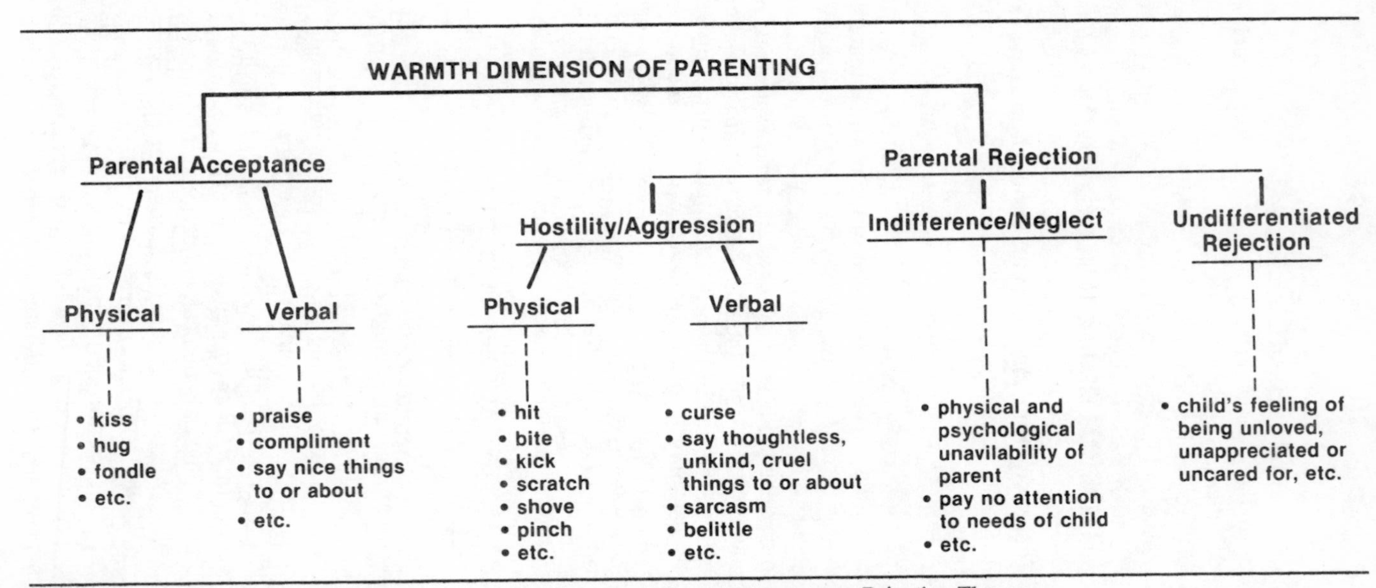

Figure 1 Conceptual Framework of Principal Parenting Concepts in Parental Acceptance-Rejection Theory

expressions of warmth and affection include hugging, fondling, caressing, approving glances, kissing, smiling, and other such indications of endearment, approval, or support. Expressions of verbal warmth and affection include praising, complimenting, saying nice things to or about a child, perhaps singing songs or telling stories to a young child, and the like. Children in most accepting families experience combinations of all these behaviors. Even the warmest of parents, however, is apt to get angry and impatient, or display other elements of rejection from time to time, although in some families children never know the satisfaction of parental affection or approval in any form.

Parental rejection—which is defined conceptually as the absence or significant withdrawal of warmth, affection, or love by parents toward children—lies at the opposite end of the warmth dimension. It takes three major forms (Rohner, 1975): (1) hostility and aggression, (2) indifference and neglect, and (3) what I call "undifferentiated rejection." Hostility and indifference are internal psychological feelings within the individual. Hostility includes feelings of anger, resentment, enmity, and ill will or malice toward the child. Indifference, on the other hand, is simply a lack of concern for the child, or not really caring about him or her. Aggression and neglect are, for the most part, behavioral manifestations of these internal states. "Aggression" refers to behaviors that have as their intention the physical or psychological hurt of another person, of oneself, or (symbolically) of an object. Aggression is differentiated behaviorally into physical and verbal forms. Physical aggression includes hitting, biting, pushing, shaking, pinching, scratching, scalding, burning, tying up, and the like. Verbal aggression, on the other hand, includes sarcasm, belittling, cursing, scapegoating, denigrating, and saying other thoughtless, unkind, cruel things to or about the child.

Whereas hostility may be the sole motive for aggression, indifference is only one possible motive for neglect. That is, parents may neglect a child for a variety of reasons, only one of which has to do with indifference. In PAR theory, neglect is expressed when parents fail to attend to the physical, medical, educational, and other needs of the child as well as when they ignore the needs, concerns, wishes, and interests of the child—either as expressed by the child or as known by the parent. One of the best single indicators of neglect is the physical and psychological nonavailability of the parent. Physical nonavailability is easy to understand: Mother and/or father are simply not there physically. The child is alone with no one to care for him or her. Psychological unavailability is more subtle. Mother or father may be physically present, but the parents do not give the child psychological access to them. The parents do not respond to the child or interact with him or her. They are inattentive to the child's requests for help when the child is in need. A commonplace scenario occurs, for example, when children approach a parent saying, "Mommie, I fell down and hurt my elbow." Mother says, "Go away, can't you see I'm busy!" while she sits watching her soap opera. Mother is there physically, but not psychologically. Such instances of neglect are often motivated by an internal state of indifference. The parent simply does not care about the child. However, many cases of neglect are motivated by anger. This sometimes happens, for example, when a child reminds the parent of a spouse or consort who walked out. Every time the parent sees the child he or she thinks of that person, and gets angry. Rather than taking out their anger on the child physically—and hitting the child, which of course happens frequently—these parents try to stay away from the child altogether.

Undifferentiated rejection (in Figure 1) is the feeling of being unloved, unwanted, or rejected without necessarily having any of the above positive indicators of rejection present. "I can't show you that my parents were mad at me. I can't say they neglected me, but I just didn't feel they cared very much about me," said one articulate child in a recent research project. "They tried, I guess, but they just didn't like me." Here is a case in which a child felt unloved, uncared for, unwanted, and unappreciated—though there were no easily discernible signs of the "differentiated" forms of rejection described above, that is, of either overt neglect or aggression expressed against her. Even though the researchers found no "objective" signs of rejection in the family, the child felt "rejected," and she responded to these feelings as PAR theory predicts rejected children everywhere are likely to respond (described later).

The difference between "differentiated" and "undifferentiated" rejection lies in the fact that "differentiated" rejection may be observed behaviorally as either aggression or neglect (or both), or it may be experienced subjectively as hostility or indifference. "Undifferentiated" rejection, on the other hand, refers exclusively to subjective experiences of being unloved without clearly observable indicators of rejection being present. (It is a question for future research to determine whether some children subjectively experience themselves to be *loved* or "accepted" in the absence of observable indicators of acceptance. For reasons described later in this chapter, my guess is that they do.)

In doing research on parental acceptance and rejection one may, I believe, work at any level of abstraction depicted in Figure 1. For example, one may ask about the differential effects of verbal versus physical aggression on children's behavior, or one may move to a higher level of abstraction and ask about the differential effects of parental aggression (of all forms) versus parental neglect, or compare the effects of these behaviors with expressions of warmth and affection. Or one can go to a still higher level of abstraction and deal with the constructs "acceptance" versus "rejection," or move to the highest level and simply talk about the "warmth dimension" (that is, overall acceptance-rejection). One may measure the endless little specifics that go on in families, or one may ask people to give an overall summary of their feelings about what goes on (or went on at an earlier time, in childhood). Which of these approaches one uses depends on one's specific interests.

VALUE IMPLICATIONS OF THE TERM "REJECTION": A CAUTIONARY NOTE

I should add a word of caution at this point. The word "rejection" is loaded with unintended, unwanted, and negative semantic implications. For most people, "rejection" means something bad, and therefore if one attaches the label "rejecting" to parents one seems to have said they were bad parents. This value judgment is not intended in PAR theory. In fact, in many societies—and historically in our own—good, responsible parents often reject and abuse their children in the sense of rejection as defined analytically here (DeMause, 1975; Kagan, 1978b; Maccoby, 1980; Rohner and Rohner, 1981b; Sommerville, 1982; Watson and Watson, 1928). I do not say these parents are bad parents. Rather, I ask the question: When parents behave toward their children in ways that are consistent with the definition of rejection used here, do the children then respond in ways predicted by PAR theory—even though the rejection process may be normatively approved within the community? This is an empirical and more or less value-neutral question.

It may be useful to observe here that in some circumstances rejection may even have socially valued consequences. (Illustrations of this point are given in Chapter 7.) Most of the time, however, rejection probably does have "negative" implications. However, with respect to the "science" of parental acceptance and rejection it is important to maintain to the greatest degree possible value neutrality about the label. Regrettably, "rejection" is the only word in the English language that conveys simply and directly, if also excessively, the phenomena addressed by PAR theory.

PHENOMENOLOGICAL EMPHASIS IN PAR THEORY

One can study parental acceptance-rejection from two contrasting perspectives: as subjectively experienced by the individual or as objectively assessed by the researcher. The two approaches often, but not always, lead to the same conclusion (Clausen, 1972; Schwarz et al., 1985; Hunt and Eichorn, 1972). For example, I recently went into a home where the parents were poised, literate, and gracious. They dressed their 11-year-old son well, and they sent him to the "right" school. Direct observations of the family and interviews with the parents led me to believe the parents were concerned, loving people. Why then was the boy a problem in school? Why did he have a record of truancy and acting-out behaviors? And why was he thrown out of three private schools in less than two years? All external indicators made this seem like a model family, but from the boy's point of view his home was an emotional refrigerator. It seemed to him that his parents were so involved in their respective professions and social lives that they had no time for him. The parents expressed love and concern for the boy but it made little difference what *they* felt because the *boy* perceived and experienced a lack of love. And as Kagan (1978b: 57) has aptly stated, "Evaluation of a parent as hostile or accepting cannot be answered by observing the parent's behavior, for neither love nor rejection is a fixed quality of behavior. Like pleasure, pain, or beauty, it is in the mind of the beholder. Parental love is a belief held by the child, not a set of actions by a parent."

Kagan's phenomenological statement helps explain why many studies do not find a significant relationship between parental behavior, as reported by parents, and child adjustment. These studies fail to take into account the child's experiences with parents' actions. The impact of parental behavior on the child is shaped by perceptual and inferential processes within the child. Empirical evidence provided by Michaels et al. (1983), Serot and Teevan (1961), and Zucker and Barron (1971) supports the view that parents and children do not necessarily see parental love, demands, or punishment in the same way, and that parents often make incorrect inferences about the way their children perceive parenting. Several other studies have pointed out that children may be more affected by how they perceive parental behavior than by the actual behavior itself (Ausubel et al., 1954; Goldin, 1969; Heilbrun, 1973; Rabkin, 1965; Schaefer, 1965).

For reasons such as these, PAR theory lays greater emphasis on a phenomenological approach than on a behaviorist approach. That is, the theory makes the controversial assumption that human behavior is affected more (but not exclusively) by the way individuals perceive, interpret, or construe events—that is, by the way they phenomenally experience them—than by the objective events themselves.[1] Thus PAR theory emphasizes more the child's subjective experience of warmth, hostility, or indifference than any "objective" determination that the child is loved or rejected—although this is a matter of relative emphasis. There are times when the objective facts of the world cannot be ignored.

The phenomenological orientation helps explain why some children who are defined as being abused or neglected do not feel rejected (Herzberger et al., 1981). The orientation also seems to be essential in working comparatively across cultural or ethnic boundaries. Almost any given "objective" behavior might be interpreted differently by people in other sociocultural systems. And that fact creates one of the central problems for cross-cultural research. For example, if an American mother wants to show that she is happy with her child, she might praise him or her. In India, for ideological and religious reasons, parents are often reluctant to praise their children, especially in front of others. Instead, a Bengali mother might express her approval by peeling an orange and removing the seeds. Bengali children correctly understand that their mothers did something special for them and they accept the gesture as a sign of approval just as American children accept their mothers' compliments as signs of approval. Had the American mother peeled and seeded an orange instead of using praise, her child would not have received quite the same symbolic message. The two forms of maternal behavior are, in their respective sociocultural contexts, equivalent symbolic expressions of parental acceptance.

PAR theory postulates that children everywhere—in America and cross-culturally—respond in consistent ways to forms of behavior they perceive as "rejecting" or "accepting." The problem, however, is to discover what behaviors are understood by individuals in various sociocultural systems as being expressions of acceptance or rejection. For example, it is possible to criticize someone in any sociocultural system, but the specific behavior connoting "criticism" can be highly variable and idiosyncratic from society to society. A specific behavior implying criticism in one sociocultural context may even be a compliment in another. For example, on the island of St. Kitts in the Caribbean, a man who hisses at a woman has complimented her. The same behavior in much of the United States is likely to be regarded as rude. This issue of "equivalence of meaning" (Sears, 1961) is a serious problem in cross-cultural comparative research on parental acceptance-rejection.

It is sometimes argued that the social comparison process (Festinger, 1954; Suls and Miller, 1977) *within* a given society may also affect one's perception of parental behavior on the warmth dimension. For instance, some social comparison theorists argue that rejection might be a more painful experience for a child in a community where the child perceives him- or herself to be the only person singled out for rejection than in a community where many children feel rejected. With this position PAR theory has no quarrel. Other social comparison theorists, however, argue that in communities where most or all children are rejected (as "objectively" reported by the investigator), children may not feel rejected because they do not have others with whom to compare themselves unfavorably. PAR theory questions this viewpoint, arguing that children's subjectively felt need for "love" tends to be so strong that even in communities where most children are rejected, any given child is likely to respond with a personal feeling of discontent about not getting as much love or "positive response" as wanted (and hoped for) from his or her own parents—rather than feel all right about this withdrawal of love because no one else is being loved either.

Additional doubt is raised about the "social comparison" hypothesis insofar as Ruble et al. (1980) are correct when they suggest that children may not begin to use social comparison information until about eight years of age, an age well beyond the time when children cross-culturally begin to respond reliably to the effects of rejection (Rohner, 1975). More specifically, evidence discussed later shows that 2- through 6-year-old children the world over respond to parental rejection as PART's personality theory predicts, even in societies where virtually all the children are reported by anthropologists to be rejected.

ANTHROPONOMY AND THE EPISTEMOLOGICAL FOUNDATIONS OF PARENTAL ACCEPTANCE-REJECTION THEORY

Anthroponomy: Widely Believed, but Rarely Achieved

Parental acceptance-rejection theory is part of a widely believed but rarely achieved interest in the behavioral sciences, an interest I have come to call "anthroponomy" (Rohner, 1980, 1984a)—the "science" dealing with the search for, discovery, and verification of cross-culturally generalizable "universals" of human behavior (that is, scientifically derived principles of behavior that can be shown empirically to generalize *across our species* under specified conditions wherever they occur). It is clear, I hope, that I do not claim here to be creating a new science of human behavior, but only to draw attention to a widely held sentiment that a major purpose of behavioral science—for many behavioral scientists, at least—is to establish valid principles of *human* behavior, that is, principles that generalize across our species. Although many behavioral scientists share this sentiment, relatively few actually work to produce such principles. I employ the term "anthroponomy" to embrace several programs of otherwise unrelated research that are devoted to establishing true *cross-culturally* generalizable principles of behavior. This growing body of research is scattered throughout the human sciences, especially in psychology, linguistics, and certain portions of anthropology and biology (see Buss, 1984). Piaget (Ginsburg and Opper, 1979), for example, worked for more than half a century on an anthroponomical theory of the development and structure of human cognitive processes. Well over a hundred cross-cultural studies support, for the most part, his ideas about the postulated stages of cognitive development, although certain features of his system have not fared too well (Dasen and Heron, 1981).

Chomsky (1965, 1966) and associates (such as Wexler and Culicover, 1980) argue that a general and universal structure underlies the idiosyncrasies of all human languages; Lenneberg (1964, 1969) and

Slobin (1972) elaborate on this argument and contend that these formal linguistic universals reveal a common biological-evolutionary foundation to humankind's capacity for language. Greenberg (1978) and others (for example, Comrie, 1981; Lloyd and Gay, 1981) provide documentation for substantive and "implicational" universals in human language. They show, for instance, that if property "x" exists in a language then property "y" must also exist. Studying universal affective or connotative aspects of language, Osgood and associates (1975) provide evidence (using the semantic differential technique) that people the world over—regardless of differences in culture or language—appear to use the same semantic standards for making affective judgments. Berlin (1970; Berlin et al., 1973; Berlin and Kay, 1969) and many others, such as Mervis and Rosch (1981) and Witkowski and Brown (1977), continue their quest to discover structural and evolutionary semantic universals in language (for example, universals in color lexicons, ethnobiological domains, and other aspects of people's semantic universes).

Ekman (1980, 1982) and associates, along with Izard (1980; Malatesta and Izard, 1984) and others, continue to demonstrate universals in basic human emotions and in the facial expression of emotion. Witkin (Witkin and Berry, 1975) and Berry (1976) search for universals in the antecedents and correlates of psychological differentiation. These topics represent but a small portion of the various programs of anthroponomical research actually attempting to discover empirically—rather than merely assert—worldwide regularities and cross-culturally valid causal-functional relationships in human behavior. Cross-cultural research in PAR theory adds to this growing body of anthroponomical research by searching for empirically valid principles about the antecedents, consequences, and correlates of parental acceptance and rejection everywhere—in the United States and cross-culturally—*regardless of variations in culture, language, race, historical period, ethnicity, or other limiting conditions.*

The Phylogenetic Perspective

PAR theory and research—as is true for much other anthroponomical research—are guided by metatheoretical or epistemological viewpoint that has, in various forms, gained wide currency in recent decades. These converging viewpoints do not yet have a generally agreed-upon name, but I have found it useful to summarize them under the labels "phylogenetic perspective" and its derivative, the "phylogenetic model" (Rohner 1976, 1978).

In its simplest and most general form the viewpoint I label the "phylogenetic perspective" asserts that the contemporary behavior and behavior-potential of *Homo sapiens* is a function in an as yet unspecified way of interactions over the millenia between humankind's biological state and experience.[2] "Biological state" refers here to the complete range of genetic dispositions found in populations throughout our species. It also includes biological structure and processes of the living body, for example, the nervous system, the endocrine system, and our senses of sight, hearing, taste, smell, and touch. From a developmental point of view, biological state is more or less synonymous with maturation or organismic growth. Overall, then, "biological state" refers to humankind's complete biological, including genetic, endowment.

The term "experience" in the schema refers to anything that individuals perceive or anything to which they react as living organisms. It includes experiences with the physical world, the social or interpersonal world, and, very importantly, with oneself, including one's inner world. Also included in experience is a person's total history of experiences, probably from the moment of conception but certainly from birth onward. And it includes the kinds of experiences called "learning," including "culture learning." By "culture learning," I refer to enculturation or the process through which one becomes a responsible adult member of a given society, as defined by the norms of that society.

If one adds an evolutionary (specifically, genetic-behavioral coevolution) perspective to the biological term "epigenetic" (the sum of all interactions between genes and environment that create the distinctive characteristics of an organism), one approximates closely the meaning of the phylogenetic perspective. Lumsden and Wilson (1981, 1983) seem to share this viewpoint to a large extent with their concept of "epigenetic rules." From an evolutionary standpoint the phylogenetic perspective implies that humankind has phylogenetically acquired, biologically based potentials for certain kinds of behavior. Actualization of these potentials, however, may be altered by experience (Ginsburg and Laughlin, 1971).

This line of argument is relevant to parental acceptance-rejection theory in that PAR theory makes the assumption—an assumption yet to be proven empirically—that humans everywhere have a fundamental need for positive response from the people most important to them. This need for positive response seems to be endogenous within our species. That is, it is probably phylogenetically acquired in the course of human evolution, and seems likely to be related in some way to the fact that *Homo sapiens* is a sociable species living everywhere in community with other human beings. This need for positive response is, no doubt, also reinforced in the context of total infantile dependency. Thus the two forces together—biology and experience—seem to interact to produce varying intensities of this need-state within individuals. In addition, PAR theory postulates that children everywhere have a phylogenetically acquired tendency to respond in specific ways when warmth, affection, love, or other forms of positive response are withdrawn from them by the people most important to them. PAR theory also postulates, however, that individual exceptions will appear to these "universals" in behavior. That is, for some of the reasons described in the phylogenetic model below, not all children respond to rejection to the same degree.

The Phylogenetic Model

Whereas the phylogenetic perspective pertains mainly to evolutionarily acquired *species* potentials and dispositions, the phylogenetic model allows one to consider the individual. The two schemas are the same except that the phylogenetic model adds another element, "cognition" or "mental activity"—which thus makes the effects of the phylogenetic model profoundly different from the phylogentic perspective.

More specifically, the phylogenetic model asserts that the behavior and development of an *individual* is a function in some unspecified way of the interaction between an individual's biological state and experience *as modified by cognition.* Cognition or mental activity includes the concept of intelligence, not in the restricted sense of IQ, but rather in the broadest sense of an individual's capacity to know, comprehend, reason, and understand. In some respects the phenomenon of cognition or mental activity as used here is also closely related to volition, and includes what philosophers call "free will," the capacity to make rational (or irrational) choices freely.[3] Unlike the phylogenetic perspective, which is primarily concerned with genotype and is useful largely from a population and evolutionary point of view, the phylogenetic model is useful from an ontogenetic or individual point of view.

Cognition in the phylogenetic model draws attention to the fact that individuals are not passive organisms governed solely by mindless forces of either biology or experience.[4] Neither are individuals limitlessly free agents.[5] Each of us is, of course, influenced greatly by both endogenous and situational factors, with a significant residue remaining of unique, individualistic mental activity and consequent action. Thus, according to the phylogenetic model, an individual's behavior is only partly predictable. It is also partly indeterminate, by its very nature. In this respect, but in more spirited language, sociobiologists Lumsden and Wilson (1983: 55) state, "On Earth at least, genes and free will are partners of necessity and not partners of convenience."

It seems quite clear to me—along with many other behavioral scientists, some of whom come to the same conclusion from different routes (for example, Wann, 1964; Hitt, 1969)—that human beings live in both an objective and a subjective world, and thus human behavior is, in important ways, both knowable and predictable in scientific terms. Yet for any given individual at any given point in time human behavior remains in its essential nature partially indeterminate and therefore somewhat unpredictable. This position is, of course, a significant challenge to the conventional positivist tradition in science that asserts that human behavior, like the physical world, is ultimately knowable through the canons of science (Kimble, 1984). This position is also the reason I argue for probabilistic universals in behavior rather than for invariants or constants. That is, I believe that universals should be thought of as forms of behavior that have a *significant probability* of occurring under specified conditions, wherever such conditions occur throughout our species, not as invariants or constants of behavior. Phylogenetically acquired behavioral dispositions always seem to have at least a small range of variation in their expression.

When one draws from the phylogenetic perspective, one generally talks about species-wide commonalities, and the ways in which all humans are alike.[6] With the phylogenetic model, on the other hand, one is asked to recognize that every individual is and must forever remain unique, in phenomenological isolation, as it were. These apparently contradictory viewpoints combine to produce a viable generalizing science of anthroponomy in the following way: All humans share a great many species traits and states of readiness in common, states and traits that have been transmitted phylogenetically from our infrahuman ancestors. It is also true, however—as Darwin pointed out over a hundred years ago—that each individual has his or her own unique genotype. Because each individual's genotype is to some degree unique, it follows that the interaction of these unique genetic, experiential, and cognitive differences must over time create unique persons who at the same time can be compared with any other person one has ever known. We recognize ourselves in all others, regardless of differences in race, class, culture, or language. It is through this line of reasoning, I believe, that one is able to move back and forth easily between the phylogentic perspective and the phylogenetic model.

Now I move this epistemological viewpoint closer to parental acceptance-rejection theory. I believe that the phylogenetic perspective, along with the universalist approach described in the next chapter, gives sufficient conceptual and methodological rationale to begin effective anthroponomical search for species-wide regularities (that is, "universals") in children's and adults' responses to the perception of parental acceptance and rejection.[7] The phylogenetic model cautions against searching for invariants, but, more important, it gives one reason for expecting that—within definable limits—individual children will respond somewhat differently to perceived rejection. Even though human beings seem to have the phylogenetically acquired predisposition to respond to rejection in specific ways, the conscious and unconscious working of the human mind can, under some circumstances, act as a kind of override mechanism affecting or altering the usually expectable outcome of rejection. Viewed another way, the phylogenetic model gives reason for suspecting that some apparent exceptions to the postulates of PAR theory (and other anthroponomically oriented theories as well) may sometimes be theoretically meaningful departures from the theory. These considerations lead me to the "probability model" in PAR theory research, discussed next.

The Probability Model in PAR Theory Research

Exceptions almost inevitably appear in behavioral science research, partly because of simple mismeasurement, imperfections in theory and research design, social desirability response bias or other sources of potential invalidity, and other such practical concerns, but also, as I argued above, because human behavior is to some extent inherently indeterminate (see also Georgoudi and Rosnow, 1985). Nearly inevitable measurement problems in conjunction with a certain degree of inherent indeterminance in human behavior lead me to adopt the "probability model," which recognizes that behavior has only varying degrees of likelihood of occurring under specified conditions. Positions similar to this have been enunciated by Brunswik (1955), Postman (1955), Royce (1982), Campbell and Stanley (1963), and Scarr and McCartney (1983).

The probability model raises doubts about the existence of absolutes, invariants, or exceptionless uniformities in behavior, as postulated by "mechanical-model" theorists. Mechanical-model theorists assume behavior is strictly ruleful, and that if the rules are determined perfectly, behavior can be predicted with perfect fidelity. Moreover, mechanical-model theorists believe that all behavior is "caused" and potentially "knowable" (Kimble, 1984). Mechanical-model theories are often stated in the form of invariants or absolutes. Logically, then, if one finds a single exception to a mechanical-model theory that exception should be sufficient to disprove the theory. In fact, however, advocates of mechanical-model theories often ignore evidence that contradicts their theories (see Kuhn, 1970; Scarr, 1985).

An illustration of a mechanical-model theory should help clarify this line of reasoning. G. Stanley Hall (1904) postulated a mechanical-model theory when he wrote about the universality and inevitability of adolescent stress—that adolescence is universally and inevitably a time of stress, conflict, tension, or rebelliousness. (More recent proponents of the "adolescent stress" thesis include Freud, 1969; Hirsch, 1970; and Josselyn, 1954.) Not only does evidence in America fail to support this contention (Gallatin, 1976; Conger, 1977), but one has to search hard for societies cross-culturally where the contention *is* true (Rohner, 1977b).

I argue in PAR theory that the mechanical model is an improper perspective on behavioral reality, that in fact behavior is not ruleful to such a great degree. Therefore, the best one can do as a behavioral scientist—not as second best or by default, but by the very nature of behavioral reality—is to deal with a world of probabilities, specifically the probability or likelihood of certain events or behaviors happening under specified conditions. Thus PAR theory researchers try to determine the probability that a sample of rejected children drawn at random from anywhere in the world will respond the way the theory predicts.

NOTES

1. This is, of course, an empirically testable point, and the theory could be shown to be wrong with respect to its greater emphasis on a "phenomenological" versus a "behaviorist" orientation.

2. The phylogenetic perspective asserts—along with most contemporary human biologists—that the ancient "nature *versus* nurture" debate is misguided. Today there seems to be little serious disagreement among professionals in the bio-behavioral sciences that environment and heredity cannot be decomposed into individual units; for all practical purposes biology and experience work in inextricable interaction (Ginsburg and Laughlin, 1971; Lumsden and Wilson, 1981, 1983). The phylogenetic perspective focuses on this interaction, specifically in the ways heredity (or biology, more generally) and experience each affected the other in the course of human evolution, shaping through their interaction what we have become as a species, *Homo sapiens.*

3. For a rich and useful discussion of the history and contemporary viewpoints in the debate within psychology regarding free will, volition, intentionality, purposiveness, and like constructs in human behavior (versus material/efficient causation models, imputed by the dominant paradigm within behaviorism, a paradigm that rejects telic or purposive explanations of behavior), see Rychlak (1980, 1983) and Westcott (1983).

4. I regard cognition in the phylogenetic model as being critical to parental acceptance-rejection theory because mental activity seems to coordinate all human experience. That is, in order to have "human" experience, the experience must be given meaning through mental activity. This mental activity—whether conscious or unconscious, intended or unintended, recognized or unrecognized—generally mediates between the biological state of individuals and their experiences, thus often modifying individuals' endogenous dispositions to respond to events in specific ways. This is what seems to happen in the case of many "copers," described later.

5. Much of the "mental activity" in the phylogenetic model seems to be susceptible to the same lawlike regularities as "biological state" and "experience."

6. Essentially elaborating on the viewpoint I call the phylogenetic perspective, Scarr and McCartney (1983), however, delineated a promising conceptual scheme (which drew heavily from prior work of Plomin et al., 1977) describing how genetic and environmental differences among individuals combine to produce *individual variations* in human development—as well as describing how genotype and experience (or "environment," in their scheme) combine to produce species-wide commonalities in human development. Apparently, then, the phylogenetic perspective can be employed effectively in the context of individual development as well as in the context of panhuman developmental tendencies.

7. These universals in the antecedents, consequences, and correlates of parental acceptance and rejection should be construed as species-wide but not necessarily species-specific. They are not, therefore, to be confused with instincts, which are commonly defined as complex, genetically determined forms of species-specific behavior such as the nest-building behavior of swallows, or the mating behavior of stickleback fish.

2

Researching Parental Acceptance and Rejection: The Universalist Approach

This chapter describes a paradigm of research for doing anthroponomical research on the antecedents, consequences, and correlates of parental acceptance and rejection. If one is serious about trying to establish transculturally valid principles of behavior, then a relevant question becomes: How does one do it in ways that will persuade reasonably skeptical people of the validity of the claimed principles? In my opinion, a complicated issue such as this requires a complex research design known as the "universalist" approach (Rohner, 1975). Key ingredients in the universalist approach include a convergence-of-procedures and preferably a convergence-of-methodologies research design in cross-cultural, comparative settings. A multimethod approach is required, I believe, because every discrete research procedure, as well as every general "methodology" in the behavioral sciences, has certain inherent weaknesses and deficiencies, and worst of all each has the potential for certain kinds of bias—in addition to strengths that prompt researchers to use each of them in the first place (Webb et al., 1966; Maccoby and Martin, 1983).

As intimated above, I make a distinction conceptually between "procedure" and "methodology." "Procedure" here refers to a specific measurement process, that is, to a single method, assessment device, or technique of data collection such as interviewing or the use of questionnaires. Each of these is a coherent, integrated procedure for collecting information. "Methodology," on the other hand, is a class or tradition of research, a research paradigm, a body of methods, rules, and postulates employed within a discipline. For example, the experimental method is a methodology in the sense used here. It is not a specific research procedure as is a questionnaire or an interview. It is a general paradigm of research that has an intellectual history. One can trace the origin and development of ideas forming the methodology. Moreover, methodologies are complex in that they have many parts, and they make specific assumptions about the world.

The various behavioral science disciplines are distinguished to some degree by their tendency to favor one or another methodology. Significant portions of psychology, for example, are wedded to the use of the experimental method. In anthropology the classic and preferred methodology is participant-observation research. It, too, has a long history, makes certain assumptions about the world, employs a specific logic, and has certain values associated with it. Many sociologists and political scientists favor survey research that involves large-scale national or regional sampling, and has a complex logic of its own. The holocultural method, yet another methodology, was started primarily in anthropology but is now used widely across all the behavioral sciences. With each of these methodologies only certain kinds of questions may properly be asked. Therefore, one's choice of methodology dictates the kind of science one practices (or, alternatively, one's science dictates the methodology to be used; Kuhn, 1970).

As I said above, every specific measurement procedure and every methodology has the potential for certain kinds of bias (Irvine and Carroll, 1980). (Bias, here, refers to a systematic error, as distinguished from random error.) In anthroponomical research, as in all other scientific research, it is essential that results achieved truly relate to the people or phenomena studied, and are not an artifact of the procedure used. But every existing procedure and methodology has potential for its own kind of bias; one cannot be certain in monoprocedure or even monomethodology research that the results are unaffected by the method(ology) used (Campbell and Fiske, 1959; Webb et al., 1966). It is for this reason that universalist, anthroponomical research calls for a multimethod(ology) or convergence-of-method(ologies) research design. That is, even though each measurement process has its own potential for bias, no two processes share exactly the same bias. Therefore, if one continues to get significant results when using a variety of different measures and paradigms of research—each of which is admittedly imperfect—then one may properly become increasingly confident that the conclusions are robust, accurate, and generalizable (Webb et al., 1966).

In addition to a convergence-of-methods (that is, convergence-of-procedures and convergence-of-methodologies) research design, I argue that anthroponomical research also requires cross-cultural comparative research, and, whenever possible, a worldwide (holocultural) sampling design (Naroll et al., 1980).[1] The rationale for this assertion is based on the fact that anthroponomical research, unlike other behavioral science research, is devoted *explicitly* to the search for species-wide generalizations about human behavior. Accordingly, it is obligatory for anthroponomists to demonstrate that their results generalize worldwide across diverse ethnic, cultural, racial, social class, and other populations. It is not sufficient in anthroponomical research to rest one's case on results achieved within a single population, no matter how elegantly the work might have been done there. This requirement has been recognized many times in cross-cultural psychology and elsewhere (Berry, 1980; Brislin et al., 1973; Dawson, 1971; Devos and Hippler, 1969; Jahoda, 1970, 1979; Sechrest, 1976; Triandis, 1977, 1980). With these prescriptions in mind I turn now to the methodologies and specific procedures used in PAR theory research.

CONVERGING METHODOLOGIES IN PAR THEORY RESEARCH

To the greatest extent practicable a two-tier approach is employed in PAR theory research. That is, I argue for a convergence-of-methodologies approach as well as a convergence-of-procedures approach, described in the next section. As shown in Figure 2, the methodologies include holocultural research, ethnographic and socialization research, and social psychological and developmental research. The strengths and weaknesses of each are described in turn, but first I want to point out that for reasons described above some of the conclusions reached in one paradigm occasionally fail to converge with results reached in one or both of the other two paradigms. (This problem is even more common across individual measurement procedures, discussed later.) Where two or preferably all three research designs converge one may find anthroponomical principles. As I said earlier, if a single conclusion survives the onslaught of two or more

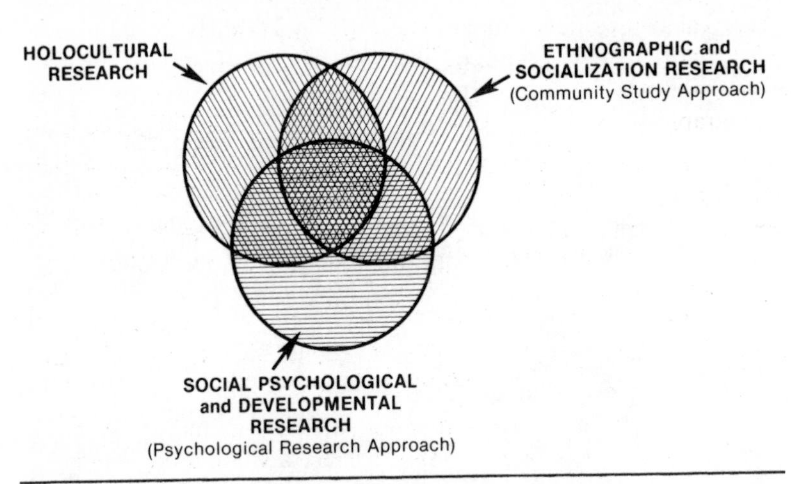

Figure 2 Convergence of Methodologies in PAR Theory Research

imperfect methodologies—each with its own flaws and imperfections—one has increased the plausibility that the results truly relate to the issue studied and are not an artifact of the methodology used. It is an entirely problematic and empirical question, however, to what extent one gets converging results in any given research project.

I do not argue that all anthroponomists must necessarily use the same three methodologies described here. These are simply the ones I choose because they are effective for this kind of research. Researchers working in other domains—for example, cross-cultural research on Piaget's theory (Dasen and Heron, 1981)—sometimes use different methodologies, but the *logic* of the universalist approach must always be retained in anthroponomical research.

Holocultural Research Paradigm

The holocultural methodology (Naroll et al., 1980) is a paradigm of research for testing hypotheses "by means of correlations found in a worldwide, comparative study whose units of study are entire societies or cultures, and whose sampling universe is either (a) all known cultures . . . or (b) all known primitive tribes" (Naroll et al., 1976: 1). By drawing on a sample of the known and adequately described sociocultural systems of the world, past and present, the holocultural methodology provides a fair representation of the human condition as it is revealed in written ethnographies.[2] (Ethnographies are anthropologists' written descriptions of the way of life of specific peoples around the world.) In order to do holocultural research one codes ethnographies in much the same manner as a researcher might code an interview, using the logic of interview coding. In PART research, computerized tests of relationships are then run between the derived codes for parental acceptance-rejection, for the personality dispositions of children and adults, and for relevant sociocultural variables. Using the holocultural method, PART researchers ask if parenting is related to the behavior of children and adults, and to sociocultural phenomena, as reported by ethnographers in the world sample.[3]

The holocultural method has one very great and essential strength: It allows one to generalize to the whole world. If a hypothesis is confirmed in the holocultural paradigm, one has reason for thinking it is probably true for human behavior everywhere, unless one suspects that the results achieved are the consequence of bias in the sampling or measurement process. Serious holocultural researchers, however, take care to rule out the likelihood of various sources of bias.[4] No other paradigm of research has the power to tell quickly whether or not a relationship is likely to generalize to humans everywhere (Rohner, 1979a).

Properly used, the holocultural method is complex and second in power (Blalock, 1979) only to the experimental method (Rohner, 1977a). It does have certain disadvantages, however. Using as it does "societies" or "sociocultural systems" as its unit of analysis, it cannot tell anything about variations in the behavior of individuals. It tells only about cultural variations and uniformities, or about the typical behavior of many individuals within each society of the world sample. Also, researchers can ask about only those issues on which ethnographers have reported in their writings. But ethnographers rarely write about certain things in detail, such as personally intimate (for example, sexual) behaviors that occur universally.

Ethnographic and Socialization Research Paradigm

Ethnographic and socialization research (hereafter referred to as the "community study" approach) complements holocultural research because it too draws from different sociocultural systems of the world. But in this paradigm the investigator (usually an anthropologist) himself or herself studies for many months—through participant observation, systematic observation, interviewing, and similar procedures—the behavior of individual parents and children within the local community. An advantage of this paradigm is that it allows one to test for relationships between variables *within* a culturally organized population (versus *across* populations, as with the holocultural method). Another of its strengths is to embed information explicitly and systematically within a cultural context (Goodenough, 1980). This is possible because anthropologists typically live in the community from six months to a year or more, often studying intensively the religious beliefs, political organization, economic system, family structure, and all the other belief and behavior systems that go into making life a sociocultural totality within a community. PAR theory researchers can then embed a sample of families and children within the rich sociocultural matrix of the total community.

One of the greatest advantages of the community study approach lies in its ability to test in a distinctive way a central hypothesis within PAR theory: Rejected children in widely divergent communities around the world—regardless of differences in culture, language, or race—develop personality dispositions more like each others' (in terms of the personality traits postulated in PART's personality theory) than like their own accepted siblings' within the same community. In other respects, siblings within a given community are more like each other than they are like any of the other children. They speak the same language, for example, believe in the same god, wear similar clothing, prefer the same foods, and so forth.

This hypothesis is displayed graphically in Figure 3, which shows that within any given society there is a range of variation in the love or rejection typically experienced by children. Children in Society A, for example, typically feel accepted, as shown by the fact that the curve in Figure 3 peaks at the acceptance end of the warmth dimension. One child (Child 2), however, feels rejected, but Child 1 falls within the modal (that is, accepted) range of parenting within the community. In Society B, parents' level of warmth tends to fall within the midrange, but Child 3 is given more warmth and affection than the average child, and Child 4 is given less. Note in Figure 3 that Children 1 and 3 (and 5) all experience the same level and form of parental acceptance. Similarly, Children 2 and 4 (and 6) all experience rejection in the same way

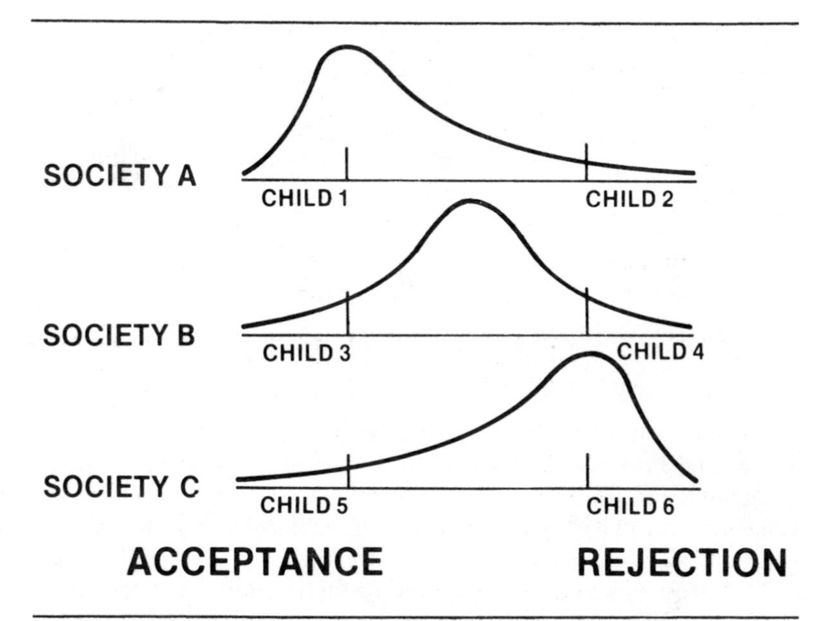

Figure 3 Parental Acceptance-Rejection in Three Hypothetical Societies

and to the same degree. In Society C parents usually reject children, but—as just indicated—Child 5 escapes this maltreatment, whereas his sibling (Child 6) is targeted along with most other children in the community.

According to the hypothesis stated above, rejected Children 1, 3, and 5 should share a constellation of personality dispositions (the personality dispositions described later in PART's personality theory), even though they live in widely separated sociocultural systems, represent different racial stocks, and speak different languages. Moreover, the personality dispositions of these children should be systematically different from those of each rejected child's accepted siblings. Unlike the holocultural method, which focuses on modal or typical behavior within a given community (for example, Society A is characterized by acceptance, but Society C is characterized by rejection), the community study approach allows one to study individual variability in behavior within the community in order to test this hypothesis and others like it.

The community study approach has its disadvantages too, however. It is, for example, time consuming and expensive. Virtually

100% of a person's time for six months to a year or more is taken up in fieldwork, and sometimes anthropologists must also hire a small research staff to assist them. A second disadvantage of the community study approach is its typically small sample size. That is, in order to gather context-rich information about parents and children within the total community, the anthropologist typically works with only a small number of people, thus seriously limiting the power of statistical analysis that is possible in large-sample research, discussed in the following section.

Social Psychological and Developmental Research Paradigm

The disadvantage of the community study approach just mentioned is remedied in the social psychological and developmental research paradigm (henceforth called the "psychological research" approach), which includes all conventional forms of psychological research recognized in the standard journals of psychology. The psychological research approach allows one to employ large samples and to incorporate powerful multivariate statistics in data analysis. A disadvantage of much of this work, however—even though the work is often done internationally—is that it usually gives little information about the sociocultural context, beyond basic demographic or social-situational statistics such as age, sex, intact versus broken family, and socioeconomic status. For this reason there are few ways in intracultural research of this type to control for possible sociocultural effects.

Only a restricted range of variation occurs in the "normal" behavior of individuals within any given nation. For example, if researchers work only in America—even though the work is done well—they may wind up with faulty anthroponomical results simply because only a limited range of normatively acceptable behavior alternatives are open to Americans, and as a result culturally approved behavior occurs within restricted ranges of variation. Those persons who exceed these limits are considered deviant or "sick," and negative sanctions are often placed on them (Becker, 1963; Scheff, 1966; Schur, 1976). Excessive or deviant behavior in one society, however, may fall within the range of acceptable and sometimes even preferred behavior in another (Benedict, 1934).

Let me illustrate this point. Studying child rearing in Kansas City some years ago, Sears and Wise (1950) found that 94% of the sample children had been weaned by 7 months of age, and no child was still being breast-fed by the time he or she was three years old. Most Americans would probably be surprised, and maybe even shocked, to see children being breast-fed for a period as long as three years, but in a worldwide sample of 37 societies Whiting and Child (1953) discovered that age of weaning cross-culturally ranges from about 12 months to 3, 4, or even 6 years in a few instances. In only two cases (about 5%) in their cross-cultural sample were children weaned as early as Americans in Kansas City, before the age of 7 months. Thus, in worldwide perspective, the weaning habits of Americans—at least as generalized from Kansas City—were extreme.

Sears and Wise examined the relationship between age of weaning and the amount of emotional disturbance expressed by infants in their Kansas City sample. The authors conclude that the older babies are when weaned the more emotional disturbance they show. Can this conclusion be incorporated into a general theory of human behavior? Is it universally true that the older children are when weaned the more likely they are to be distressed by weaning? Whiting and Child (1953) show that people who generalize from Sears and Wise's study will be misled, even though the Kansas City study was well done. Because the vast majority of children in Kansas City were weaned by the age of 7 months, the researchers had a very restricted time period on which to base their conclusions. Drawing on the greater variability of normal behavior cross-culturally than we find in the United States or in any other single sociocultural system, however, Whiting and Child discovered that Sears and Wise were correct in applying their conclusions to children aged 13 to 18 months: Children are more likely to become disturbed the older they are when they are weaned. Beyond 13 to 18 months, however, children show steadily fewer signs of emotional distress at weaning. Thus a curvilinear relationship—not a linear relationship—seems to exist between age of weaning and emotional distress. The curvilinear relationship could not have been discovered had Whiting and Child not had access to the greater variability in "normal" behavior found cross-culturally than within the United States.

I should also point out that knowledge about the relationship between age of weaning and emotional disturbance would be incomplete without data provided by Sears and Wise because only two societies in Whiting and Child's transcultural sample fell within the time range (that is, weaning at birth to 7 months) reported in the Kansas City study. Without intracultural information such as this, one would have no way of knowing what the effects of weaning are at the lower age limits. This fact shows the complementary nature of intracultural and cross-cultural comparative research. It is, nonetheless, also important to remember that a significant disadvantage of intracultural psychological research is that one can rarely be sure—even when the research is done impeccably—to what extent results can be generalized to panhuman behavior (Rohner, 1977c). The same conclusion has been reached recently by Triandis (1978), Touhey (1981), and others.

The distinction between community study research and psychological research can sometimes be fairly fine, the main distinction being that community study research has an in-depth component lacking in most social psychological/developmental research. Psychological research is often a kind of survey research, sampling several hundred children and their parents through questionnaires or interviews on a one-shot basis. But doubt about the psychological research paradigm begins to fade when converging results emerge from work done in several different nations or societies using the same methods, made appropriate to each sociocultural setting.

CONVERGING PROCEDURES IN PAR THEORY RESEARCH

Earlier in this chapter I said that I use a two-tier approach in PAR theory resarch, that is, a multiprocedure approach as well as a multimethodology approach. I will now describe advantages and disadvantages of specific procedures and instruments used in this research.

As shown graphically in Figure 4, PAR theory researchers use a convergence-of-procedures approach whenever possible within both the community study paradigm and the psychological research paradigm. (The logic of holocultural research does not allow for a multiprocedure orientation in the sense used here.) More specifically, PAR theory researchers use self-report questionnaires, interviews, and systematic behavior observations. Self-report questionnaires, however, have been by far the most commonly used method employed

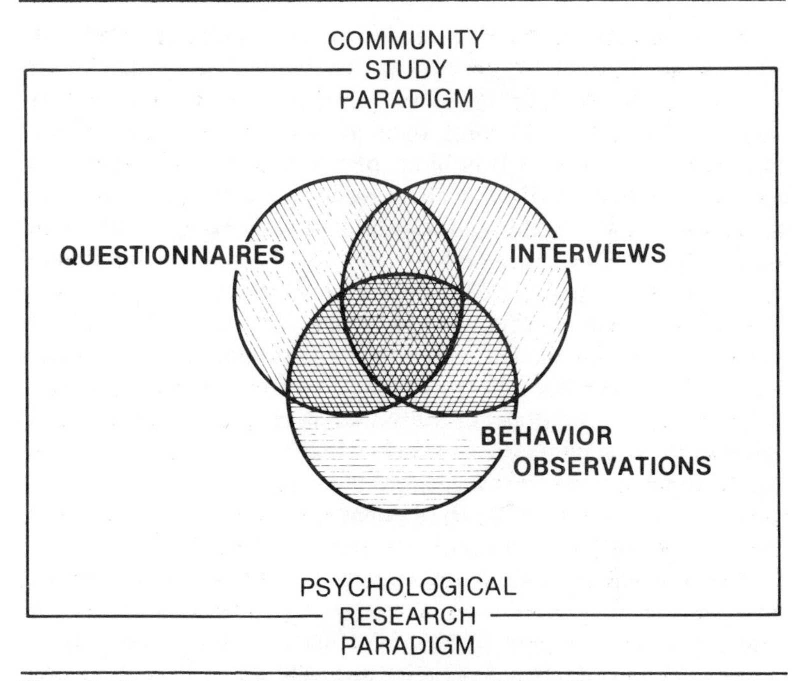

Figure 4 Convergence of Procedures in PAR Theory Research

by researchers internationally, especially in the psychological research component.

Self-Report Questionnaires: The PARQ and the PAQ

Two different sets of questionnaires in more than a dozen languages are available for this work. These questionnaires are the Parental Acceptance-Rejection Questionnaire (PARQ) and its complement in PAR theory, the Personality Assessment Questionnaire (PAQ). The PARQ is designed to elicit respondents' assessments of their childhood (or their children's socialization) experiences in terms of perceived parental "warmth" (that is, acceptance-rejection). Three versions of the PARQ have been developed (Rohner, 1984a): (1) Parents (usually mothers) respond to the Mother PARQ according to their perceptions about the way they treat their children. (2) The Adult

PARQ asks adults to reflect on the way they were treated when they were about 7 through 12 years old. (3) The Child PARQ asks children to reflect on the way their primary caretakers (usually their mothers) now treat them.[5] In all three versions respondents assess parental *behavior* (rarely attitudes) in terms of the same four scales: (a) perceived warmth and affection, (b) perceived hostility and aggression, (c) perceived indifference and neglect, and (d) perceived undifferentiated rejection. (As indicated earlier, "undifferentiated rejection" refers to conditions in which parents are perceived as withdrawing love from a child—that is, the child interprets his or her parents' behavior as rejection—but in which such rejection does not clearly reflect either perceived or "objectively" measured hostility, neglect, or indifference, as defined in the preceding chapter.) All versions of the PARQ (and PAQ described below) are virtually identical except for the pronoun referent (for example, "My mother . . . ," versus "My child . . . ,"), and all use the same response options, thereby maximizing a comparability of responses across all versions.

The second self-report questionnaire, the PAQ (Rohner, 1984a), complements the PARQ in that it assesses respondents' perceptions of themselves with respect to the seven personality and behavioral dispositions postulated in PART's personality theory to be associated with parental acceptance and rejection. These personality and behavioral descriptions are as follows: (1) hostility, aggression, passive aggression, and problems with the management of hostility and aggression; (2) dependence; (3) self-esteem; (4) self-adequacy; (5) emotional responsiveness; (6) emotional stability; and (7) worldview. Three versions of the PAQ have been developed: (1) Mother PAQ, in which parents (usually mothers) respond according to their perceptions about their children's behavior in terms of the seven personality dispositions. (2) The Adult PAQ asks adults to reflect on their perceptions of themselves with respect to the same seven behavioral dispositions. (3) The Child PAQ asks children to reflect on themselves with respect to the same dispositions. All versions of the questionnaires are provided in Rohner (1984a), but the Child PARQ and the Child PAQ are also included in Appendix B of this volume.

The validity and reliability of the PARQ and PAQ have been assessed in several sociocultural settings, and both questionnaires have been found repeatedly to be psychometrically adequate. Internal reliabilities (coefficient alpha) of scales on the Adult PARQ, for example, ranged in the United States from .86 to .95; internal reliabilities (coefficient alpha) of scales on the Adult PAQ ranged in the United States from .73 to .85. Factor analyses of items on each questionnaire tended strongly to yield the expected factors (that is, theoretically expected scales), thus providing further evidence regarding the construct validity of the theoretical constructs underlying PARQ scales and PAQ scales, respectively. Other measures of concurrent, discriminant, and convergent validities of scales on both instruments are also satisfactory, suggesting overall reliability and construct validity of both self-report questionnaires. A detailed discussion of the validity and reliability of the PARQ and PAQ may be found in Rohner (1984a).

The Parental Acceptance-Rejection Interview Schedule

In addition to the self-report questionnaires, two interview schedules have been developed, one for children and one for adults. Both complement the PARQ in that they ask about the same content areas tapped by that questionnaire (as measures of the convergent validity of responses on the Mother PARQ and Child PARQ). Unlike individual versions of the PARQ, however, both versions of the Parental Acceptance-Rejection Interview Schedule (PARIS) ask about the mother's warmth (that is, acceptance-rejection as defined by the same forms of perceived behavior assessed on the PARQ) and the father's warmth. Moreover, both versions of the PARIS ask about the form and degree to which mothers and fathers control their children's behavior (that is, the extent to which parents are permissive or strict). Finally, both versions contain sections dealing with the ability of children to cope with parental acceptance-rejection and control. The adult version also contains a section for determining who the major caretaker of a child is. With this exception (that is, regarding major caretakers) the child version of the PARIS elicits the same information as the Adult PARIS, but from the child's own perspective.

Behavior Observations and the Background Data Schedule

The converging-methods approach recommended here calls for systematic time-sampled and behavior-setting sample behavior observations (see Longabaugh, 1980) within each family, insofar as is practicable. That is, as an additional, "objectively" determined measure of parental warmth (acceptance-rejection) and of the behavioral dispositions of children, PART researchers often try to observe the actual interaction between major caretaker(s) and the sample child within each family. Finally, the Background Data Schedule (BDS) is used with every family participating in the research. The BDS (included in Appendix B) is used to collect basic social-demographic data, such as the age and sex of the household members, ethnicity, major language(s) spoken, religious preference, educational attainment, occupation and employment status, marital status, family stress experienced, and recreational preferences. The BDS contains two main sections, one to be completed by or about the child's mother or major female caretaker (if any), and one to be completed by or about the child's father (or whoever is the most significant adult male in the child's life), if any. The full set of instruments, procedures, and other materials needed for empirical studies of parental acceptance and rejection in America and internationally is available in the *Handbook for the Study of Parental Acceptance and Rejection* (Rohner, 1984a).

Advantages and Disadvantages of Each Class of Procedure Used

Each of these research methods—interviews, behavior observations, and questionnaires—has its own distinctive advantages and disadvantages. Use of questionnaires, for example, is cost-efficient. In less than a morning's time researchers can administer the PARQ and PAQ to several hundred respondents congregated together. Moreover, psychometric properties including validity and reliability of these instruments can be ascertained explicitly for each sociocultural system where they are used. Although much more time-consuming, and therefore costly, interviews have an advantage over questionnaires in that they allow researchers to probe for richer detail than possible in questionnaires. Some behaviorist-oriented researchers, however, criticize all forms of self-report procedures (such as questionnaires and interviews) because of their susceptibility to social desirability response bias, unconscious distortions, and other such problems (Hilgard, 1949; Webb et al., 1966; Averill, 1983).[6] These researchers favor direct observation of family interaction and child personality. In PAR theory research, one runs the risk of spending many hours observing a family but seeing only a few minutes of behavior relevant to the theory. This, of course, is an inefficient use of research time. Moreover, families can just as easily alter their behavior in socially desirable ways for the benefit of the observing stranger as they can present themselves in socially desirable ways on questionnaires or interviews. These problems of bias, mismeasurement, and other sources of error constitute a major reason for adopting the logic of the multimethodology and multiprocedure approach. The phenomenon studied must be fairly robust to survive the onslaught of multiple imperfect measures, especially if these measures are made in widely different sociocultural contexts.

NOTES

1. The logic of the universalist approach is laid out more completely in Rohner (1975).
2. Detailed guidelines for using the holocultural method are provided in Naroll et al. (1976), and in Rohner et al. (1978). Barry and Schlegel (1980) assembled into a book-length work the most commonly used holocultural sample, the standard cross-cultural sample (Murdock and White, 1969)—along with fourteen bodies of coded data using the standard sample. Levinson and Malone (1980) provide a monograph summarizing and assessing the theoretical findings of over 300 studies coming from this and numerous other holocultural samples.
3. In Chapter 1, I said that PAR theory draws primarily from a phenomenological perspective, but holocultural data are not necessarily phenomenologically oriented. That is, it is not always clear to what extent any given ethnography describes observable manifestations of parental acceptance or rejection, or children's (or parents') phenomenologically perceived experiences of acceptance-rejection. This fact constitutes one of the problematics of holocultural studies in PAR theory research, but from a pragmatic viewpoint it does not seem to be a serious limitation because holocultural research usually yields the same results in PAR theory research as the more phenomenologically oriented methodologies. In fact, holocultural research generally seems to be the most cost-effective method available in many different programs of research for identifying relationships that will emerge ultimately as valid anthroponomical principles.
4. The great majority of societies included in most holocultural studies represent Third World or tribally organized societies. Only a minority are industrialized nations. Some critics of the holocultural method argue that this fact represents a sampling bias, and, as such, limits the generalizability of results coming from holocultural research. This may be an apt criticism for some holocultural studies, but a comparison of industrialized and nonindustrialized societies in the two holocultural samples on which most PART research has been based (discussed later) shows no tendency for results in industrialized nations to be significantly different from results in nonindustrialized societies.

5. The Child PARQ, which assesses the child's perceptions of his or her mother's behavior, can be changed easily to assess the child's perception of his or her father's behavior, or the behavior of any other major caretaker.

6. For a more complete discussion of the "response bias" criticism of self-report procedures, specifically as it pertains to PAR theory research, see Rohner (1984a: 80-86).

3

PART Within the Whole: The Sociocultural Systems Model

In this chapter I enlarge the perspective adopted up to now. I show here and throughout the remainder of the book how the effects of parental acceptance-rejection permeate the entire sociocultural system, as well as the personality of the individual. To accomplish this objective I utilize the convergence-of-methods approach described in the preceding chapter, and I take as a given the probability model described in Chapter 1. I begin this chapter with a description of PART's "sociocultural systems model," which provides a way of thinking about the antecedents, consequences, and correlates of parental acceptance-rejection within individuals and society. Following that I discuss evidence bearing on three sets of relationships within the model: (a) the relationship between acceptance-rejection and the natural environment, and (b) the relationship between acceptance-rejection and maintenance systems, including household structure, and the availability of fathers as major caretakers. The third topic is an evolutionary perspective on the relationship between acceptance-rejection and subsistence economy.

PAR THEORY'S SOCIOCULTURAL SYSTEMS MODEL

The sociocultural systems model employed in PAR theory (shown in Figure 5) dates back in various forms to the 1930s. The ancestral

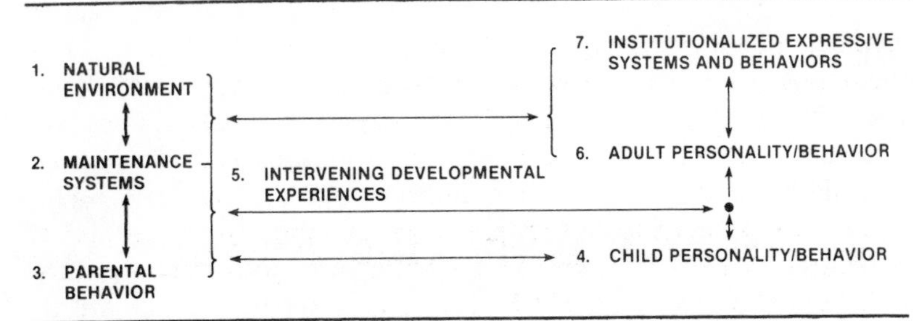

Figure 5 Parental Acceptance-Rejection Theory Sociocultural Systems Model

form of the model was created in 1939 by Abram Kardiner, a psychiatrist with strong interest in anthropology. Whiting and Child (1953) revised Kardiner's model in 1953, and subsequently Whiting and Whiting revised the model several times. Drawing stimulus from Kardiner (1939, 1945a, 1945b) and Whiting and Child (1953), the PAR theory version of the model was created in 1966, but it was published for the first time in 1975 (Rohner, 1975). The sociocultural systems model attempts in a generalized way to show interrelationships among categories of variables within sociocultural systems. This schema attempts to connect children's socialization experiences with personality, and in turn to connect these to sociocultural processes.

The model shown in Figure 5 contains seven elements: (a) the natural environment, (b) maintenance systems, (c) parental behavior, (d) child personality and behavior, (e) intervening developmental experiences, (f) adult personality and behavior, and (g) institutionalized expressive systems and behaviors. *Natural environment* refers to climate, terrain, flora and fauna, altitude, temperature, and the availability of minerals—in short, to all those things pertaining to the physical world humans live in, adjust to, and are affected by. Human beings in turn also affect the natural environment, especially through their technology, which is part of society's "maintenance systems." This relationship is indicated in Figure 5 by the double-headed arrow joining "natural environment" with "maintenance systems." (Elements in the model joined by double-headed arrows are believed to have mutual influences.) The mutual interdependency between environment and maintenance systems is sometimes referred to as the "ecological system."

Maintenance systems within society are those features of a sociocultural system that ensure the survival of the family and members of the community, and they help maintain the integrity of the population in its physical and cultural sense (Whiting and Child, 1953). Maintenance systems include the ways people make a living, ensure social control, and ensure the procreation and successful rearing of children. Phrased in common anthropological parlance, these include such social institutions as economic organization, political structure, systems of defense, family structure, household organization, settlement pattern, and so forth—all the things that bear directly on the survival of a culturally organized population within its environment.

Parental behavior refers to the caretaking behaviors and beliefs of parents. PAR theorists, of course, are especially interested in the warmth dimensions of parenting, but also in parental control and similar dimensions.[1] As indicated earlier, I am most interested in explaining why some parents are warmer than other parents—why some parents are accepting and some are rejecting. Do features of the natural environment or maintenance systems predict reliably whether or not parents everywhere tend to be warm or not warm toward their children? As indicated by the double-headed arrow pointing from maintenance systems toward parental behavior, PAR theory predicts that features of the maintenance systems (for example, household structure, and some subsistence economies) do tend to be associated with certain forms of parenting described in the next chapter. The double-headed arrow also indicates that some aspects of parental behavior may affect some maintenance systems. For example, if enough parents prohibit their offspring from frequenting local video game arcades or other recreational facilities, the facilities (that is, maintenance-systems elements within the local economic structure) will be forced out of business. Parental behavior, too, may directly or indirectly affect curriculum and school activities (that is, the educational institution, which is also an element within societal maintenance systems).

The interaction between parental behavior and *child personality/behavior* is often more directly evident than the relationship just discussed, and is the focus of the latter part of this chapter.

If PAR theory dealt only with a simple "parent effect" perspective (Bell, 1968), the social systems model would have a single arrow pointing from parental behavior to child personality. In reality, however—as everyone who deals with children knows—children constantly initiate action and interaction with their parents. A great part of being a parent is responding to stimulation from one's children, not just initiating to children (Yarrow, 1977; Lewis and Rosenblum, 1974). A significant part of children's behavior and personality is self-produced, or self-initiated (Bell and Harper, 1980). This point of view is opposed to the classic Freudian or psychodynamic orientation—sometimes referred to in the developmental literature as the "social mold" theory or development—which says, in effect, that children are empty vessels to be molded, shaped, or filled by their parents.

A child's endogenous temperament is also a source of stimulation to parents (Buss and Plomin, 1975; Bates, 1980; Strelau, 1983; Thomas and Chess, 1977; Thomas et al., 1968). Some infants and children, for example, are more excitable than others, some are relatively phlegmatic or active, quiet or irritable, impulsive or controlled, sociable or shy and withdrawn. Temperament theorists such as Buss and Plomin (1975) argue for the primacy of factors such as these in the parent-child dyad. So far, however—except when employing the "multivariate approach" to research discussed later—PAR theory has concentrated little on the *reciprocal* influence between children and parents. Like the vast majority of developmentalists, PART researchers have tended to focus more on the presumed "causal" influences flowing from parent to child. This is recognized as a limitation in the work accomplished so far—but it is a limitation of the work completed, not of the theory itself.

The principal concern of PART's personality theory is the relationship between acceptance-rejection and a constellation of seven personality characteristics in children, a cluster of dispositions that are outcomes of varying degrees of parental acceptance-rejection experienced by children. As described more fully later, these personality dispositions include manifestations of hostility and aggression, dependence or defensive independence, self-esteem, self-adequacy, emotional responsiveness, emotional stability, and worldview. Moreover, PAR theory's "coping theory" tends to concentrate on a cluster of social-cognitive attributes, including sense of self, self-determination, and personalizing. No doubt as the theory continues to be developed other social-cognitive and personality dispositions will become featured.

Referring again to Figure 5, the double-headed arrow above "child personality/behavior" rises to a dot, joining two additional elements in the sociocultural systems model, namely, "intervening developmental experiences" and "adult personality/behavior." A single-headed arrow lies above the dot. That arrow reveals the only nonreciprocal relation in the system, namely, the inevitable truth that having lived one's life, one cannot go back in time to alter it in the slightest detail. The double-headed arrow above "child personality" denotes the fact that as people mature from childhood to adulthood they interact not only with parents, but with increasingly larger portions of the sociocultural system—the maintenance systems, expressive systems, and natural environment. This interaction is portrayed in the schema as *intervening developmental experiences* connecting the developing child with all other aspects of the sociocultural system. This segment of the sociocultural systems model implies the time dimension, though in fact the whole model should also be conceived as moving through time, as individuals and societies change.

Intervening developmental experiences are important in PAR theory as potential sources of change, altering the usual outcome of the rejection process. For example, PAR theory predicts that the effects of rejection may be muted insofar as the rejected child is able to establish a warm, trusting relationship with someone, such as a peer, a teacher, a neighbor, or the other, nonrejecting parent. In the absence of such benign intervening experiences, PAR theory predicts that the constellation of personality and behavioral dispositions affecting rejected children are likely to affect *adult personality/behavior.* Many adults, however, seem to have rewarding experiences to some degree as they grow up, experiences that deintensify expected outcomes of perceived rejection. Moreover, there may be an endogenous, phylogenetically acquired, self-righting directional tendency in human development. Sameroff and Chandler (1975: 235) elucidate this possibility:

> The human organism appears to have been programmed by the course of evolution to produce normal development outcomes under all but the most adverse of circumstances (Waddington, 1966). Any understanding of deviances in outcome must be seen in the light of this self-righting and self-organizing tendency which appears to move children towards normality in the face of pressure towards deviation.

As viewed in the sociocultural systems model, institutionalized expressive systems and behaviors originate as extensions or expressions of personality, but, once created, the expressive systems also react back onto thought and behavior of people. This postulation is shown in Figure 5 by a double-headed arrow connecting "adult personality/

behavior" and "institutionalized expressive systems and behaviors." Institutionalized expressive systems and individualized expressive behaviors are ubiquitous but essentially nonutilitarian features of a sociocultural system. They are called "expressive" because, as I said earlier, they are believed to express or reflect people's internal psychological states. From an anthropological point of view, institutionalized expressive systems include the religious beliefs of a people, their recreational preferences, their artistic and musical traditions, their games, folklore, certain medical beliefs, and the like. For example, why do some people in some cultural systems believe in the evil eye as a source of illness and death, and people in other such systems do not? Within a given society why do some believe that God is harsh and punitive whereas others believe God is warm and loving—and still others do not believe in God at all? These are expressive beliefs that covary with other life experiences, including the experience of parental warmth or rejection in children.

It is important to remember that institutionalized expressive systems are believed in PAR theory to be symbolic creations of many individuals over time, and as people change, expressive systems and expressive behaviors also change. Sometimes, expressive systems change very slowly and when such occasions arise participants in the system may experience increasing tension or dissatisfaction. The great religious traditions of Christianity, Judaism, Islam, and Hinduism provide cases in point. All have been codified in writing for centuries. By referring to the written scriptures, vested religious authorities can dictate at any time how things should be. Paradoxically, this "strength" can also be a weakness. Occasionally, the written scriptures are perceived by the believers to be inconsistent with or nonsupportive of the lived-in world experienced day to day. But because the religious beliefs are cast in stone, as it were—and have the weight of authority and history behind them—they tend to change grudgingly, if at all. They therefore may no longer satisfy the expressive needs of the believers. Nonwritten religious traditions, transmitted by oral history from elders to young people, are more susceptible to gradual and steady reformulation over time, and hence they tend to be more in tune with psychological and material reality perceived by the members of society.

At any given point in time, institutionalized expressive systems exist before children reach adulthood. And, as I said earlier, although expressive systems are human creations, once created they affect the subsequent behavior of humans. For example, some populations believe in sorcery and witchcraft. Knowledge that powerful others have the ability to manipulate events in malevolent ways influences individuals' behaviors in certain contexts. Indeed, important features of the maintenance systems, parental behavior, and other aspects of sociocultural systems may be shaped in significant ways by the institutionalized beliefs in sorcery, witchcraft, or a malevolent supernatural. Otterbein and Otterbein (1973), for example, found just that in their interviews with twenty caretakers in the Bahama Islands: Eleven parents there who believed in the malevolent supernatural treated their children more harshly than the nine parents interviewed who believed in a more benevolent supernatural.

One final set of observations about the sociocultural systems model seems in order. As the caption to Figure 5 suggests, sociocultural systems tend to be systems in which sets of beliefs and institutionalized behaviors are related to each other in such a way that if a change is made in one element a change in at least one other element is likely to occur. There may also be places in a sociocultural system where a major change will reverberate throughout the entire system. There is, then, interconnectedness within a sociocultural system, very loose interconnectedness in some places and very tight in others, but overall I imagine a sociocultural system to form a "system"—and that is what the model in Figure 5 tries to convey.

If this line of reasoning is correct, then behavior in any given segment of the model should correlate significantly with behavior in other segments of the model, especially those behaviors noted by the arrows shown in the model. PAR theory focuses on the implications of this conception as they relate to the antecedents, consequences, and correlates of the warmth dimension. I begin that task by examining the empirical relationship between parental acceptance-rejection and the natural environment.

PARENTAL ACCEPTANCE-REJECTION AND THE NATURAL ENVIRONMENT

Throughout history—from the time of ancient Greeks such as Aristotle and Pliny the Elder to the recent past—claims have been made about the governing influence of climate and other environmental forces on people's lives (see Netting, 1971; Sahlins, 1964). I doubt that natural environment very often has a directly determining effect on such things as a population's child-rearing practices, but environment certainly may influence other aspects of a sociocultural system such as a people's subsistence economy, and, in turn, it may have a second-order effect on parenting.

Little empirical evidence exists about the direct impact of environment—that is, of flora, fauna, climate, terrain, and the like—on acceptance-rejection, beyond a weak tendency for parents in comfortably warm, dry climates to accept their children to a slightly greater degree, on the average, than do parents in hot, humid, tropical climates ($r = .18$, $p < .10$; Rohner, 1975). Why this relationship exists is unclear. I suspect, though, that future research will show it to be an artifact of some third, currently unidentified and unmeasured, variable.

PARENTAL ACCEPTANCE-REJECTION AND MAINTENANCE SYSTEMS

Parents behave as they do toward their children for many reasons: because that is the way they themselves were raised, because that is the way the sociocultural norms say children should be raised, because of idiosyncratic personality dispositions of the parents in response to the specific behavior of the child, and the like. Maintenance systems within a society also dispose parents to behave one way or another—sometimes undisguisedly so, sometimes subtly; sometimes parents are consciously aware of the influence, sometimes they are not.

Parental Acceptance-Rejection and Household Structure

Household structure, for example, is universally (cross-culturally) an important maintenance system affecting styles of parenting (Levinson and Malone, 1980). The single-parent family—which is typically a mother-child household—is the simplest form of family structure anywhere, and, as shown later, this household form is also at greatest risk for rejection, especially if the mother is socially isolated with one or more children.

The "nuclear" family household, in which fathers live with their wives and children, is the preferred form of household structure throughout most of the United States and the next most common familial unit found widely throughout the world. The voluntary presence of fathers in households the world over is a significant predictor of greater acceptance toward children (Rohner, 1975) in part because fathers can relieve mothers of the burden of continuous child care. The next most common family form found around the world is the three-generation "stem" family household, in which a nuclear family lives with one set of grandparents (Murdock, 1949). It tends to be associated with the greatest parental acceptance (Rohner, 1975) because the mother is provided a live-in alternative caretaker—a grandparent—usually the grandmother, who herself is frequently past childbearing age and is often no longer economically productive. Continual availability of grandparents to help with child care frees the mother from the tension of unremitting interaction with young children. Family structures beyond the stem family—for example, the "joint" family of India—become increasingly complex. Forces other than frequency and intensity of interaction determine whether the children are accepted or rejected in these families (Minturn and Lambert, 1964).

The possibility of reducing continuous interaction with children seems to be the primary structural factor having predictive power for acceptance-rejection in different forms of households (Colletta, 1981). Parents are likely to become irritable and to withdraw some of the warmth they normally feel whenever they are trapped over a long period of time in isolated confinement with one or more small children. Millions of mothers the world over find themselves in just such isolation, brought about by culturally stipulated household structure; by divorce, death, or desertion; and by other social, cultural, and personal factors.

For reasons such as these one would expect to find less acceptance in mother-child families than in any other form of household. Nuclear family households should be intermediate in parental acceptance, and stem family households should be associated with the greatest acceptance. Cross-culturally this is precisely what was found in a holocultural sample of 35 societies (Rohner, 1975). As reported by Kellam et al. (1977), these trends also seem to hold true in the United States. That is, these authors found that mother-child households in the United States entail the highest risk in terms of social maladaptation and the non-well-being of children.[2] Moreover, according to these authors, mother-grandmother households in the United States are nearly as good in terms of parental acceptance as nuclear families with mother, father, and children in residence together. Social isolation, they conclude, is a more significant risk factor in maternal behavior than absence of the father. This conclusion has been affirmed repeatedly in the child abuse literature in North America and elsewhere (Gerbner et al., 1980). The child abuse literature (for example, Elmer, 1967; Garbarino, 1976; Garbarino and Crouter, 1978; Gil, 1970) repeatedly suggests that one of the significant risk factors associated with child maltreatment is the isolated parent's sense of loneliness and alienation from the surrounding community and other possible sources of social and emotional support.

A variety of conditions other than household structure per se can affect the form, frequency, and intensity of maternal interaction with children. For example, in addition to bringing people into the home (as happens with the creation of stem families) or losing people (as often happens in the creation of the mother-child household in America), the mother can send her children out (for example, to day care) or she herself can go out (for example, to work). All these options can reduce isolation effects. Moreover, the number of children in a family can significantly affect the warmth that children experience. Drawing from a sample of 28 college females, for example, Lavigne (1984) found that even though all the women reported a substantial amount of maternal acceptance at home, college women who came from families with four or more siblings perceived significantly less overall maternal acceptance as measured by the PARQ than women who came from families with one to three siblings (Fisher's exact, $p = .01$). Nuttal and Nuttal (1971) found the same effect in Puerto Rico, where they worked with a sample of 5370 students attending public and private schools.

Parental Acceptance-Rejection and the Presence of Fathers

Earlier, I said that the willing presence of fathers in a household is a significant predictor of acceptance. I will now amplify on that assertion. The relation between "importance of father" as a major caretaker and parental acceptance-rejection was examined in two holocultural studies. Both studies show that the more important fathers are as caretakers, the more children are likely to be accepted. The first study of 78 societies (Rohner, 1975) shows a significant relationship between overall parental acceptance and importance of fathers ($r = .40$, $p = .0005$). The second study used the Standard Cross-Cultural Sample of 186 societies (Rohner and Rohner, 1982). The authors of this study divided the acceptance-rejection dimension into three components, and showed that paternal warmth is correlated worldwide with importance of fathers ($r = .57$, $p < .001$); paternal indifference was negatively correlated with fathers' importance ($r = -.51$, $p < .001$), that is, the more important fathers are as caretakers, the less indifferent they are; paternal hostility, however, was not related significantly to fathers' caretaking importance ($r = .27$, $p =$ n.s.). These results become more significant in view of the fact that "importance of mothers" as caretakers cross-culturally correlated less well than did "importance of fathers" with overall parental acceptance-rejection ($r = .29$, $p = .005$).

Neither maternal warmth nor maternal hostility related significantly to mothers' importance as caretakers ($r = .10$, $p =$ n.s., and $r = .05$, $p =$ n.s., respectively). Maternal indifference, however, was related firmly to mothers' importance in that the more indifferent mothers around the world are toward their children, the less important they tend to be as primary caretakers ($r = -.50$, $p < .001$). I might also note here that the more important mothers are as primary caretakers transculturally, the more controlling they tend to be ($r = .42$, $p < .01$), but no such relationship holds for fathers ($r = -.17$, $p =$ n.s.) (Rohner and Rohner, 1982).

Additional evidence also points to the importance of fathers in the acceptance-rejection process. For example, in a holocultural sample of 26 societies, the relative "presence" of fathers in households (from a minimum presence, where, for example, fathers sleep in a men's house with the other men of the community, to maximum presence, where the father is almost always available to the child) was correlated positively with overall parental acceptance. That is, parental acceptance increases insofar as the fathers are maximally available in the household (Rohner, 1975). I should caution, however, that the fathers are effective caretakers only to the degree that they are willing caretakers. Fathers who are involuntarily confined at home because of unemployment or illness may resent being there and may resent having to deal with their children. Child abuse and other literature shows how vulnerable families may be to all forms of intrafamily disruption and violence when the father is unwillingly confined at home (Gelles, 1980; Elder, 1985).

AN EVOLUTIONARY PERSPECTIVE ON ACCEPTANCE-REJECTION AND SUBSISTENCE ECONOMY

In this section I will shift focus and discuss how "occupation," or the ways people make their livings (that is, subsistence economy), can shape accepting versus rejecting and other behaviors toward children. Barry et al. (1959) were the first to address this question holoculturally. They studied the child training practices of "low versus high food-accumulating" societies (hunters and gatherers and fishermen versus argiculturalists and pastoralists, respectively). They found in a sample of 104 societies that parents in low food-accumulation societies tend to be assertive—that is, to be self-reliant and achievement oriented. Parents in high food-accumulation societies, on the other hand, put greater pressures on their children than in low food-accumulation societies to be compliant—that is, to be obedient and responsible ($p = .001$).

A subsequent study looked at the relationship between parental acceptance-rejection and subsistence economy (Rohner, 1975). Specifically, hunters were compared with pastoralists (Murdock, 1967). The rationale for such a comparison was essentially this: Pastoralists have a guaranteed food supply as long as they keep their livestock alive, but food supplies for hunters are less assured. Many hunters have to forage for food day to day, and it is often impossible to accumulate a safe reserve. So, overall, hunters may be more vulnerable in that their survival is often in greater jeopardy than is the survival of agriculturalists and pastoralists. Results of this comparison showed that none of the hunters in the sample rejected their children, whereas a few of the pastoralists did. A review of world ethnography uncovers no true hunting society anywhere where children are typically rejected.[3] Hunters can be demanding disciplinarians, and they can be quite controlling, but they all seem to be reasonably warm and accepting. Parents in all other economic systems (for example, industrialism, agriculture, pastoralism, fishing) do sometimes reject their children.

Why should such a difference exist between hunting and other forms of economy? I believe that true hunters such as the Eskimo or the Plains Indians in the United States during aboriginal times—the Cheyenne Indians, for example—not only did not reject their children, but could not reject them if that kind of society was to survive, because rejection produces characteristics that are probably maladaptive for successful hunting. It seems plausible, for example, that personality dispositions such as emotional stability, positive feelings of self-adequacy and self-esteem, a sense of self-determination, and a positive worldview—all of which are associated with parental acceptance—are more adaptive in a hunting context than are their contraries. Persons who have these dispositions can, psychologically, more easily leave the security of the campsite to go on a food quest in an often hazardous, demanding, and uncertain environment. Insofar as they are successful, their families are likely to survive, their children are more likely to reach reproductive age, to marry, and to bear children of their own—and to raise their children in the way they had been raised, with warmth and affection.

Hunters who have been seriously rejected do not have this constellation of adaptive personality traits. As a result, one might expect the families of these people to fare less well over time than families of accepted hunters who have a selective advantage, in a Darwinian sense (Konner, 1982). Fewer offspring of the rejecting hunter reach child-bearing age. Those who do and who treat their own children as they have been treated (that is, rejected) place their offspring at risk. As the generations pass, fewer and fewer of these people survive to perpetuate the rejection cycle. The net effect is—if rejecting hunters ever existed in the course of human evolution over the past several million years—they have now vanished in favor of the adaptive "accepting" style of parenting.

Insofar as this line of reasoning is correct, it has implications for the history of rejection and child abuse. Humankind has spent about 99.7% of its existence (since the time of the australopithecines 4.5 million years ago) as hunters and foragers. For reasons described above, humankind was also presumably fairly warm and accepting toward their children during this hunting stage. It was not until about 12,000 years ago that agriculture was invented, and industrialization has existed for only about 200 years. History amply documents rejection, abuse, and violence against children since the beginning of the Industrial Revolution, and even to the time of Christ, 2,000 years ago (Payne, 1916; deMause, 1982; Despert, 1970). It is unclear, however, whether rejection goes back 12,000 years to the time of incipient agriculture in the Western world. The archaeological record can probably never tell us, but from the evolutionary perspective of 4.5 million years, even this date is very recent—and so too, presumably, is rejection.

The plausibility of the argument regarding the evolutionary recency of parental rejection is enhanced when one considers that the evolution of sociocultural systems has been marked by development from simpler forms (such as hunting societies) to more complex forms (such as industrialized nations) (Erikson, 1977; Murdock and Provost, 1973; Naroll, 1973; Naroll and Divale, 1976)—and that parental acceptance-rejection correlates significantly with cultural complexity ($r = .30$, $p = .025$). The more complex a sociocultural system is, the less warm parents in general tend to be (Rohner, 1975); not dramatically less warm, but measurably so. This raises a troubling question in terms of increased human suffering: At what cost have contemporary humans created technologically complex but impersonal, and violence-prone, industrialized societies?

NOTES

1. The two dimensions of parental warmth and parental control are emphasized here because they have been shown repeatedly in factor-analytic studies to explain the greatest percentage of the variance in parents' behavior toward children (see Rohner and Pettingill, 1985). Warmth (that is, acceptance-rejection) and control (that is, permissiveness-strictness) factors seem to emerge consistently in these factor-analytic studies, regardless of whose point of view is studied, including the following: parents' accounts of their treatment of (versus attitudes toward) children (Sears et al., 1957; Peterson and Migliorino, 1967a, 1967b); parents' attitudes toward (versus actual treatment of) children (Cline et al., 1963; Nichols, 1962; Schaefer, 1959); direct observation of parental-child interaction (Baldwin et al., 1949); adults' retrospective reports of the treatment they received as children (Roe and Siegelman, 1963; Seigelman, 1965a); and childrens' reports of parental behavior (Renson et al., 1968; Schludermann and Schludermann, 1970, 1983; Saavedra, 1977; Seigelman, 1965b, 1966).

These factor-analytic studies also suggest that, overall, parental warmth and parental control are more or less independent of each other (Goldin, 1969; Martin, 1975; Maccoby and Martin, 1983; Schwarz et al., 1985). That is, on the average, knowing how warm parents are toward their children gives no basis for predicting how controlling they are: Warm parents can be very strict or they can be very permissive, and the same holds true for rejecting parents. Warmth and control seem to have different effects on children, however, and they seem to interact with each other in important ways to produce distinctive outcomes in children and youths. For example, many "acting out," aggressive, noncompliant delinquents seem to come from extremely permissive, rejecting homes (Nielson, 1984; Becker, 1964; Duncan, 1971; Glueck and Glueck, 1950), whereas children from punishing or restrictively controlling and rejecting homes often display certain psychiatric problems of social withdrawal (Becker, 1964; Seigelman, 1968), turning anger against themselves, and, perhaps, depression (Goldin, 1969).

2. Similarly, in a study of 558 seventh-, eighth-, and ninth-grade students, Rosenthal et al. (1980) found that single-parent households are associated with more impaired self-

concept of youths than are two-parent households. Bilge and Kaufman (1983), however, offer a proper cautionary note about overemphasizing the potential hazards of single-parent households.

3. I specify here "true" hunters. Many sociocultural systems include some hunting in their subsistence activities, but they are called "true" hunters in this work only if hunting per se contributed 50% or more to their subsistence (Murdock and Morrow, 1970). The other 50% might be contributed by gathering, or by some other economic activity.

4

PART's Personality Theory and Its Historical Antecedents

The preceding chapter dealt with the first two elements in PART's sociocultural systems model. This chapter focuses on the third through sixth elements in the model—that is, on the relationship between parental behavior and personality of children and adults—and to a modest extent on experiences intervening between childhood and adulthood (for example, peer-group relations over time). More specifically, I will concentrate here on a discussion of the expectable personality outcomes of parental rejection as postulated in PART's personality theory. First, however, I will briefly review salient historical work that ultimately led me to develop PART's personality theory. I will also review other consequences of rejection not highlighted currently in the theory.

HISTORICAL ANTECEDENTS TO PARENTAL ACCEPTANCE-REJECTION THEORY

Although systematic research on parent-child relations began in the 1890s (Stogdill, 1937), it was not until the 1930s that a substantial body of empirical work appeared regarding the antecedents and especially the effects of parental acceptance-rejection and parental control. Much of the impetus for this early work came from psychoanalytic theory and from clinical settings where disturbed children were treated (see, for example, Bender and Yarnell, 1941; Bowlby, 1940, 1944; Burlingham and Freud, 1944; Ferenczi, 1929; Horney, 1937; Levy, 1943).

A major program of research that included the warmth dimension during the 1930s came from the Fels Research Institute, where, in 1937, Champney (1941) developed the Fels Parent Behavior Rating Scales.

These scales were used extensively from the 1930s into the 1960s (see, for example, Baldwin et al., 1945, 1949; Becker 1960; Medinnus, 1959, 1961; Peterson et al., 1959; Roff, 1949; Waters and Crandall, 1964). During the 1930s the Smith College Studies in Social Work also produced a long and useful series of research papers on the effects of parental acceptance-rejection (see, for example, Cole, 1933; Foley, 1932; Franchot, 1941; Knight, 1933; Witmer et al., 1938). And toward the close of the decade Symonds (1939) published an important book-length conceptualization of parental acceptance-rejection and parental control (see also Symonds, 1949), in which he reviewed the existing literature regarding the then current thinking and research on acceptance-rejection and parental control, and their effects on children's behavior.

A major result of much of this early work was the documentation of the wide variety of different personality and behavioral problems associated with parental rejection. Rarely, however, did one study follow from or build logically upon prior research. The net effect was a laterally spreading versus hierarchically cumulative body of knowledge about the antecedents and effects of parental acceptance and rejection. This state of affairs has tended to continue over the succeeding decades, but at an accelerating rate. The 1930s through the 1960s, especially, saw an acceleration in the production of publications on parental acceptance-rejection: About two dozen articles and books were written in the 1930s on issues related to acceptance-rejection, but by the 1960s this number had risen to well over 100. Since then, however, the level of involvement in parental warmth-related research has declined slightly.[1]

Of particular note during the late 1950s and the 1960s was the publication of several seminal and trend-setting series of papers. Especially noteworthy was the work of Schaefer and associates, who formulated and documented an important conceptual framework for understanding parental behavior (see, for example, Bayley and Schaefer, 1960; Renson et al., 1968; Schaefer, 1959, 1961, 1965; Schaefer and Bayley, 1960, 1967; Schaefer and Bell, 1957). More specifically, through the use of factor analysis, Schaefer (for example, 1959, 1961) shows clearly the salience of the warmth and control dimensions of parenting. Schaefer's program of research using the Children's Report of Parent's Behavior Inventory was continued into the 1970s and 1980s by Schludermann and Schludermann (1970, 1971, 1983).

Also noteworthy from the 1960s onward is Siegelman's research dealing with effects of perceived parental acceptance-rejection and perceived parental control on children's and youths' behavioral dispositions (see, for example, Roe and Siegelman, 1963, 1964; Siegelman, 1965a, 1965b, 1966, 1973, 1974).

My own research leading ultimately to the formulation and testing of parental acceptance-rejection theory was instigated in 1960 by a statement made by Coleman (1956: 117):

> In general, . . . rejected children tend to be fearful, insecure, attention-seeking, jealous, hostile, and lonely (Wolberg, 1944). Many of these children have difficulty in later life expressing and responding to affection.
>
> When the parents are actively rejecting, a highly emotional, nonconformist attitude is typically engendered, with open rebellion against the pressures and restrictions of the environment, and various antisocial patterns such as lying, stealing, promiscuity, or other delinquent behavior (Baldwin [et al.], 1945). Probably all conditions of rejection are conducive to self-devaluation and to an evaluation of the world as an insecure and dangerous place, thus inhibiting normal spontaneity and the confident reality testing essential for normal development.

As I read this I wondered if these claims were true for humans everywhere, or whether they might be culture bound, so I conducted a small holocultural study using nineteen societies scattered widely around the world (Rohner, 1960b). I was electrified to find that Coleman's claims about rejected children tending to be more hostile and aggressive and tending to have more negative worldviews than accepted children were apparently true, not simply in the United States but all over the world. The relation between parental rejection and self-esteem emerged in this holocultural study as being more problematic.

These results prompted me to undertake a more thorough inquiry into the cross-cultural antecedents and consequences of parental acceptance-rejection, but at that time no adequate theory or methodology existed to guide my research in the cross-cultural domain. So, my first problem was to find out how parental acceptance-rejection is expressed by parents in different sociocultural settings, and then to develop a set of procedures for studying the warmth dimension appropriately in cross-cultural comparative contexts (including holoculturally), as well as intraculturally. This quest led to a detailed intracultural analysis of parental rejection in three societies of the Pacific (Rohner 1960a), and to a large, methodologically detailed holocultural study employing a representative sample of 101 known and adequately described sociocultural systems of the world (Rohner, 1975). Results of these two studies—as well as of several smaller, intervening cross-cultural studies, not to mention the many other studies already completed in the United States by other researchers—persuaded me that the warmth dimension of parenting did indeed have consistent effects on children and adults everywhere, regardless of variations in class, race, ethnicity, culture, or time period.

EFFECTS OF PARENTAL REJECTION: AN OVERVIEW

Children who perform poorly on IQ tests also tend to do poorly in school, but children who score well on IQ tests do not necessarily do well in school. By the same token, children who perceive themselves to be rejected tend to develop certain social, behavioral, and emotional problems. Knowing that children feel accepted, however, is not always sufficient for predicting positive psychological adjustment. Unrelated events can intrude into the lives of loved children and lead them into difficulties. Exceptions notwithstanding, it seems quite clear from research going back to the 1930s that, on the average, parental rejection by itself is often sufficient to produce specific outcomes in children's behavior. Rejection is also a "lurking" variable in many behavioral disorders in that it is implicated, though not always directly, in a great many social, emotional, and cognitive problems of both children and adults.

About 800 studies have been completed since the 1930s on parental acceptance-rejection and their antecedents, but especially their consequences. Many of these studies were reviewed by Rohner and Rohner (1975) and by Rohner and Nielsen (1978). In that literature it seems quite clear that the effects of rejection often but not inevitably have serious consequences for personality development and personality functioning. For example, rejection has been implicated directly and indirectly in the etiology of acting out and conduct disorders (see, for example, Becker, 1960; Nielsen, 1983; Peterson et al., 1961; Salama, 1984), vandalism (Shulman et al., 1962), delinquency (Ahlstrom and Havighurst, 1971; Bachman, 1970; Conger and Miller, 1966).[2] Parental rejection has also been found repeatedly in the family background of drug and alcohol abusers (Campo, 1985; Baer and Corrado, 1974; Frank, 1980; Linblad, 1977; Tec, 1970).[3] Moreover, rejection has been found to antedate developmental and personality issues such as impairment in the development of moral reasoning and moral behavior (Hoffman, 1970; Bilbro et al., 1979), disturbed body image (Schonfeld, 1966), stuttering (Kinstler, 1961), and a wide variety of specific personality dispositions (see Rohner and Nielsen, 1978, for an extended annotated bibliography of relevant publications).

Rejected children have often been found to have greater academic and intellectual-performance problems than accepted children: They tend to perform less well on standardized achievement and IQ tests (Chan, 1981; Manley, 1977), for example, and they tend to perform less well in school (see Sheintuch and Lewin, 1981; Starkey, 1980). In relation to accepted children and adults, rejected persons also tend to have greater interpersonal-relations problems, including disturbed friendship and peer relations (Levy, 1943), more anxious introversiveness (versus extraversion) (Roe and Siegelman, 1964; Siegelman, 1965a), to report less satisfaction in marital relations (Sadeghi, 1982), and to report more negative changes in marital adjustment in the transition to parenthood (Belsky and Isabella, 1985).

Finally, parental rejection has been reported in a wide variety of mental and physical health issues. For example, rejection has been implicated in several psychophysiological problems such as allergies (Miller and Baruch, 1948, 1950), asthma and other respiratory ailments (Jacobs, et al., 1972), and hypertension (McGinn, 1963). Rejection has also been implicated in numerous forms of psychiatric disorders, including neuroses (Horney, 1937, 1945; Jacobs et al., 1972), emotional adjustment disorders (Adler, 1963; Goldin, 1969; Salama, 1984), and perhaps schizophrenia (Heilbrun, 1973; Kohn, 1973; Nielsen, 1983). As more and more evidence is found for genetic predispositions for schizophrenia (Rosenthal, 1970), however, there is increasing doubt that rejection is related to the illness in a directly causal way. The stress generated by rejection may simply be one of several classes of elements that is associated with the onset of schizophrenia. Autism is also an area in the clinical literature where historically rejection has figured prominently, and where currently there is increasing doubt about its causal primacy (Cohen and Shaywitz, 1982; Schreibman and Koegel, 1975). When these profoundly withdrawn children come to clinics at approximately 2 to 4 years of age, clinicians often observe cold, withdrawn parents who have trouble coping with their anger. At one time clinicians assumed that small children became autistic as a way of coping with cold, withdrawn, angry parents (Kanner 1943, 1949). As time has passed, however, it has become increasingly clear that coldness and emotional withdrawal may be the parents' way of trying to cope with a child who, unlike most infants, does not cuddle, make eye contact, or do the other things that seem to be so important in the parental bonding process. After a while parents may begin to ask, "What have I done? What have I created? Why isn't my child like other children?" Parents may cut off their affect toward the child, and then ultimately come to the clinic and appear cold and unresponsive, that is, rejecting.

PERSONALITY DISPOSITIONS EMPHASIZED IN PART'S PERSONALITY THEORY

It is obviously infeasible in a single theory or program of research to incorporate all these disparate correlates and consequences of parental acceptance and rejection, so PART's personality theory focuses instead on a limited constellation of personality dispositions that seem to characterize rejected children and adults the world over. These dispositions include dependence or defensive independence, depending on the degree and form of rejection; emotional unresponsiveness; hostility, aggression, passive aggression, or problems with the management of hostility and aggression; negative self-esteem; negative self-adequacy; negative worldview; and emotional instability.

Listing these personality dispositions in the way I do here highlights the "negative" end of the personality continua, the end most closely associated theoretically with rejection (versus acceptance). An essential point here is that each of these personality dispositions falls on a continuum of "more" or "less" (for example, more or less emotionally responsive or unresponsive). Humans everywhere can be placed somewhere along each of these seven continua. All of us are, for example, more or less emotionally responsive or unresponsive, more or less dependent or independent, and so forth.

The Seven Personality Dispositions Defined

Because these seven dispositions are central to PART's personality theory, it is important to explain what they mean within the context of the theory. With that thought in mind I shall define and describe each disposition somewhat more fully here, and then I shall discuss the theoretical connections between acceptance-rejection and these characteristics.

Dependence. This is probably the most controversial and complicated of the seven personality dispositions associated with parental acceptance-rejection, partly because the developmental literature itself is inconsistent on the meaning of the term. The word "dependence" is sometimes used to mean one thing and the word "independence" is used to mean a qualitatively different phenomenon (for example, Beller, 1955; Heathers, 1955). In personality theory, however, dependence is used to define one end of a behavioral continuum with independence defining the other end. Conceptually, "dependence" refers to the *emotional* reliance of one person on another for comfort, approval, guidance, reassurance, and the like. "Independence," at the other end of the continuum, refers here to the essential absence of such emotional reliance on other people, or at least freedom from the need or wish to make these bids very frequently. Operationally, dependence is revealed by the bids children (and adults) make for positive response. Children do not always bid for *positive* response, of course; sometimes their behavior is simply an attention-getting attempt, and can be very negative and disruptive. Insofar as children seek emotional comfort, affection, approval, support, or reassurance, however, they are by definition being dependent.[4] Other behavioral indicators of dependence among children include clinging; attention-getting behavior; becoming anxious, insecure, whiny, or weepy when separated from the parent; and waiting for or demanding a nurturant response of someone, usually the parent.

Adults too are dependent in varying degrees, and their dependence is measured by essentially the same behaviors as children's. Specific manifestations vary, but include the seeking of comfort, nurturance, reassurance, approval, support from others—especially people who are important to the individual, such as friends and family members. To make all this more personal, let me ask, To what extent do *you* solicit or enjoy getting sympathy, consolation, encouragement, or affection when you are not feeling well, or when you are having some difficulty? To what extent do you seek help when you are having personal problems? Do you like having people feel sorry for you or make a fuss over you when you are sick? These are all indicators of dependence in which normal people engage—in varying degrees—all the time.

The independent person is one who does not often rely on others for emotional support, encouragement, reassurance, comfort, and so forth, who does not often feel the need to make these bids for positive response, who does not feel the need to seek or try to evoke sympathy from friends and family when troubled or hurt, and the like. Emotionally healthy adults are able to make these bids from time to time. The important issue is how often and how intensely one feels the need for such positive response.

The developmental literature not infrequently confuses "independence" with "self-reliance." Indeed, the two terms are often used interchangeably. In personality theory, however, a distinction is made between them in that "self-reliance" is used to refer to *instrumental* needs, whereas "independence" is used to refer to *emotional* needs. More specifically, "self-reliance" refers to task-oriented behaviors, as, for example, when you seek out someone to help you complete a task or to make decisions about tasks, activities, and actions. Every now and then, when she was a young child, my daughter approached me saying, "Daddy, help me take the knot out of my shoestring." Insofar as that was purely a request for help with a task, it pertained to low self-reliance, but when it was an attempt to get attention from me it became dependence. The distinction is sometimes subtle and is often difficult to make. The critical difference, however, is that one incident deals with instrumental activities or task-oriented behaviors, and the other deals with emotional responses.

Emotional Responsiveness. This is an easier and more straightforward disposition to describe than dependence. It refers to a person's ability to express freely and openly his or her emotions, for example, feelings of warmth and affection toward another person. Emotional responsiveness is revealed by the spontaneity and ease with which a person is able to respond emotionally to another person, the extent to which the individual—adult or child—feels comfortable forming warm, intimate, involved, lasting, and nondefensive attachments with other people, attachments that are untroubled by emotional wariness, constriction, or lack of trust. The ease with which persons are able to express their sympathy, affection, concern, and other such feelings, for example, has to do with emotional responsiveness. The interpersonal relationships of emotionally responsive people tend to be close and personal, and such people have little trouble responding to the friendship advances of others.

In contrast, emotionally unresponsive people are emotionally insulated from others. They have restricted and often only defensive emotional involvements with others. They may, however, be sociable and friendly, but friendliness is not to be confused with the ability to enter into a genuinely intimate relationship. Some people who are friendly are incapable of having intimate, involved, nondefensive relationships; their relationships tend to be nonpersonal and somewhat distant emotionally. Sometimes emotionally unresponsive people are cold, detached, aloof, and unresponsive; they may lack spontaneity, and they may have difficulty both giving and receiving normal affection. In extreme cases, emotionally unresponsive people may be emotionally bland, affectless, and apathetic. Of course, all these personality dispositions are matters of degree. As I said before, we are all more or less emotionally responsive or unresponsive, and so forth.

Hostility and Aggression. Hostility is an internal or emotional feeling of enmity, anger, or resentment. Aggression is the behavioral manifestation of anger or hostility, and is defined as the intention to hurt somebody (or something) physically or psychologically. Aggression is here distinguished from assertiveness in that assertiveness refers to individuals' attempts to place themselves in physical, verbal, or social equality with or superiority over another person (see also Gelles and Straus, 1979). The assertive individual may attempt to direct a group's activities, to dominate a conversation, or to stand up for his or her own rights—in other words, to thrust him- or herself forward physically or verbally without the intention of hurting the other person physically or emotionally. When one does intend to hurt the other, then the act becomes one of aggression. Of course, individuals sometimes assert themselves without any intention of hurting, but the other person *perceives* the act as one of aggression, thus the distinction between aggressiveness and assertiveness is at times a matter of interpretation or inference. Americans sometimes use the word "aggression" in a positive way. A businessman, for example, may be described as "a really aggressive guy! He's a go-getter." Rarely does the speaker mean that the person is truly aggressive as defined here. He may be, of course, but the speaker usually means the man is assertive, active, or forceful. Obviously, then, "being aggressive" has multiple meanings in English, but as used in PART's personality theory "aggression" is defined by the intent to hurt, or, at least, the inference or interpretation of the intent to hurt someone, something, or oneself.

Passive aggression is a less direct expression of aggression. It takes such forms as pouting, sulking, procrastination, passive obstructionism, and stubbornness. Imagine, for example, someone standing in a doorway you want to get through. You know the other person is aware you want to pass, but he continues to stand there anyway. That is one possible expression of passive aggression. The individual is not actually trying to injure you, and he is not saying the hostile things he may be thinking, but it is an act that is intended to annoy or irritate, that is, to "hurt" you. Passive aggressive individuals do not always consciously recognize their own motivation, however.

As intimated above, both children and adults sometimes have conscious or unconscious—recognized or unrecognized—difficulty coping with or managing their feelings of anger, hostility, or resentment, and have trouble expressing these feelings. People who have trouble expressing their hostility and aggression overtly often reveal their anger in disguised and symbolic forms, such as passive aggression, worried preoccupation about aggression, either their own or other people's; aggressive fantasies, daydreams, or dreams; anxiety over their own real or fantasied aggression; or unusual interest in hearing about or talking about aggressive or violent incidents. Some people, for example, get private pleasure from reading about or viewing fights, violent accidents, crimes of violence, and the like.

Individuals' responsiveness to incidents such as these may symbolically express problems coping with their own feelings of hostility and aggression. An illustration of this point might be helpful. As described by Bateson and Mead (1942) and by Mead (1939), the people of highland Bali are a paradox. On the one hand, they are widely thought of as a nonviolent, relaxed, peaceful, and happy people. On the other hand, one finds in Bali—at least in the mountainous countryside described by Bateson and Mead—signs of suppressed rage and the attendant psychological problems of rage management. This paradox seems to be embedded in the interaction between cultural ideology and tendencies for humans everywhere to respond to rejection in basically the same way. More specifically, the Balinese prize an equable temper and fear the direct expression of aggression. Adults put pressure on children not to express anger even though parents, especially mothers, play a teasing game designed to arouse intense emotions of rage, jealousy, or fear.

In this game, which is often referred to as the "borrowed baby game," a mother borrows a neighbor's young infant and gives it her breast expressly for the purpose of teasing her own 18- to 48-month-old child. When her child cries or has a tantrum the mother returns the "borrowed" baby, but ignores her own child. If her child then attempts to regain reparation with her, she often retakes the infant and reenacts the same teasing sequence. A variation of this pattern is to borrow a neighbor's infant and place it over the head of her own older child—an indecorous act according to the normative standards of this age- and sex-stratified society. The woman's own child is likely to recognize the impropriety of this behavior and go into a jealous rage. As a third method of teasing her child, the mother may hand the child to a neighbor and threaten to leave him or her. If the child bursts into tears, she may pick the child up without looking at him or her. At no point in these sequences does the mother allow an emotional climax to occur, nor does she herself become involved. In fact, Balinese mothers typically remain more or less impassive and withdrawn during these teasing episodes. Typically, according to Bateson and Mead (1942) and Mead (1939), this apparently rejecting behavior results in the alienation of mother-child ties. And, not surprisingly, one finds Balinese children responding to these forms of maternal treatment as PAR theory predicts.

Because the direct expression of aggression is frowned upon in Bali, one finds people with psychological problems managing their hostility and aggression. It is, therefore, probably no accident that one of the common forms of psychopathology there is running amok. "Running amok" means that affected persons—who have usually been depressed, withdrawn, and sleepless, and have suffered loss of appetite for a few days prior to this time—erupt into a frenzied episode of uncontrolled violence, destroying everything and anyone around them—dogs, chickens, children, mothers, anybody—until they themselves are brought down. At one time in Bali persons who went amok were killed by members of the community, but when the Dutch came into Indonesia around the turn of the century they mandated that amok persons were to be captured and subdued. When they regained control of themselves—as they eventually did—they were tried in court for whatever crimes they committed while in the amok state, and then sentenced to varying periods of hard physical labor. After enforcement of this legislation for some years, the incidence of amok in Bali dropped dramatically, according to Gregory Bateson (personal communication, April 1960). It is almost as if running amok had been, at an earlier time, a suicidal mission, as if people had unconsciously recognized what the end result was to be—their own destruction. Being sentenced to hard labor, however, did not have the same desired psychological outcome, so amok declined in incidence. This is conjecture, of course, but according to Bateson (personal communication, April 1960), it does seem to be the case that the incidence of amok dropped substantially after the Dutch entered the area.

A second behavioral disposition of the Balinese described by Bateson and Mead (1942)—their unusual preoccupation with cockfights—also suggests that the people have trouble coping with their own hostility and anger. As expressed in Bali, this preoccupation is related to the unusual distractability of adults, to their emotional withdrawal, and to the ease with which they go into trance. Balinese adults often withdraw into themselves and walk about in a dreamlike state, "forgetting," as Bateson and Mead (1942) say. This "withdrawal into vacancy" is characteristic of the highland Balinese, and probably accounts for the tranquil picture often painted of these people. The attention span of these adults is quite short, as seen by the fact that they do not attend to any activity for long. A wood-carver working on a puppet, for example, works for a short while then withdraws into vacancy, sitting for a few moments with eyes and mouth open slightly. After interacting with her child for a few moments a mother too may abruptly withdraw into herself, ignoring her child totally. One of the few things that holds a Balinese's attention relentlessly, however, is a cockfight. Two cocks are placed in a pit and roused to fight until one destroys the other. Adults stand motionless, enraptured and riveted until the violence is completed, and then they walk away in a dreamlike state, "forgetting"—until the next fight begins.

Why should cockfights be so transfixing for the Balinese? It seems plausible that this rapt involvement is an expression of—and perhaps a symbolic release of—the Balineses' problems managing hostile and aggressive impulses developed, in part at least, as a result of early socialization experiences of rejection.

Self-Evaluation (Self-Esteem and Self-Adequacy). As construed in personality theory, self-esteem and self-adequacy are both expressions of a more generalized phenomenon called "self-evaluation." Self-evaluation consists of feelings, attitudes, and perceptions about oneself falling on a continuum from positive to negative. As one semi-independent component of self-evaluation, self-esteem is a global emotional judgment that individuals make about themselves in terms of worth or value. Feelings of positive self-esteem imply that one likes oneself; that one approves of, accepts, and is comfortable with oneself; that one is rarely disappointed in oneself; and that one perceives oneself to be a person of worth and worthy of respect. Negative self-esteem, on the other hand, implies that one dislikes or disapproves of oneself; that one devaluates oneself and sometimes feels inferior to others; that one perceives oneself to be a worthless person or worthy of condemnation. All of us can place ourselves somewhere along this continuum.

Self-adequacy, on the other hand, refers to judgments we make about our own competence: Am I competent to perform tasks adequately, to cope satisfactorily with problems, to satisfy my own instrumental needs? Feelings of positive self-adequacy imply that one views oneself as capable of dealing satisfactorily with problems; as a success or capable of success in the things one sets out to do; as self-assured, self-confident, and socially adequate. Feelings of negative self-adequacy, on the other hand, are feelings of incompetence, the perceived inability to meet day-to-day demands successfully, feelings that one cannot compete successfully for the things one wants.

Self-esteem and self-adequacy sometimes show up as separate factors in factor analyses, and sometimes they do not. In correlational studies, however, they are almost always related to each other significantly. It becomes a matter of scientific or clinical judgment whether one wants to keep them separated or combine them. In personality theory I keep them separated because they seem to be related somewhat differently to parental acceptance and rejection.

Worldview. Worldview is a little known concept in the clinical and research literature (except Coleman, 1956), yet it is a significant element in the personality repertoire of humans everywhere. As used in PART's personality theory, "worldview" refers to a person's (often unverbalized) overall evaluation of life, of the universe, of the very essense of existence as being essentially positive or negative. A person with a positive worldview sees life as basically good, secure, friendly, happy, or unthreatening, or has some other positive valence. For a person with a negative worldview, on the other hand, life is seen as essentially bad, insecure, threatening, unpleasant, hostile, uncertain, and/or full of many dangers. Worldview, then, is a judgment individuals make about the quality of existence. It is not to be confused with one's empirical knowledge of social, economic, and political events. One may know, for example, that the local political system is corrupt, or that humanity is potentially on the brink of global destruction, or that one cannot trust one's boss. This "knowledge" may be empirically derived, but it is not the same thing as worldview. Worldview goes to a different level; it concerns one's feelings or perceptions of the quality of existence, as being in some degree "good" or "bad."

Emotional Stability. The seventh personality disposition of concern in PART's personality theory is "emotional stability," which refers to an individual's steadiness of mood, his or her ability to withstand minor setbacks, failures, difficulties, and other stresses without becoming upset emotionally.[5] Emotionally stable persons tolerate minor stresses and strains of day-to-day living without becoming emotionally upset, anxious, nervous, or tense. They are able to maintain composure under minor emotional stress, and they are not easily angered. They are fairly constant in their basic mood state, and they generally revert quickly to that state following those occasions when they have experienced great stress or have been exceptionally provoked. The unstable person, on the other hand, is subject to fairly wide, frequent, and often unpredictable mood shifts that swing from pole to pole, perhaps being cheery one moment and gloomy or depressed the next, happy to unhappy, content to dissatisfied, anxious to calm, or warm to hostile. Emotionally unstable people are upset easily by small setbacks, difficulties, and disappointments. If they expect something to happen but it does not, they are apt to become angry or dejected. And they often lose their composure under stress.

These seven personality dispositions in their "negative" expressions represent a constellation of interrelated characteristics that are predicted in personality theory to result from the experience of rejection in all cultures, races, and languages of the world. These are regarded as species-wide but not necessarily species-specific response tendencies.

PART'S PERSONALITY THEORY

Dependence and Defensive Independence

In the largest sense of the word, "dependence" is an *emotional* need or wish for response, especially positive response, from other people. Behaviorally, "dependent behavior" refers to the bids for positive response that children (and adults) make to persons important to them. The capacity for dependence is distinctively, though probably not uniquely, human. Some other higher primates also seem to share this capability. Moreover, the need for positive response takes somewhat different forms as children mature from infancy to adulthood, and, correspondingly, individuals' reactions to the withdrawal of positive response (that is, rejection) vary somewhat with increasing maturity.

Dependence is sometimes viewed by Americans as a negative quality to be eliminated in children. This belief is ill-founded, I believe, because a child's ability to reach out to others is one indicator of normal psychosocial development. The person who has lost the capacity to make bids for positive response from significant others is a person in emotional trouble, perhaps to a greater degree even than someone who is excessively dependent.

The predicted relationship between dependence and love withdrawal, or rejection, is complex and curvilinear, as shown in Figure 6. The shape of the curve has not yet been determined precisely, but PART's personality theory postulates that it looks roughly like the curve in Figure 6, which shows that under normal circumstances the accepted child is midrange dependent—neither very dependent nor excessively independent. (This fact is depicted in Figure 6 by the point at which the "normal dependence" line enters the vertical axis, that is, the dependence axis.) Thus the accepted child is generally one who is at least moderately dependent. As parents become increasingly rejecting, the child is likely—up to a point—to intensify bids for positive response, that is, to become increasingly dependent. Beyond that undefined point on the parental rejection scale, the child is likely to make fewer and fewer bids for positive response. He or she will then appear to be independent, but this apparent independence is not "healthy independence." Rather, it is what I call "defensive independence." Severely rejected children long for positive response, but it is commonly too painful for them to continue seeking love from chronically hostile or indifferent parents. These children often withdraw into themselves (that is, they become less emotionally responsive, described later), and insofar as they become emotionally insulated they make fewer dependency bids. Under the conditions of extreme rejection these children are also likely, metaphorically at least, to say to their parents, "To hell with you! I don't need you anyway!" In anger and hurt they may turn away from their parents—they may counterreject their parents (Nye, 1958; Ritchie, 1957; Beaglehole and Ritchie, 1961)—and perhaps turn into themselves, or sometimes act out their hurt and anger in socially inappropriate ways.

This apparent "independence" (that is, defensive independence) of seriously rejected children is a way of defending themselves against further hurt, of trying to cope with the pain of rejection in a situation over which they have little control. For many children, defensive independence, emotional unresponsiveness, and counterrejection are basic organismic responses, perhaps primitive, but effective as ways of pro-

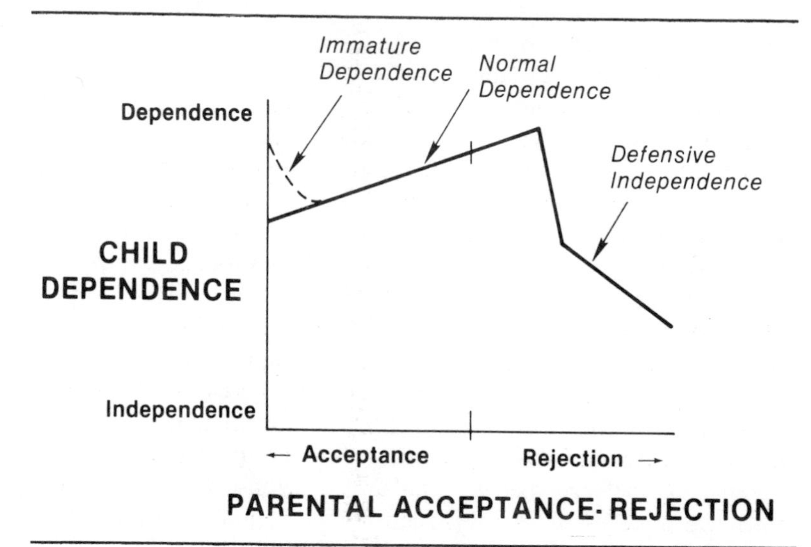

Figure 6 Expected Relationship Between Parental Acceptance-Rejection and Dependence

tecting themselves to some degree from further hurt of love withdrawal, parental aggression, and other forms of rejection.

The point at which rejected children shift from increasing dependency to defensive independence (shown as the crest of the main curve in Figure 6) probably varies from child to child in a complex, interactive way with the duration, form, and severity of rejection. For example, many children react at first to mild rejection with increased efforts to regain warmth, but after a period of time, in cases of severe rejection, the hurt of continuing to try to get positive response may be too great, so the child makes fewer bids for response, that is, becomes defensively independent. No doubt children also vary to some degree in their initially (that is, the prerejection period) felt need for positive response, thus introducing yet another factor in the complex equation explaining variations in dependence/defensive independence.[6] The hostile parent generates anger in the child and provides the child with a hostile model to emulate. This adds to the likelihood of anger in the child, and anger (or problems with the management of hostility and aggression) is frequently another important part of defensive independence.

The relationship between dependence and acceptance-rejection is further complicated by the fact that both parental warmth (that is, love and affection) as well as definite expressions of rejection (for example, hostility, indifference, and undifferentiated rejection) seem to heighten children's dependency, up to a point. In the context of parental acceptance, children's dependency needs are reinforced by warm and responsive parents (Finney, 1961). Children are provided an approachable model to emulate. Parental warmth and affection combined with intrusive parental control—that is, moment-by-moment control over and manipulation of a child's behavior—are likely to produce an especially noticeable spiking in the dependency curve. I have labeled this spiking "immature dependence" in Figure 6 because this form of parenting denies children the opportunity of doing the many things young, curious, active children are inclined to do. If the parent is always present, saying in effect, "Sweetie, don't do that. You might hurt yourself! Oh, Dear, let mommy help you!" then the child never fully develops a sense of competence, mastery, and a realistic sense of his or her own limits. The child is continuously reinforced in immature dependency. I call the form of parenting producing this immature dependency "smother love." The child is smothered with infantilizing, affectionate control (see also Levy, 1943).

Smother love raises the question of whether or not children can receive too much love (Bronfenbrenner, 1961; Adler, 1927). I am asked about this frequently, but as far as I know I have never seen a case in which children receive too much love per se. It is not love that does the damage; it is the other behaviors going on in the family (for example, intrusive control or inconsistent discipline) while love and concern are also being expressed.

Children's responses to perceived rejection have much in common with their responses to grief associated with the anticipated or expected loss of a significant person (Averill, 1968). In both contexts children (and adults) subjectively experience intense distress; both contexts may be associated with psychological changes; and both are associated with certain behavioral reactions, including an intensified effort to reestablish the former, warm relationship. With both anticipatory grief (Averill, 1968) and the perceived rejection the individual resists strenuously the loss or disruption of the relationship. Moreover, both grief and rejection are associated with a substantial amount of anxiety, insecurity, and other painful emotional reactions. Sometimes, however, the anxiety, insecurity, and other emotions normally associated with grief and rejection are overlaid with or replaced by anger or rage. This seems to be the case especially with defensive independence. Similar reactions have been described by Bowlby (1969, 1973), Ainsworth, (1973), and others (for example, Maccoby, 1980) in the context of attachment theory. Parallels such as these between PAR theory and other areas of inquiry have yet to be explored fully.

Emotional Unresponsiveness

Seriously rejected children have not learned how to give love because they have not known loving parents after whom they may model their own behavior, and even though they crave affection they have difficulty giving or accepting it. In order to protect themselves from further emotional hurt, rejected children tend to withdraw emotionally, to make fewer bids for positive response, to encyst their emotions. Ultimately, they may stop trying to get positive responses from the people who are most important to them, but through it all they maintain an often unrecognized and sometimes vehemently denied wish or yearning for love. In this way, rejected children may become emotionally insulated, unable to form warm, intimate relations with others freely and openly. Their attachments tend to be troubled by emotional constriction or defensiveness, and in extreme cases they may become apathetic or emotionally bland or flat.

Hostility and Aggression

Rejected children are also apt to become resentful of or angry at their parents. They may act out their anger directly or they may keep it bottled up, creating problems with its management. According to PART's personality theory, rejected children are especially likely to become hostile, aggressive, or passive-aggressive if parental rejection takes the form of hostility and aggression. Under these conditions children are provided a hostile model to emulate (Bandura and Walters, 1963) and in this way their aggressive dispositions may intensify. Sometimes, however, parents do not let their children express their anger overtly. These children are apt to develop problems managing their hostility. Suppressed, overcontrolled anger is often expressed in such disguised or symbolic forms as worried preoccupation about aggression, aggressive fantasies or dreams, or an unusual concern about the real or imagined aggression of others. The Balinese's fascination with cockfights described earlier, for example, illustrates one symbolic expression of individuals' problems managing their aggression. I should point out that even under optimal conditions one does not expect to find total absence of aggression in children (or adults). Indeed, normal children (and adults) everywhere are likely to display irritation, anger, and other forms of hostility and aggression from time to time (Rohner, 1976). Children who never seem angry or aggressive may be in psychological trouble to the same degree as but in a different way from hyperaggressive children.

Negative Self-Evaluation (Self-Esteem and Self-Adequacy)

Self-evaluation is construed in PART's personality theory to include two closely related dimensions: self-esteem and self-adequacy. The first deals with feelings of self-worth, and the second with feelings of competence. Children who feel rejected say, metaphorically, "My mother doesn't love me, therefore I'm not worthy of love. I'm no good!" This reaction to parental rejection comes about, according to symbolic interaction theorists (Cooley, 1902; Mead, 1934), because children tend to view themselves as they think "significant others" see them. And if their parents, as the most significant of others, do not love them, then it follows that they are apt to view themselves as unlovable and therefore unworthy and inadequate human beings. These self-attributions are the essence of negative self-esteem.

Children who think of themselves as worthless, no good, and worthy of condemnation easily generalize these feelings to beliefs about personal incompetence and inability. These children feel they have little control over important events in their lives. Indeed, insofar as being loved or unloved is one of the most important events in human life, these rejected children are correct in their appraisal. But they also tend to generalize incorrectly these feelings of negative self-adequacy to other domains. These children become caught in a self-fulfilling prophecy: Insofar as they feel less competent and less masterful, they may in fact behave that way. Others then evaluate them more negatively, and this negative evaluation feeds back onto their impaired feelings of self-esteem and self-adequacy. No doubt this pernicious spiral is implicated in the poorer academic performance of rejected children compared to accepted children. And no doubt the spiral is implicated in adults' occupational and other task-oriented choices, described later in this book.

Negative Worldview

One's psychological construction of reality—or image of life and of the world—seems to be shaped to a large extent through childhood experiences in the home, especially experiences of acceptance and rejection. Rejected children—children who experience great psychological hurt at the hands of their parents—are likely to be anxious, insecure, dependent or defensively independent, angry, and emotionally unresponsive, and to devaluate their feelings of self-esteem and self-adequacy. It is a small step for them to attribute these painful family experiences and internal feelings to the very essence of life and the universe: "That's what life is. It's hurtful, untrustworthy, treacherous!" In the view of many rejected children, the world is, in its essential nature, an unfriendly, hostile, insecure, unpleasant place. Rejected children often expect little more from life. That is, they develop a negative worldview that, once established, often bullies them throughout life.

Emotional Instability

Because of the psychological damage brought about by rejection, children who feel unloved are likely to have less tolerance for stress than accepted children. They have, as many clinicians say, less "ego strength" (English and English, 1958), and as a result they tend to be less emotionally stable than accepted children. That is, they are more prone to react to minor daily stresses with emotional upset, fits of anger, and the like. Of course, accepted children also become emotionally upset from time to time. As with all these personality dispositions, the difference between accepted and rejected children is one of degree, not of kind.

So far in this chapter I have emphasized "negative" outcomes of the rejection process rather than the usually more "positive" outcomes of parental acceptance. I have done this because parental rejection by itself seems to be sufficient in most instances to produce the described effects, whereas parental acceptance is not. That is, even though accepted children usually develop "positive" expressions of the personality dispositions described here, they do not always do so. Accepted children may be aggressive or have impaired feelings of self-esteem, for example, for reasons that have nothing to do with parental rejection. It is unlikely, however, that accepted children will develop the full constellation of personality characteristics described for rejected children. If they do develop them, then one has grounds for suspecting that the children themselves do not feel accepted. Probably few of even the most loved and healthiest children fall at an idealized, optimal level on all these personality continua. Accepted children often report varying but usually moderate degrees of these "negatively" phrased dispositions.

Insofar as rejected children tend to be aggressive, emotionally unstable, defensively independent, and the like, one of rejection's malignant by-products is the creation of children who are less easy to be with than accepted children. This in turn can trigger a response in a susceptible parent of even further rejection, and a vicious interactive spiral is created that becomes even harder to interrupt. In effect, rejected children often become unwitting provokers of their own subsequent rejection or abuse (Erchak, 1981). The personality constellation associated with rejection also reduces the likelihood that rejected children will develop fully satisfying peer relations (Levy, 1966) or satisfying relations with teachers or other nonfamily members (see discussion of element 5 of Figure 5). And so the rejected child's already-damaged senses of self-adequacy and self-esteem are further diminished.

PART's personality theory predicts that in the absence of positive counteracting developmental experiences (such as the ability to establish a successful friendship with someone), rejected children are likely to mature into adults who are dependent or defensively independent; somewhat emotionally unresponsive; hostile, aggressive, or passive-aggressive; or who have problems managing their hostility and aggression; suffer a loss in positive self-esteem and self-adequacy; have a negative worldview; and are less emotionally stable than adults who have been accepted as children. Moreover, personality theory expects these adults to have strong needs for affection (that is, needs for positive response) but they are often impaired in their ability to accept affection or to return it. Thus another of the malignant by-products of rejection is produced in the tendency for these adults who become parents to perpetuate the rejection cycle with their own children—along with the constellation of personality characteristics just described. They are also probably people with less satisfying marital relations (Sadeghi, 1982).

In summary, then, PART's personality theory postulates that each of the seven personality dispositions described in this chapter will appear significantly more often among rejected children and adults the world over—regardless of variations in culture, race, language, or other such conditions—than among accepted children and adults. Dependence or defensive independence, hostility and aggression, negative self-esteem, negative self-adequacy, negative worldview, emotional unresponsiveness, and emotional instability by no means exhaust the roster of personality consequences of parental acceptance-rejection—as indicated earlier—but these are the major ones included in personality theory at this time.

NOTES

1. More specifically, about 27 studies on acceptance-rejection were published in the 1930s. This number nearly doubled during the 1940s, but by the 1950s the number had risen to nearly 2½ times as many relevant publications as in the 1930s. This number, in turn, nearly doubled in the 1960s, but after that the growth rate declined appreciably, to about 90 studies in the 1970s. The 1980s do not appear to show any significant increase over the 1970s.

2. References cited in this section are illustrative only. A complete listing of significant sources could lead to two dozen or more citations for some topics. Moreover, the topics themselves are merely illustrative of the many behavioral, personality, and developmental issues in which parental rejection has been found to be a significant antecedent.

3. In this context, Campo's (1985) research is especially illuminating. Employing a hierarchical discriminant function analysis he was able to demonstrate that maternal and especially paternal rejection (as assessed by the adult PARQ described in Chapter 2), along with psychosocial functioning (assessed by the Adult PAQ), correctly distinguished with 92.5% accuracy a group of forty substance abusers from a matched group of forty nonabusers. Adding the variable "level of education" raised the classification accuracy to 98.75%.

4. This conception of dependence seems to be consistent with Hartup's (1963: 333) definition, which says that dependence is revealed "whenever the individual gives evidence that people, as people, are satisfying and rewarding."

5. It is interesting to note that Goldberg (1981) argues that "emotional stability" is one of at least five personality dispositions that are probably universally encoded in all natural languages of the world. This point is yet to be confirmed empirically.

6. This internally felt need for positive response probably varies (from individual to individual) as a function of the interaction between biology (for example, temperament) and experience, as described earlier in the phylogenetic perspective and the phylogenetic model.

5

Converging Evidence on PART's Personality Theory

Much of this chapter deals with converging evidence bearing on the major postulates of PART's personality theory. I will focus especially on evidence coming from worldwide, holocultural research, and from psychological research conducted in the United States and internationally.[1] Prior to discussing the results of statistical analyses about the relationship between parental acceptance-rejection and personality, I will provide information about the methods and samples used in this chapter and describe the overall quality of parental care (in terms of acceptance and rejection) experienced by children cross-culturally. The chapter ends with a longitudinal study of "unwanted" (rejected) versus "wanted" (accepted) children in Czechoslovakia.

SAMPLES AND PROCEDURES

Holocultural Research

The holocultural paradigm described in Chapter 2 employs two representative, stratified samples of the adequately described sociocultural systems of the world, past and present. The sample of 101 societies employed originally in *They Love Me, They Love Me Not* (hereafter referred to as the *Love* sample) is described in detail in Rohner (1975); the standard cross-cultural sample (hereafter referred to as the *Standard* sample) is described in detail in Murdock and White (1969) and, as used in this research, in Rohner and Rohner (1981b).

Specialists in holocultural research generally recognize at least four classes of methodological problems that should be addressed in rigorous holocultural studies (Naroll et al., 1976; Levinson and Malone, 1980; Rohner et al., 1978). These methodological problem areas include attention to (1) characteristics of the sample, including attending to possible sampling bias; (2) cross-culturally generalizable conceptual definitions and adequate cross-cultural operationalizations of variables; (3) the coding process and code characteristics, including possible coder bias (see Rohner and Rohner, 1981a); and (4) problems of data quality control, specifically, testing for possible ethnographer bias in original fieldwork and report writing. Each of these methodological issues was assessed in detail in the Love sample, and each was shown in Rohner (1975) to be nonproblematic. Indeed, research based on the Love sample is widely regarded as an exemplar of holocultural research (Levinson and Malone, 1980). All these methodological problem areas—except for systematically assessing possible ethnographer bias—were also assessed for the Standard sample. The Standard sample itself as well as codes in this research using the sample have been found by Murdock and White (1969), Rohner and Rohner (1981b), Levinson (1977), and Barry (1980) to be adequate.

In the holocultural research reported here two independent raters coded each parental-behavior and personality variable in the sample ethnographies, following procedures dictated in Rohner (1975). All variables in the Love sample were coded on a 5-point scale. After determining that the level of interrater reliability was appropriately high (following procedures detailed in Rohner, 1975) the two raters' codes for each variable were summed, creating 9-point scales ranging—in the Love sample—from 2 through 10, where a code of 2 reveals (a) low parental acceptance (high rejection), and (b), in terms of personality dispositions, low aggression, low dependence, negative self-evaluation, negative worldview, emotional unresponsiveness, and emotional instability.[2] A code of 10 on rating scales in the Love sample reveals (a) high parental acceptance, and (b), for personality, high aggression, high dependence, positive self-evaluation, positive worldview, emotional responsiveness, and emotional stability. All child personality and parental behavior codes in the Love sample are based on children from the ages of 2 through 6, or, in the case of the parenting codes, for as long before age 2 or after age 6 as the child-training practices in that society remained approximately constant with respect to the behavior being coded. Other methodological details pertinent to coding the Love sample are provided in Rohner (1975).

Similar procedures were used for coding parental behavior in the Standard sample. That is, two independent raters coded each variable on a 4-point scale. After determining that interrater reliability coefficients were appropriately high (see Rohner and Rohner, 1981b), the raters' codes were summed, creating a 7-point scale ranging from 2 through 8. Point 2 on the scale reveals that parents are "rarely" hostile, indifferent, or rejecting, or, alternatively stated, that they are "almost always" warm and accepting; a code of 8 means that parents are "almost always" hostile, indifferent, or rejecting, or that they are "rarely" warm and accepting.[3] In the Standard sample the emphasis in ratings was placed on children from 3 through 6 years of age, or for as long before age 3 or after age 6 as the treatment of children remained approximately constant with respect to the specific behaviors being coded (for example, parental warmth, aggression, and neglect). Other methodological details pertinent to coding the Standard sample may be found in Rohner and Rohner (1981b).

Intracultural Psychological Research

Fifteen psychological studies regarding children's perceptions of parental acceptance and rejection are reported here for eight nations (ten language groups), including Canada (French- and English-speaking samples), Czechoslovakia, India (Bengali-, Hindi-, and Telegu-speaking samples), Korea, Nigeria (Hausa, Yoruba, Ibo, and Tiv tribal/ethnic groups), Puerto Rico, and the United States. Eight international studies reported here involve adults' retrospective reports of their own acceptance-rejection experiences in childhood. These various studies involve 2200 children and about 800 adults. The children range in age from 6 through 19 years, but most typically they were about 9 through 13 years of age. They were approximately evenly distributed by sex. As shown later, in Table 2, adults in several of the studies were mothers of the sample children, so overall sex distribution among adults tends to be skewed toward females. Both children and adults tended to come from either working-class (for example, skilled or semiskilled labor) or middle-class (for example, business or professional) backgrounds, although some of the Tiv and Puerto Rican children came from wealthy, upper-class, elite families in their respective sociocultural milieus. Some of the Indian children and adults were rural peasant agriculturalists, and consequently difficult to classify according to social class. More specific information about numbers and age characteristics of the various samples internationally are shown in Tables 1 and 2.

In every psychological-research sample reported in this chapter the Parental Acceptance-Rejection Questionnaire (PARQ) was administered in respondents' native languages. In some studies, noted later, the Personality Assessment Questionnaire (PAQ) was also administered. In each nation the instruments were subjected to a series of translation and back-translation (Brislin, 1970, 1976) procedures to assure that the wording was appropriate to the linguistic idiom used by respondents.[4] Efforts also were made to assess the validity and reliability of instruments used in several of the languages (see, for example, Rohner 1984a; Saavedra, 1977; Rohner and Chaki-Sircar, n.d.). In every case the PARQ and PAQ were found to be psychometrically adequate.

General characteristics of the PARQ and PAQ were described in Chapter 2, but more detail will be helpful here for interpreting the tables in the remainder of this chapter. The PARQ contains 60 statements to which children and adults respond in terms of how well each statement describes (or described) the way their major caretakers (mothers and fathers) treat (or treated) them. Examples of scale items on the Child PARQ are as follows: "My mother makes me feel wanted and needed" (perceived warmth/affection); "My mother goes out of her way to hurt my feelings" (perceived hostility); "My mother ignores me as long as I do nothing to bother her" (perceived indifference/neglect; "My mother does not really love me" (perceived undifferentiated rejection). Subjects repond to statements such as these on a 4-point, Likert-type scale ranging from "almost always true" to "almost never true." The PARQ ranges from a possible low score of 60 (revealing maximum perceived acceptance, or minimum perceived rejection) to a high of 240 (revealing maximum perceived rejection). A score of 150 or higher on the PARQ reveals that the respondent perceives, overall, more maternal or paternal rejection than acceptance.[5] Other properties of the PARQ are detailed at length in Rohner (1984a).

The Child PAQ contains 7 scales with 6 items each, for a total of 42 items; the Adult PAQ contains the same 7 scales, but with 9 items each, for a total of 63 items. The scales are designed to measure the personality characteristics described in PART's personality theory: hostility/aggression, dependence, negative self-esteem, negative self-adequacy, emotional unresponsiveness, emotional instability, and negative worldview. On both versions of the PAQ, subjects respond in terms of how well they believe each item describes them. Examples of scale items on the Child PAQ are as follows: "I have trouble controlling my temper" (hostility/aggression); "I like my mother to give me a lot of attention" (dependence); "I feel that I am no good and never will be any good" (negative self-esteem); "I feel I cannot do many of the things I try to do'' (negative self-adequacy); ''It is hard for me when I try to show the way I really feel to someone I like'' (emotional unresponsiveness); ''I feel cheery and happy one minute and gloomy or unhappy the next'' (emotional instability); and ''I see the world as a dangerous place'' (negative worldview).

Subjects respond to statements such as these on the same 4-point scale described for the PARQ. The Child PAQ ranges from a possible low score of 42 (revealing ''positive'' mental health associated theoretically with perceived acceptance) to a high of 168 (revealing ''negative'' mental health associated theoretically with perceived rejection). Similarly, the Adult PAQ ranges from a possible low score of 63 to a possible high score of 252. In addition to computing the total PAQ score, investigators usually compute each scale score separately, and correlate that with the total PARQ score and with individual PARQ scale scores. Other properties of the PAQ are detailed at length in Rohner (1984a). The Child PARQ and Child PAQ are both provided in Appendix B, along with sample scoring sheets for the instruments.

CHILDREN'S EXPERIENCES CROSS-CULTURALLY WITH ACCEPTANCE AND REJECTION

The Love and Standard samples described above show that on the average—and with notable exceptions discussed in Rohner (1975) and in Rohner and Rohner (1981b)—children around the world are generally treated with warmth and concern by their parents. In fact, as measured in the Love sample, children in these 101 societies on the average fall at point 8 on a scale ranging from 2 through 10, revealing quite high acceptance (Rohner, 1975).

Converging evidence regarding this conclusion is found in intracultural data within each of eight nations (ten language groups) where children responded in their own languages to the child version of the PARQ. As shown in Table 1, children in fifteen samples within these eight nations reported a wide range of variation in perceived parental acceptance-rejection, but in all samples except Monterrey, Mexico, children perceived themselves overall to be accepted by their parents. In fact, omitting the Mexican sample, in which children on the average perceived themselves to be rejected, the cross-national mean score in perceived warmth is 107.1. Converting this to the holocultural scale described above yields a score of approximately 7.9, a score remarkably similar to the worldwide code of 8 in the holocultural Love sample.

TABLE 1
Cross-National Mean Scores in Children's Perceived Acceptance-Rejection (Child PARQ)

Nation (Language Group)	*Acceptance-Rejection* $\bar{X}$	*SD*	*N*	*Ages (in Years)*
Canada				
Quebec City (French)	101.0	27.50	68	($\bar{X}$ = 11)[a]
Newfoundland (English)	100.1	23.80	24	7-10
Czechoslovakia				
Prague (Czech)	108.1	24.73	151	16-17
Southern Bohemia (Czech)	98.3	20.90	228	11-12
India				
Andra Pradesh (Telugu)	126.2	23.94	107	7-14
Madhya Pradesh (Hindi)	102.8	22.68	40	($\bar{X}$ = 10)[b]
West Bengal (Bengali)	109.8	14.82	50	6-12
Korea (Korean)	112.1	25.10	124	15-18
Mexico				
Monterrey (Spanish)	151.5	24.06	174	8-15
Nigeria (Tiv)	115.8	19.09	92	9-12
Puerto Rico (Spanish)	100.7	26.07	208	13-19
United States				
Enfield, CT (English)	104.6	28.00	316	8-12
Vernon, CT (English)	106.1	24.20	227	6-11
Washington, D.C. (English)	106.5	29.20	220	9-11
Korean-Americans (English)	108.9	23.85	171	7-12

a. The age range of French Canadian children was not reported by Salamé. Consequently, the mean age of these children is recorded here.
b. The age range of Hindi-speaking children of Madhya Pradesh was not reported by Prakash. Consequently, the mean age of these children is recorded here.

The Love sample included an American community (Fischer and Fischer, 1966) that was coded 7 on the 9-point holocultural scale. Evidence from the social psychological/developmental research component in America is consistent with this ethnographic report. Specifically, 764 school-aged middle-class and working-class American children in three separate samples responded to the child version of the PARQ. The children averaged an overall score of 106 on the PARQ, equivalent to about 7.95 on the Love sample coding scale. Thus it seems that, on the average, American children feel accepted within their families to about the same extent that children elsewhere in the world do.[6]

A similar portrait can be drawn for adults' childhood experiences. Using the adult version of the PARQ in eight samples representing five nations and five language groups, Table 2 shows the mean level of acceptance-rejection experienced by adults in their childhood. As was true of children, adults in these sociocultural systems recall having experienced in childhood a fairly wide range of variation in parental warmth. Nonetheless, in all but one of the groups adults perceived themselves to have been accepted as children.[7] The single exception was that of adults in the Washington, D.C., sample, who reported more rejection (Adult PARQ, $\overline{X}$ = 159, S.D. = 33.00) than did adults in any other nation. In fact, these Americans perceived themselves to have been more rejected as children than accepted. (Remember, a score of 150 or higher on the PARQ reveals significant rejection.) Some behavioral scientists are inclined to dismiss as unreliable adults' retrospective recollections of their childhood experiences. Data from the long-term Berkeley Growth Study, however, suggest that adults do report accurately their childhood experiences from more than thirty years earlier (Clausen, 1972; Hunt and Eichorn, 1972).

Omitting the anomolous Washington, D.C., sample, the mean Adult PARQ score for these eight groups is 102, which is approximately equivalent to 8.1 on the Love sample holocultural scale. Thus, as with children, adults internationally seem in general to feel that they were accepted, as children, by their parents.

Comparing Tables 1 and 2, it is worth noting that even though both children and adults in various parts of the world tend to report a substantial degree of parental acceptance in their lives, children within any given nation tend, in general, to perceive somewhat less acceptance than do adults within that nation. This generalization fails to hold, of course, in Washington, D.C., where adults reported having experienced more rejection than did children. Why this should be true is unclear.

RELATIONSHIP BETWEEN PERCEIVED ACCEPTANCE-REJECTION AND CHILDREN'S PERSONALITY

Overall, the postulates of PART's personality theory discussed in the previous chapter are supported by converging evidence from the two holocultural studies, numerous psychological studies conducted in the United States, and several psychological studies internationally. A summary of much of this evidence is provided in Table 3, which presents data from the two holocultural studies and from a composite of three major psychological studies in the United States (hereafter called the

TABLE 2
Cross-National Mean Scores in Adults' Retrospective Reports of Acceptance-Rejection Experienced in Childhood (Adult PARQ)

Nation (Language Group)	*Acceptance-Rejection* $\overline{X}$	*SD*	*N*	*Ages (in Years)*
India				
Andra Pradesh (Telugu)	111.7	28.20	99	20-35
Madhya Pradesh (Hindi)	100.4	24.90	40	(mothers of sample children)
West Bengal (Bengali)	96.4	16.73	51	(mothers of sample children)
Canada				
Newfoundland (English)	91.4	18.47	23	28-57
Nigeria (English)	103.1	16.00	301	17-29 (college students)
Sweden (Swedish)	93.9	25.74	71	average age approximately 20 (college students)
United States				
Enfield, CT (English)	115.3	42.40	66	(mothers of sample children)
Washington, D.C. (English)	159.0	33.00	147	18-43 (college students)

All-America sample).[8] The table shows correlations between parental acceptance-rejection and children's personality dispositions relevant to personality theory.

Several observations must be made about Table 3. First, emotional unresponsiveness, negative worldview, and emotional instability were uncodable for children in the Love sample because ethnographers in that sample reported on those personality characteristics too infrequently. These variables were coded with difficulty in the Standard sample, but in that sample correlations between parental-rejection and negative worldview (r = .26) and between rejection and emotional instability (r = .26) did not achieve statistical significance at the 5% level; the correlation between rejection and emotional unresponsiveness (r = .31) was significant at the 5% level. As I just said, part of the problem with these variables in holocultural research is that ethnographers do not often observe them carefully among children.

Second, as indicated earlier, self-esteem and self-adequacy were combined into a single measure of overall self-evaluation in both holocul-

TABLE 3
Holocultural and Intracultural-American Correlations
Between Parental Rejection and Children's Personality

Child Personality Disposition	*Holocultural Samples*		*All-America Sample*[c]
	Love Sample[a]	*Standard Sample*[b]	
Dependence	.31**	.25*	.01
Emotional unresponsiveness	–	.31**	.47***
Hostility/aggression	.49***	.36***	.41***
Negative self-esteem	{ .72***[d]	.42***[d]	.38***
Negative self-adequacy	{ –	–	.41***
Negative worldview	–	.26*	.44***
Emotional instability	–	.26*	.35***

NOTE: All correlations are computed using Pearson's r. Correlations are keyed in the direction of parental rejection (e.g., as rejection increases, emotional unresponsiveness also increases).
a. Data in this column were reported previously in Rohner (1975). Correlations here are based on different sized samples: correlations involving dependence, n = 42; hostility/aggression, n = 60; self-esteem, n = 11.
b. Data in this column were reported previously in Rohner and Rohner (1981). Correlations are based on 53 societies that could be coded for both acceptance-rejection and each personality disposition of children from the ages of approximately 3 through 6 years.
c. Data are based on the heretofore unpublished composite of 764 school-aged (7 through 11 years of age) children's total scores on the Child PARQ and Child PAQ in three separate samples in the United States.
d. Self-esteem and self-adequacy were combined in the holocultural samples to form a measure of overall self-evaluation.
*p < .10 (two tailed); **p < .05; ***p < .01.

tural samples because coders were unable to distinguish reliably between them in ethnographic reports. Finally, the weakest relationship in Table 3 was the correlation between parental rejection and dependency in the All-America sample (r = .01, p = n.s.), which is based on children's responses to the PARQ and the PAQ. The reason this coefficient approximates zero is discussed later. With the exception of these problems, all correlations in the table support the postulates of PART's personality theory. That is, parental rejection is associated significantly in the United States and cross-culturally with emotional unresponsiveness, hostility/aggression, negative self-evaluation, negative worldview, and emotional instability.

Table 4 shows the results of three cross-national studies of the relationship between perceived acceptance-rejection and children's personality dispositions. These studies were completed using the Child PARQ and the Child PAQ, translated as needed into languages of the sample children. Overall, the pattern of correlations in these three socio-

TABLE 4
Correlations Between Perceived Rejection (Child PARQ) and Personality Dispositions (Child PAQ) Among Indian and Korean-American Children

			Personality Dispositions					
Sociocultural System	*Aggression*	*Dependence*	*Negative Self-Esteem*	*Negative Self-Adequacy*	*Emotional Unresponsiveness*	*Emotional Instability*	*Negative Worldview*	*Overall PAQ Score*
Andra Pradesh, India (Telugu)[a]	.58***	.21*	.44***	.46***	.35***	.45***	.58***	.58***
Korean-Americans (Korean and English)[b]	.55***	–.11	.52***	.49***	.51***	.37***	.46***	.63***
West Bengal, India (Bengali)[c]	.17	–.11	.15	.35**	.43**	–.16	.23*	.29*

a. N = 106 7- through 14-year-olds. Language of testing was Telugu.
b. N = 171 7- through 12-year-olds. Children chose individually whether to be tested in Korean or English.
c. N = 50 6- through 12-year-olds. Language of testing was Bengali.

cultural systems supports findings in the holocultural research component and in the American psychological research component of the universalist paradigm. As in the All-America sample, the relationship between dependence and rejection emerges as problematic in these three sociocultural systems.

The last column of Table 4 presents the relationship between perceived acceptance-rejection and children's overall PAQ scores in the various sociocultural systems. Insofar as one agrees that emotional instability, negative self-esteem, emotional unresponsiveness, and other such personality dispositions are mental health-related issues, then children's total responses to the PAQ may be taken as an estimate of their "mental health" status. The correlations between total PAQ scores and perceived acceptance-rejection (total PARQ scores) are significant in the three sociocultural systems described in Table 4 ($r = .58$, $p < .001$, for Andra Pradesh, India; $r = .63$, $p < .001$, for Korean-American immigrants; $r = .29$, $p < .05$, for West Bengal, India). The relationship between total PARQ and total PAQ in the All-America sample, shown in Table 5, is also robust ($r = .57$, $p < .001$), thus providing further confirmation for claims in personality theory about the relationship between perceived acceptance-rejection and children's mental health status. Additional supportive evidence reported in Rohner and Rohner (1980) is provided from Mexico, Puerto Rico, and elsewhere.

Table 5 provides a more detailed look at the pattern of correlations between scales on the Child PAQ and scales on the Child PARQ. There, each PARQ scale is independently correlated with each PAQ scale in the All-America sample. Table 5 shows a weak but significant tendency for parental warmth (the warmth scale) to correlate positively with children's dependence. The table also shows that different forms of acceptance-rejection seem to have somewhat different effects on various behavioral dispositions. For example, parental "coldness" (that is, low warmth) does not generate the same degree of hostility and aggression in children as do "positive" expressions of rejection such as perceived hostility/aggression, indifference/neglect, and undifferentiated rejection. Indeed, on the average, the warmth scale is not as strongly correlated with children's responses to the total PAQ as are parental hostility/aggression, indifference/neglect, and undifferentiated rejection. Drawing from a sample of 316 American and 174 Mexican 8- to 15-year-old children in the United States and Mexico, respectively, Rohner et al. (1980) supported this conclusion when they reported that perceived

TABLE 5
Intercorrelation of Scales on Children's PARQ and Children's PAQ in the All-America Sample

Child PAQ Scales (Personality Variables)	*Child PARQ Scales (Parental Behavior Variables)*				
	Warmth	*Hostility*	*Indifference*	*Undifferentiated Rejection*	*Total PARQ*
Aggression	–.16***	.48***	.33***	.45***	.41***
Dependence	.16***	.11**	–.01	.12***	.01
Negative self-esteem	–.32***	.35***	.31***	.30***	.38***
Negative self-adequacy	–.36***	.35***	.38***	.29***	.41***
Emotional unresponsiveness	–.40***	.41***	.44***	.37***	.47***
Emotional instability	–.15***	.41***	.28***	.39***	.35***
Negative worldview	–.35***	..41***	.39***	.36***	.44***
Total PAQ score	–.37***	.58***	.49***	.53***	.57***

NOTE: N = 764 American children 7 through 11 years old.
*p < .05; **p < .01; ***p < .001.

parental rejection (as measured by the three "rejection" scales on the PARQ—hostility, indifference, and undifferentiated rejection) was associated with approximately 46% of the variance in American children's reported personality dispositions as measured on the PAQ; parental warmth, however, was associated with only 26% of the variation in American children's reported personality dispositions. Perceived rejection was associated with approximately 42% of the variance in Mexican children's reported personality dispositions; perceived warmth was associated with only 29% of the variation in their personality dispositions. Similar trends have also been found among Czechoslovakian children, Telegu-speaking children of India, Nigerian college students, and Korean-American schoolchildren (unpublished data, Center for the Study of Parental Acceptance and Rejection [CSPAR]).

These results are brought into sharper focus among 316 American schoolchildren who responded to the Child PARQ and the Child PAQ. (This is a subsample from the All-America sample.) Using the Child PAQ as a measure of children's emotional adjustment, it is possible to estimate the relative contribution of various parenting styles to children's overall mental health status. From data presented in Table

6, it appears that the greatest social-emotional damage is produced by "cold" (nonwarm) and "rejecting" parents (parents who are hostile/aggressive, indifferent/neglecting, and undifferentiated rejecting). A very close second, however, are "warm" but "rejecting" parents. In fact, in this sample there is no statistically significant difference between these two parenting styles. (The concepts of "cold," "warm," "rejecting," and "nonrejecting" are operationalized in the notes to Table 6.) All other pairs of parenting styles shown in the table are associated with significantly different mental health outcomes for children. In summary, these data suggest the following hierarchy of most to least damaging forms of parenting: cold and rejecting; warm and rejecting; cold and nonrejecting; and warm and nonrejecting.

Some statisticians criticize the use of multiple t tests such as those employed in Table 5, arguing that this procedure heightens the probability of making a type I error. In this regard, I should note that with alpha set at .01, the chance of a single type I error appearing in Table 6 is very small, about .06. Thus it is unlikely that results in that table are in error. Nonetheless, to be safe, Cournoyer (1985) reanalyzed the issue of "most damaging to least damaging styles of parenting" using the All-America sample of 764 children. He employed two widely used multiple-means tests, the Duncan's (1975) multiple range test, and the Waller and Duncan (1969) K-ratio test. Both of these multiple-means tests supported the conclusions drawn from Table 6. Use of two other, conservative, type II error-prone tests—the Tukey-Kramer test (Tukey, 1953; Kramer, 1956) and the Scheffé (1959) test—however, raised doubts about whether "cold and nonrejecting" parenting in the All-America sample led to *significantly* more negative personality consequences than did the "warm and nonrejecting" style of parenting. From these analyses it appears that questions about the effects of different styles of parenting are in need of additional research before fully confident answers can be reached.

RELATIONSHIP BETWEEN PERCEIVED ACCEPTANCE-REJECTION AND CHILDREN'S AGE, SEX, AND SOCIAL STATUS

Before discussing the relationship between perceived parental acceptance-rejection and adults' behavioral dispositions, I want to add information about the relation between perceived acceptance (as measured by the PARQ) and children's age, sex, and socioeconomic status. In

TABLE 6
Most Damaging to Least Damaging Parenting Styles

Parenting Style (Most to Least Damaging)	Children's Mean PAQ Scores[a]			Significance of Difference Between Groups		
	$\overline{X}$	*SD*	*n*	Groups	*t*	*p*
(1) Cold and rejecting[b]	119.4	19.93	10	1 vs 2	.83	n.s.
(PARQ, $\overline{X}$ = 183.3)				1 vs 3	2.22	$< .05$
(2) Warm and rejecting[c]	113.8	11.62	23	1 vs. 4	4.19	$< .001$
(PARQ, $\overline{X}$ = 152.2)				2 vs. 3	2.56	$< .02$
(3) Cold and nonrejecting[d]	102.7	9.36	7	2 vs. 4	8.62	$< .001$
(PARQ, $\overline{X}$ = 139.1)				3 vs 4	2.97	$< .01$
(4) Warm and nonrejecting	91.4	13.52	276			
(PARQ, $\overline{X}$ = 96.9)						

NOTE: This table is drawn from a sample of 316 8- through 12-year-old American schoolchildren.
a. The higher the PAQ score, the poorer the child's emotional adjustment or overall mental health status.
b. "Cold" refers to warmth-scale scores at or below the scale midpoint ($\leqslant 50$); "rejecting" refers to the sum of scores on the hositlity/aggression, indifference/neglect, and undifferentiated rejection scales that are at or about the midpoint for the summed scales (i.e., $\geqslant 100$).
c. "Warm" refers to warmth-scale scores above the scale midpoint of 50.
d. "Nonrejecting" refers to the sum of scores on the hostility/aggression, indifference/neglect, and undifferentiated rejection scales that are below the midpoint of the summed scales (< 100).

the United States, perceived acceptance does not vary with age, at least among children 6 through 12 years of age. The same holds true for sample children in Southern Bohemia (Czechoslovakia) and West Bengal, and among Korean-Americans: Younger children in these samples are no more or less likely than older children to report themselves to be accepted or rejected (unpublished date, CSPAR). Younger children in the Mexican sample, shown in Table 1, however, did tend slightly to perceive themselves to be more rejected than did the older children shown there ($r = -.22$, $p < .05$). Similarly, younger mothers (but not fathers) in the Bengali sample shown in Table 2 tended to report more rejection in their own childhood than did older mothers ($r = -.32$, $p < .05$; Rohner and Chaki-Sircar, n.d.) (Ages among sample Bengali mothers ranged from 20 through 70 years.) Why these age differences exist in perceived rejection among Mexican children and Bengali mothers is not yet clear.

Sex differences in perceived acceptance-rejection are also variable. Boys in the United States do not generally report more or less acceptance than girls. Similarly, Nigerian college students failed to show sex differences in perceived rejection. But Korean-American boys perceive themselves to be slightly but significantly more accepted than do Korean-American girls (unpublished data, CSPAR).

India is a complex nation with respect to sex differences in perceived acceptance. As measured by the PARQ, children in southern India—for example, Andra Pradesh, shown in Table 1—tend not to experience differences in acceptance-rejection according to sex (unpublished data, CSPAR), but as one moves further north boys appear to become increasingly favored, especially in rural areas. Boys in central India—West Bengal, for instance (see example shown in Table 1)—tend to perceive slightly more maternal warmth than do girls (as measured by the PARQ; Rohner and Chaki-Sircar, n.d.) and, according to Miller (1981) and Poffenberger (1981), girls in rural north India experience significantly greater neglect—sometimes to the point of death—than do boys. (Neglect in this context, however, is not measured by the PARQ but rather refers to such matters as parents waiting longer before attending to girls' medical problems or parents investing fewer scarce family resources when a girl becomes ill.) It is not altogether clear to what extent this so-called neglect is *perceived* by girls as a form of rejection.

Social class and other social status attributes in society are often significant predictors of parental acceptance or rejection. Overall, perceived acceptance as measured by the PARQ does not seem to vary significantly in mainstream working-class versus middle-class America, but perceived acceptance does vary in different social classes among some ethnic minorities. For example, in a sample of sixteen middle-class and nine working-class Korean-American families, working-class Korean-American children perceived their parents to be less warm ($t = 3.1$, $p < .01$), more hostile ($t = 6.2$, $p < .001$), more neglecting ($t = 2.7$, $p < .05$), more undifferentiated rejecting ($t = 5.3$, $p < .001$), and more overall rejecting ($t = 5.4$, $p < .001$) than did middle-class Korean-American immigrant children (Rohner et al., 1980). In the Mexican sample shown in Table 1, however, middle-class children perceived their parents to be less warm ($t = 3.2$, $p < .002$), more aggressive ($t = 2.1$, $p < .03$), more neglecting ($t = 3.6$, $p < .001$), and more undifferentiated rejecting ($t = 3.48$, $p < .001$) than did their working-class counterparts (Rohner et al., 1980).

In India there are sometimes caste differences in perceived acceptance-rejection. Children's perceived acceptance (as measured by the Child PARQ) in the Bengali sample, for example, varies inversely with parents' caste status (Rohner and Chaki-Sircar, n.d.): The higher the caste of the child, the less the perceived maternal warmth ($r = -.26$, $p = .08$) and the more perceived maternal neglect ($r = -.29$, $p < .05$) children report experiencing. (Maternal hostility, undifferentiated rejection, and overall rejection perceived by Bengali children, however, are unrelated to caste standing.) These results are supported by mothers' own reports about their treatment of their children. That is, mothers' reports about their warmth toward and overall acceptance of their children (as measured by the Mother PARQ) vary inversely with their caste standing: The higher the caste of the child, the less the maternal warmth ($r = -.47$, $p < .001$) and the less overall maternal acceptance ($r = -.34$, $p < .02$) reported by mothers. (However, in mothers' reports about their behavior toward their children, caste status is unrelated to maternal hostility, neglect, and undifferentiated rejection.)

The meaning of these correlational data becomes clearer when one compares the lowest castes (Untouchables) with high castes (Brahmin and Sudra castes) in the Bengali sample. Here (Rohner and Chaki-Sircar, n.d.), high-caste children, in comparison with Untouchables, perceive their mothers (as assessed on the Child PARQ) to be significantly less warm ($t = 2.81$, $p < .007$), more neglecting ($t = 2.69$, $p < .01$), and more overall rejecting ($t = 2.24$, $p < .03$). Again, these results are supported by mothers' reports about their own treatment of their children as assessed by the Mother PARQ: In comparison with Untouchable mothers, high-caste mothers report being significantly less warm ($t = 4.45$, $p < .0001$) and more overall rejecting ($t = 2.02$, $p < .05$) toward their children. I must caution, however, that most children, as well as their mothers, in all caste levels within the Bengali sample report substantial amounts of maternal acceptance. Differences reported here in maternal behavior between caste groupings are mostly matters of emphasis within the range of accepting behaviors on the PARQ.

RELATIONSHIP BETWEEN PERCEIVED ACCEPTANCE-REJECTION AND ADULTS' PERSONALITY

Less work has been done with adults' retrospective recollections of parenting than with children's reports. Therefore, adult data in the United States and internationally are not as complete as for children. Nonetheless, available evidence shown in Table 7 suggests that in both the worldwide Love sample and in an American sample (Washington, D.C.) parental hostility (one of the principal expressions of overall rejection) is related significantly to the same cluster of personality dispositions in adults as overall rejection is for children, shown in Table 3. In general, the magnitude of the correlations among adults is similar to the magnitude among children in both the holocultural sample and the American sample—further suggesting convergent validity of results in PART's personality theory.

Several differences between Table 7 and Table 3 should be noted. In the holocultural sample for adults (Table 7)—unlike for children (Table 3)—it was possible to code emotional unresponsiveness, negative worldview, and emotional instability. All these variables correlate significantly with parental hostility. Moreover, as with the child sample, adult self-esteem and self-adequacy in the holocultural sample were combined to form an overall measure of self-evaluation. One further observation should be made from Table 7: Adult dependence in both the holocultural sample and the American sample are correlated significantly with parental hostility—unlike children's data in the All-America sample (Table 3).

Further evidence supporting PART's personality theory comes from three additional samples shown in Table 8 (unpublished data, CSPAR). First, a sample of 301 college students represents three tribal groups in Nigeria—the Hausa, Ibo, and Yoruba; another represents 71 col-

TABLE 7
Holocultural and Intracultural-American Correlations Between Parental Hostility and Adults' Personality[a]

Adult Personality Disposition	*Holocultural (Love) Sample (N = 101)*	*American Sample (Washington, D.C.)*[b] *(N = 147)*
Dependence	.39** (36)	.17*
Emotional unresponsiveness	.55*** (64)	.33***
Hostility/aggression	.41*** (67)	.44***
Negative self-esteem	.49***[c]	.46***
Negative self-adequacy	(32)	.44***
Negative worldview	.46*** (59)	.24**
Emotional instability	.73*** (34)	.36***

NOTE: All correlations are computed using Pearson's r. Numbers in parentheses in the holocultural sample column refer to the sample size. Data reported for the Love sample were published originally in Rohner (1975).
a. The parenting variable used in this table is parental hostility only, not all variables associated on the PARQ with a full measure of parental acceptance-rejection.
b. Data for the American sample have not been published heretofore. They are based on the Adult PARQ and the Adult PAQ.
c. Self-esteem and self-adequacy were combined in the Love sample to form a measure of overall self-evaluation.
$*p < .05$; $**p < .01$; $***p < .001$.

lege students in Sweden; and the third represents 47 Bengali mothers in a peasant village in India. Using the Adult PARQ, participants in these studies reflected on the maternal acceptance-rejection they experienced earlier in their families of origin; using the Adult PAQ, they evaluated their own personality dispositions. As shown in Table 8, perceived rejection in all three international samples correlates significantly with all personality dispositions except dependence. That is, insofar as respondents in the three samples perceive themselves to be rejected (which only a small minority of all respondents do, in varying degrees), they also report themselves to be somewhat aggressive, to have impaired feelings of self-esteem and self-adequacy, to be somewhat emotionally unresponsive, and emotionally unstable, and to have a somewhat negative worldview.

TABLE 8

Correlations Between Perceived Rejection (Adult PARQ) and Personality Dispositions (Adult PAQ) Among Nigerian and Swedish College Students, and Among Bengali Women

			Personality Dispositions					
Sociocultural System	*Aggression*	*Dependence*	*Negative Self-Esteem*	*Negative Self-Adequacy*	*Emotional Unresponsiveness*	*Emotional Instability*	*Negative Worldview*	*Overall PAQ Score*
Nigeria (English)[a]	.34***	.04	.41***	.34***	.28***	.30***	.38***	.45***
Sweden (Swedish)[b]	.28*	.11	.30*	.37**	.33**	.35**	.35**	.45***
West Bengal (Bengali)[c]	.57***	–.10	.29*	.37***	.51***	.52***	.71***	.64***

a. N = 30 Nigerian college students. Language of testing was English.
b. N = 71 Swedish college students. Language of testing was Swedish.
c. N = 47 Bengali mothers. Language of testing was Bengali.
$*p < .05$; $**p < .01$; $***p < .001$.

CROSS-CULTURAL GENERALIZABILITY OF PART'S PERSONALITY THEORY

Evidence presented here from holocultural research, from psychological research conducted in the United States, and from several international studies tends to converge on the same conclusion: Perceived acceptance-rejection seems to be related in a consistent way to the postulated set of personality dispositions of children and of adults—regardless of differences in race, language, culture, historical period, or other such limiting conditions. These results are reassuring because, following the logic of the universalist approach, to the extent that PART is a robust theory, the same conclusions should emerge from intracultural research—which measures *interindividual* variations in behavior within different nations—as emerge from holocultural research—which measures *intersocietal* variations in behavior cross-culturally.

"DEPENDENCE" IN PART'S PERSONALITY THEORY: A QUESTION MARK

Several times in this chapter I have commented on the weak correlation between parental rejection as measured on the PARQ and self-reported dependence as measured on the PAQ. A major reason for the consistently low correlation between these variables probably lies in the fact that the PAQ dependence scale seems to be an incomplete measure of the theoretical construct "dependence" described in personality theory. That is, the PAQ seems to assess only a portion of the full conceptual meaning of dependence described earlier in this book. Specifically, the PAQ dependence scale emphasizes individuals' desire for sympathy and encouragement from persons close to them when they are sick or having trouble. It does not assess other important indicators of dependence, such as approval seeking or proximity seeking—that is, the desire to be near or in physical contact with a significant other person. And, very importantly, the scale is not an overall measure of the extent to which an individual relies emotionally on significant others. (Perhaps for these reasons the PAQ dependence scale might be relabeled "succorance" and dropped from subsequent theory testing in PART's personality theory.)[10]

In the face of holocultural evidence in which the fuller conceptual definition of dependence was employed, the suspicion is heightened slightly that PAQ's truncated measure of dependence contributes to its low correlation with perceived rejection: The correlation between rejection and dependence in the Love sample is reasonably high and significant ($r = .31$, $p < .05$), but the correlation between dependence and rejection in the Standard sample, though reasonably high ($r = .25$), is significant at less than the 10% level. I should note here that few of the societies in either world sample fell into extremely rejecting ranges in which defensive independence (that is, major curvilinearity in Figure 6) is expected to emerge.

This matter of the expected curvilinearity of the relationship between rejection and dependence suggests another reason that the simple correlation between PARQ scales and the PAQ dependence scale might often be low. That is, because dependence is thought to have a curvilinear—not a linear—relation to perceived rejection, investigators should normally use a coefficient of curvilinearity rather than a coefficient such as Pearson's r, which assumes a linear relation between variables. Pearson's correlation coefficient was used throughout this chapter, however, because—as shown in Table 1—the distribution of PARQ scores in the international samples studied so far (except in Mexico) falls within the "accepted" range of the warmth dimension—the range in which dependence scores are expected to be more or less linearly related to acceptance (the "normal dependence" section of Figure 6).

It is clear that more work must be done on the dependence variable before any confident conclusions can be drawn about its empirical (versus theoretical) relationship to parental acceptance-rejection. One of these areas of work involves a careful analysis of the relationship between dependence and each of the PARQ scales separately, especially the warmth scale, which sometimes correlates positively and sometimes negatively with dependence. More specifically, maternal "coldness" (the PARQ "low-warmth" scale) correlates weakly but *positively* and significantly with child dependence in the southern Bohemia sample ($r = .18$, $p < .01$), and with adult dependence in the West Bengal sample ($r = .34$, $p < .01$). On the other hand, maternal "coldness" correlates weakly and *negatively,* but significantly, with child dependence in the All-America sample ($r = -.16$, $p < .001$), among the Korean-American children ($r = -.17$, $p < .05$), and in the Mexican sample ($r = -.40$, $p < .001$); maternal coldness correlates weakly and *negatively,* but significantly, with adult dependence among the Nigerian college students ($r = -.15$, $p < .01$). On all other PARQ scales—for children as well as for adults—when dependence correlates significantly with one of the PARQ scales (namely, maternal hostility, neglect, undifferentiated rejection, or overall rejection) it correlates positively—except in the Mexican sample, in which all four PARQ scales correlate negatively with dependence, as does overall rejection.

Why the direction of correlations between dependence and the PARQ warmth scale is so variable is not yet clear, but what is clear is that—within any given sample—a negative correlation between dependence and the warmth scale in conjunction with positive correlations between dependence and all other PARQ scales must, mathematically, pull down the apparent correlation between dependence and overall rejection. Thus one is likely to conclude erroneously that dependence is unrelated to overall perceived rejection when in fact it may be related to different aspects of the rejection process in qualitatively different ways.

One final problem in this context is worthy of note. Dependence may sometimes relate to maternal coldness (low warmth) among boys differently from the way it relates to maternal coldness among girls. This sex difference emerged in the Telegu-speaking sample of Andra Pradesh, India. There, the overall correlation between dependence and maternal coldness for both sexes combined was $r = -.09$ (p = n.s.), but when the sample was partitioned by gender a different picture emerged: The correlation between dependence and maternal coldness among girls rose significantly to $r = -.21$ ($p < .05$), but the correlation remained nearly zero for boys ($r = .01$, p = n.s.) (unpublished data, CSPAR). No other personality characteristic on the PAQ showed such inconsistency in its relation with individual PARQ scales or with total PARQ scores.[11]

PARENTAL REJECTION AND THE LIVES OF UNWANTED CHILDREN: LONGITUDINAL EVIDENCE

Some issues that are related to the warmth dimension of parenting do not show up easily on the sociocultural systems model, or they sometimes become masked in static correlations between the PARQ and the PAQ. Abortion and its sequelae constitute one such issue. Populations the world over know about birth control procedures of one kind or another, including abortion (Ayres, 1954). In some societies women may freely have abortions without negative social sanction. Indeed, women are sometimes encouraged or even required to have abortions under certain conditions. In other societies the very suspicion that a woman might have attempted an abortion could be reason enough for public censure, reprisal, ostracism, and perhaps death. The range of sentiment about and penalties for abortion is wide indeed.

How do variations in the severity of punishment for abortion relate to parental acceptance-rejection? This issue produces one of the strongest correlations yet found in holocultural research ($r = -.76$, $p < .01$): The more severe the penalties for abortion, the less likely children are to be loved and accepted after birth (Rohner, 1975). In effect, severe penalties for abortion constrain women from having abortions, but as a result many unwanted children are born. An unwanted child is a child at risk. Alternatively, one can say that in societies with no penalties or slight penalties for abortion, only wanted children are born—and, as shown in the Love sample, wanting a child is a fair cross-cultural prognosticator of subsequent love and affection ($phi = .63$, $p = .001$; Rohner, 1975).

Matějček et al. (1978, 1980) and associates (David and Matějček, 1981) confirm and amplify these conclusions in their long-term longitudinal study of unwanted children in Czechoslovakia. The government of Czechoslovakia liberalized its abortion policy in 1957, permitting district abortion commissions to approve requests made by pregnant women to terminate unwanted pregnancies during the first three months of gestation. Through fortuitous circumstances it became possible for the researchers to gain access to the 1961-1963 records of the Prague Appellate Abortion Commission, and subsequently to match 220 children (110 boys and 110 girls) born to women who had been denied abortion on two occasions for the same pregnancy with 220 children of mothers who had not sought pregnancy termination. The fact that women in the unwanted-pregnancy group petitioned a second time to terminate their pregnancies—after having the first application disapproved—suggests that these women truly did not want to carry their pregnancies full term. I should note, however, that some women who were determined not to give birth probably found nonlegal means of terminating their pregnancies, and some mothers gave up their infants for adoption or to the permanent care of relatives. In this way extreme cases of "unwantedness" were probably eliminated from the study.

Insofar as possible, the 220 unwanted children in the study were matched child for child with the 220 wanted children in terms of age, sex, birth order, number of siblings, and grade in school. Mothers were matched for age, marital status, presence of fathers in the home, and socioeconomic status as determined by the husband's occupation. The research was initiated in 1971 when the children were between 8 and 10 years old. All 440 children were thoroughly examined medically and psychologically by members of the research team, who did not know to which group any given child belonged. For each matched pair the research team collected psychological, sociological, medical, and educational records, as well as psychological and sociological data based on interviews with the children themselves, their parents, teachers, and peers. Overall, more than 400 different measures were taken on each child. Based on 60 of the most significant measures, the researchers developed an overall "maladaptation score" for each child. The higher a child's score on the maladaptation scale the more at risk developmentally the child was believed to be.

As mentioned earlier, the research was initiated in 1971, when the children were, on the average, 8 to 10 years old. Even after so many years following the children's birth, Matějček et al. found significant differences between the wanted-pregnancy and unwanted-pregnancy groups (hereafter referred to as *wanted* and *unwanted* children). For example, the researchers reported a significantly greater incidence of "negative relationship between mother and child" in the unwanted group than in the wanted group ($p < .001$).

Unwanted-pregnancy mothers described their children as being naughty, stubborn, and bad-tempered more often than did the mothers of wanted children. Overall, families of the unwanted children were less stable, as determined by their greater unhappiness and greater divorce rate ($p < .025$), than the other group of families.

Matějček et al. provided little information in 1978 on the personality characteristics of concern to PAR theory, but they did indicate other tendencies consistent with the expectations of the theory. For example, the unwanted children performed less well in school than the wanted children, and the unwanted children were "rejected as friends" in school sociometric ratings more often than the wanted children ($p < .05$). Unwanted children were also ascribed less desirable social chracteristics by peers.[12] Moreover, both teachers and parents judged the unwanted children to be less intelligent than the wanted children. This judgment about differences in intelligence is particularly revealing in view of the fact that the two groups of children performed almost identically on the Wechsler Intelligence Scale for Children (WISC). (The mean WISC score for wanted children was 103.3; for the unwanted children it was 102.4.)

Given these experiences, it is not surprising that the unwanted children as a group disliked school more than did the wanted children ($p < .005$), and that in the face of frustration the behavior of the unwanted children was significantly less adaptive ($p < .05$) than that of their wanted counterparts. Overall, the unwanted children—especially the boys—scored higher than the wanted children on the maladaptation scale described earlier ($p < .005$). Differences among girls in the two groups were less marked, but overall differences were less favorable for the unwanted girls. Significant differences were noted for "only children" ($p < .01$): They had the lowest maladaptation score among the wanted children and the highest among the unwanted children. In this research it appears that an only child born of an unwanted pregnancy may be at maximum social risk. I should note, however, that few of the differences between the two groups—wanted and unwanted—are dramatic. Differences are often statistically significant but not numerically large.

I should also point out that some of these unwanted-pregnancy children later became wanted children—that is, they became loved and accepted. Similarly, there is no reason to think that at least a few of the wanted-pregnancy children were not later rejected by their parents. Simply wanting a child before birth is not, by itself, sufficient to guarantee that child's acceptance following birth, although, as noted before, there is a worldwide tendency for "desire for children" to be associated with subsequent acceptance.

In 1977, Matějček et al. (1980) followed up on these children, who were then 14 to 16 years old. Remarkably, 216 of the original 220 unwanted children were still available to be studied, along with 215 of the wanted children. In this phase of the work, the researchers collected questionnaire and rating-scale data from the families and from the schools, and they administered the Children's Report of Parental Behavior Inventory (CRPBI; Schludermann and Schludermann, 1970) to the children. These tests showed that the unwanted-pregnancy children perceived less positive maternal interest than did the wanted-pregnancy group ($p < .05$), but there was no significant difference between groups in the amount of hostility perceived. In comparison with the wanted-pregnancy children, the unwanted group also reported either greater maternal neglect or more intrusive maternal control. Fathers' behavior was experienced by both groups as similar to that of mothers, but to a less marked degree.

The adolescents continued over the years to react to these perceived differences in parenting. School performance, for example, worsened for the unwanted-pregnancy group, especially for the males. It was not that the unwanted youths were failing in school, but that they were considerably underrepresented in the "above-average" and "outstanding" groups. This trend is related to the fact that teachers more often rated the unwanted youths as having less desirable working skills. Those in the unwanted group were also judged by teachers as well as by mothers to be less conscientious ($p < .05$), more excitable (emotionally unstable?) ($p < .02$), and less obedient ($p < .05$). And from the teachers' point of view the unwanted group, especially the girls, tended to be either undersociable (withdrawn?), hypersociable or hyperactive. By this time, 43 of the unwanted adolescents (31 males and 12 females) had come to the attention of child psychiatric or school counseling centers in Prague. Of the wanted youths, 30 (18 males and 12 females) had also come to clinical attention, but those in the latter group were seen primarily for minor developmental deficits or for referral to special schools, remedial treatment, or delayed school entrance. The unwanted adolescents, on the other hand, were seen more often for serious behavior disorders requiring educational or psychological therapy.

Finally, two years later (in 1979) Matějček and associates (David and Matějček, 1981) again studied the youths, who were by then 16 and 18 years old. Among other instruments, the researchers administered the Child PARQ. Unwanted males (but not females) perceived themselves to be neglected or rejected by their mothers more often than by their fathers. This conclusion was supported by Matějček's Childhood, Marriage and Family Questionnaire, which suggested that the emotional gap between unwanted males and their mothers was widening and deteriorating over time. The relationship between unwanted females and their mothers seemed to remain stable or improve.

The Prague study shows that the social, emotional, and educational effects of parental rejection/unwantedness are apt to persist at least into adolescence. Future follow-up studies will tell to what extent these effects persist into adulthood, and perhaps get passed on to the next generation. The Prague study also suggests that boys may be more endangered developmentally by the effects of unwantedness than girls. This conclusion is echoed by recently emerging evidence in the United States and other parts of the world; for example, Rutter (1970b, 1979b, 1983) and others (Dunn et al., 1981; Hetherington, 1980; Wallerstein and Kelly, 1980) have found boys to be more vulnerable to the effects of stress than girls. I must add a word of caution before ending, however. In the aggregate, developmental differences between wanted and unwanted children are significant, but for individual children the differences are often difficult to detect. Indeed, as one would expect from coping theory, discussed later, some of the unwanted children in the Prague study coped very well despite their rejecting family experiences.

NOTES

1. Data from the community study component of this program of anthroponomical research on parental acceptance and rejection are presented in a separate book on a peasant agricultural village in West Bengal, India (Rohner and Chaki-Sircar, n.d.). Additional community study research is planned for the future.

2. Ethnographers seldom report the kind of information needed to code self-esteem and self-adequacy as separate constructs in holocultural research. Therefore, these two variables were combined into a more general construct called "self-evaluation."

3. Codes for sex differences in parents' (mothers' versus fathers') and others' behavior toward boys versus girls are reported for the Standard sample in Rohner and Rohner (1981b).

4. The "back-translation" process involved translation of the PARQ and PAQ into the target language by a bilingual speaker of that language and English. A second bilingual speaker back-translated this version into English, and the two English versions were then compared. The process was repeated until an appropriate version of the questionnaire was created for the target language. Subsequently, other procedures were used to make the questionnaire as culturally appropriate as possible.

5. As with many other questionnaires of its kind, the PARQ is sometimes susceptible to social desirability response bias. Investigators should often question PARQ scores that fall into the 60s or maybe even the 70s. In the relatively infrequent cases in which PARQ scores fall this low, the investigator may suspect that the respondent is intentionally or unintentionally portraying his or her family in an unrealistically idealistic way. This idealistic portrayal of the parent may reveal "denial" on the part of the respondent. In support of this view, it is worth mentioning that Nielsen (1984b) found that sexually violent adolescents reported their mothers as perfect 10s on his acceptance-rejection scale (perfect acceptance), but further inquiry showed that this portrait of the mother represented massive denial on the adolescents' part.

6. In this context it is also worth mentioning that between 7% and 10% of the American children who respond to the Child PARQ score 150 or higher, revealing that they perceive themselves to be rejected. This 7% to 10% range is also common in international studies of parental acceptance-rejection.

7. Averaging PARQ scores as I have done is risky, and masks the fact that substantial variability exists in children's and adults' perceptions of acceptance-rejection cross-culturally. It may be true that most children are accepted in most societies, but in some societies most children are rejected. And within any given society—regardless of the typical modal style of parenting—some children are treated with greater nurturance than others.

8. The pattern of correlations in the three American samples was strikingly similar (another indication of convergent validity of PAR theory); therefore, the samples were combined for ease of presentation.

9. Aggression, negative self-esteem, and emotional instability among Bengali children also emerge in Table 4 as being nonsignificantly related to perceived rejection. I have no explanation at this time for these unusual results.

10. Ironically, the frequent failure of the PAQ dependence scale to correlate significantly with perceived acceptance-rejection has a latent advantage: It raises doubts about the argument made by critics that the PARQ and PAQ correlated with each other not for the theoretical reasons postulated, but only because of shared "response bias" (see McCord, 1979). That is, some critics assert that rejected (or accepted) children do not respond in differentiated ways to the true item content of self-report questionnaires such as the PARQ and PAQ; rather, children respond on the basis of some underlying and unassessed disposition such as "negativity" (or "positivity"). Some children are more "negativistic" than others, and, accordingly, they may respond to items on the PARQ and PAQ in a negative way; positively disposed children might respond positively, the claim is made, to items on these questionnaires—rather than responding to the true personal significance of the individual items. Insofar as children (or adults) have general dispositions to respond negatively or positively to the questionnaires, spurious correlations can be created that have no relation to individuals' true experiences with themselves or their parents.

A variety of sources of evidence cast doubt on this interpretation regarding the PARQ and PAQ (see Rohner, 1984a: 38-39, 83-86), but here I shall merely point out that if response bias were a major factor affecting the relationship between PARQ scales and PAQ scales, then the dependence scale would probably correlate with the PARQ at least as well as the other PAQ scales. To the extent that this line of reasoning is correct, perhaps PAQ's dependence scale can be used as a measure of response bias.

11. As described earlier, personality theory postulates that dependence varies not only with the form and severity of rejection measured on the PARQ, but also with the length of time that the child has experienced rejection, and with the consistency or inconsistency of parents' rejecting behaviors. Including the variables of "chronicity" and "inconsistency" in the scheme might improve the correlation between perceived rejection and dependence. Up to this point, neither the PARQ nor holocultural research, however, has measured chronicity or inconsistency directly. These are examples of additional areas in which more work is needed.

12. The unwanted children also experienced a greater number of acute illnesses ($p < .05$) than the wanted children, but not long-term diseases, accidents, or hospitalizations.

6

Parental Acceptance and Rejection in Life-Span Perspective

Two related classes of questions are addressed in this chapter. First, what effect does parental rejection seem to have when it is experienced for the first time at specific stages in life—infancy, childhood, adolescence, adulthood, and old age? Second, is there a period in human development when a person is especially vulnerable or susceptible to the effects of rejection? In certain respects both questions are shrouded in uncertainty and controversy because insufficient empirical evidence exists to settle the issues. Nonetheless, I believe it is important to expose the issues, and to lay out briefly my position with respect to them.

INFANCY

Children seem to experience, process cognitively, and respond to parental rejection in qualitatively different ways during the three major development epochs prior to adulthood: infancy, childhood, and adolescence. Many people, especially those who draw from psychoanalytic theory (for example, Freud, 1949, 1959; Berman, 1958; Bowlby, 1940, 1951, 1969; Erikson, 1950), believe that the experiences of infancy have lifelong developmental implications. Nielsen (1984: 1) provides a clear and recent illustration of this belief:

> Both theory and clinical research . . . suggest that the first year of life plays a unique and crucial role in establishing the basis of personality

> development and later behavior, e.g., the establishment of trust and empathic abilities, upon which all later emotional development will be dependent. Individuals who have traumatic disruptions during this period are often described like a well constructed house built upon a cracked and faulty foundation. They don't do well under later stresses and pressures, regardless of its source.

Although widely believed, little empirical evidence (see, for example, Bayley and Schaefer, 1960; Clarke and Clarke, 1976; Kagan, 1976; Rutter, 1972) supports popular assertions such as this about the long-term effects of rejection and maternal deprivation resulting from infancy, that is, during the first year or so of life.[1] This should not be very surprising, however, because rejection is a symbolic process in that it requires understanding or comprehension of something equivalent to "Mother doesn't love me." This in turn seems to require the development of a sufficiently articulated sense of "self" and of "other." In other words, it appears that there must be a "me," and there must be recognition of that "other" person, mother or father. This is a complex developmental phenomenon that does not seem to occur fully until after the first year of life. Kagan (1974: 93) echoes this viewpoint: "We must acknowledge an important discontinuity in the meaning of acceptance-rejection for the child prior to eighteen months of age, before he symbolically evaluates the action of others, in contrast to the symbolic child of three or four years." Indeed, according to Kagan (1978a: 73), the infant's first experiences may be permanently lost: "The infant's mind may be more like a sandy beach on a windy day than a reel of recording tape."

Claims regarding the primacy of the infancy period are often confounded insofar as researchers and clinicians retrospectively trace the development of children from infancy into early childhood. When they find rejected children (for example, 9 years old) responding the way PAR theory predicts, they sometimes argue that this represents evidence that the effects of rejection begin in infancy. However, the clinician/researcher has no way of knowing for certain when the behavioral effects of rejection begin to appear for the first time. In all likelihood, the most significant effects do not emerge until after the first year of life. This controversy regarding the significance of infancy will probably continue until appropriate longitudinal data are collected, ideally on samples in which infants are rejected during their first year and then subsequently accepted.[2]

Although appropriate longitudinal data are absent regarding the long-term effects of rejection occurring during infancy only, a holocultural study provides modest evidence on the issue. Drawing a subsample of thirty societies from the Love sample (Rohner, 1975), coders rated variations in parental acceptance-rejection typically expressed toward infants (under 12 months of age) around the world. The coders also rated the behavioral dispositions of 2- through 6-year-old children in the sample societies. Correlations between parental behavior in infancy and children's personalities were weak and statistically nonsignificant. That is, variations in parents' behavior toward infants were not related to the personality characteristics of young children. One cannot claim too much from this study, however, because the sample was small, though representative. Nonetheless, the results are suggestive and consistent with the expectations of PAR theory and with the conclusion by Rutter (1970a), who found from his critical review of the developmental and clinical literature that behavioral characteristics of infants during the first six months of life are essentially nonpredictive of subsequent behavioral characteristics of children or of adults.

I want to add a word of caution at this point. My argument here is only that the expected consequences of rejection are not likely to persist into middle childhood if the rejection ceases before earliest childhood, that is, before 1½ to 2 years of age. I do not argue that the effects of other forms of parenting might not persist for some years following infancy, though many experts in the past several years have cast doubt on that too (Clarke and Clarke, 1976; Kagan, 1976; Turkington, 1982). Also, I do not suggest that the physical effects of some forms of rejection such as battering might not persist through life. Fractures, ruptures, and other physical traumas resulting from battering obviously can have lifelong implications.

I use the age of 1½ to 2 years as the approximate threshold distinguishing infancy from early childhood. If such a thing as a "sensitive period" exists when children are most susceptible developmentally to the effects of rejection, this age probably marks its onset. This age range should be viewed as a rough marker only, however, not as an absolute threshold. The age of heightened vulnerability varies from child to child. I use 18 to 24 months as an approximate criterion, because by 2 years of age children usually are competent in language. Language per se may not be important for rejection—given that many forms of rejection are not linguistic—but the capacity for language signals a level of cognitive development that is probably required before the rejection process has its full symbolic impact.

CHILDHOOD

For my purposes in PAR theory, childhood is construed as the period from 2 through 12 years. It is during this time, I suspect, that rejection is likely to have its most pronounced impact. If there is such a thing as a period of heightened vulnerability to rejection, this is probably it. Although complex cognitive, social, emotional, physical, and other forms of growth and development occur in children from 2 to 12 years, there do not appear to be significant differences in children's responses throughout the period to perceived rejection, at least with respect to the personality dispositions of major concern to PART's personality theory (except possibly in very earliest childhood, when it is difficult to assess some of the PART-related personality dispositions of children). Generally, however, 6-year-olds seem to respond to rejection in the same way as 12-year-olds—with the exception, of course, of individual differences within and across age groups (unpublished data, CSPAR). Some 6-year-olds, for example, have a more clearly differentiated sense of self than other 6-year-olds, or even than some 7-, 8-, or 9-year-olds (Maccoby, 1980). And, as I observe later in Chapter 7, a differentiated sense of self seems to be one of the social cognitive factors that helps children cope with perceived rejection.

What makes childhood, versus infancy and adolescence, the time when humans are most vulnerable to rejection? No doubt it has to do with the fact that children, unlike infants, are capable of complex linguistic and nonlinguistic symbolizing. Young children are in the process of constructing a sense of "self" and "nonself," but they still tend to be quite egocentric in that they do not yet seem able to see the world as others see it. That is, they cannot yet take the perspective of the other person (Selman, 1976; Selman and Byrne, 1974; Rubin and Pepler, 1980). As Piaget has put it, they cannot assume points of view different from their own, so when their mothers or fathers snarl at them after getting disappointing news that an anticipated event has been canceled, young children often seem unable to understand that their parents are not really angry at them, but simply disappointed about the cancellation (Ginsburg and Opper, 1979). Apparently, many children develop the capacity for such perspective-taking and depersonalizing only in late childhood or adolescence (Shantz, 1975), and some individuals never develop the understanding. For reasons such as this the lives of young children are in many symbolic respects different from the symbolic world of adolescents and adults, as Piaget (Ginsburg and Opper, 1979) and others have shown in recent years (see, for example, Maccoby, 1980). Moreover, very young children have fewer cognitive, social, or emotional resources than older children to fend—psychologically or physically—against the acid mist of day-to-day yelling, belittling, hitting, emotional coldness, and other forms of rejection.

ADOLESCENCE

What happens if the rejection process begins *for the first time* during adolescence? How are youths of this age affected in relation to younger children? Well-researched empirical evidence on this question is scanty, but I expect that the effects of rejection beginning for the first time in adolescence are likely, in most cases, to have less severe long-term effects than the effects of rejection that begins in childhood. In other words, the effects of rejection in adolescence often seem to be truncated in relation to the effects in childhood. Why? Because adolescents frequently have cognitive (Shantz, 1975) and other psychological as well as physical resources available to them that younger children do not. Adolescents often have a fairly well-developed sense of self—or sense of identity (Erikson, 1968; Conger, 1977)—which can (as described more fully in Chapter 7) help shield them to some degree from the negative effects of rejection. Moreover, they often have more or less positive self-esteem, and feelings of self-adequacy; they are more or less emotionally stable and emotionally responsive, and if they had been accepted as children, they are likely to have developed in a more or less "positive" direction the other personality dispositions pertinent to PART's personality theory. Rejection may temporarily disrupt these characteristics, especially if it becomes chronic during adolescence, but dispositions often seem to return to their former, more stable, level when the rejection has passed, or when the adolescent has left the rejecting family. Moreover, as mentioned above, adolescents often have social-cognitive capabilities that are usually unavailable to younger children, capabilities that help them cope mentally and emotionally with perceived rejection. (These social-cognitive attributes are discussed at length in Chapter 7.)

Still another class of factors helping adolescents deal more effectively with rejection than younger children is the fact that extrafamilial influences have generally assumed greater salience around this time. The direct and immediate impact of the family is thus diluted by peers and peers' families, by teachers, and by other extrafamilial people and agencies. Finally, the adolescent is often big enough and strong enough to block some forms of rejection. For example, as a child, an adolescent that I know had been knocked around physically by his father. After reaching adolescence, the youth said, on one occasion when his father was threatening him, "Knock it off! If you touch me again I'll flatten you!" The father was startled by the realization that his son now had the physical capacity to stand up for himself, to fight back if necessary. It seems clear, then, that neither the subjective nor the objective world of adolescents is the same as it is for younger children.

ADULTHOOD

Rejection can occur at any point in the life cycle, and it occurs in many relationships other than parent-child relationships (for example, among friends, between lovers, and between spouses). Probably all contexts of rejection in which a primary relationship is ruptured produce some of the same effects as parental rejection—at least for a short time. The breakup of a marriage, for example, may be associated with anger, defensive independence, impaired self-esteem, emotional instability, and so forth. Rejection in contexts such as these is probably much more common among adults than is *parental* rejection (that is, rejection of an adult offspring by parents). I know of no information about the effects of parental rejection when it begins for the first time in adulthood, but one can speculate that the effects would vary according to the importance of the relationship to the individual. For those adults who still have a primary relationship with the rejecting parent—who continue to care a great deal about what the parent does and thinks—the rejection process is no doubt painful. But for normal adults the effects are not likely to be long-lasting, at least with respect to the characteristics of major concern to PART's personality theory.

Rejection extending from early childhood into adulthood is another matter. Here, as I have said before, the outcome may be felt for a lifetime. Even though most people seem to have some positive experiences as they mature from childhood to adulthood—experiences that may help mute the more traumatic consequences of rejection—adults who were rejected as children are nonetheless apt to carry some of the scars into adulthood. And, for reasons described earlier, such people tend to perpetuate the rejection cycle onto the next generation (see Horney, 1933; Gelles, 1980; Straus et al., 1980).

These conclusions about the effects of childhood rejection extending into adulthood find support in holocultural research using the Love sample (Rohner, 1975). These data show that adults tend to display the expected constellation of personality characteristics in societies where they have been rejected as children.[3] That is, these adults tend, more than adults who have been accepted as children, to be hostile, aggressive, or passive-aggressive or to have problems with the management of hostility and aggression, to be more dependent, to have impaired self-evaluation, to be less emotionally responsive and less emotionally stable, and to have a more negative worldview. More fine-grained evidence regarding the long-term effects of childhood rejection comes from the longitudinal research conducted in the United States. Analyzing data in the Berkeley Growth Study (in which study members were born in the late 1920s), for example, Block and Haan (1972) found that parental warmth, stability, and overall acceptance (or rejection) in childhood tended to affect individual's development and performance at all age levels over the subsequent half century—but substantial personality changes also occurred well beyond childhood (see also Moss and Susman, 1980).

OLD AGE: AS YOU SOW, SO SHALL YOU REAP

Rejection of the elderly is not uncommon in America (Costa, 1984; Gelles and Cornell, 1985), and sometimes occurs cross-culturally (see, for example, Koyama et al., 1980). The reason may sometimes be summarized by the aphorism, "As you sow, so shall you reap." That is, as shown in the following studies, adult offspring who have been rejected as children tend worldwide to reject their own parents in turn when the parents reach dependent old age.

Birmingham (1982) provided cross-cultural evidence on this issue. Using the Love sample of 101 societies, she coded the treatment of the elderly cross-culturally. She then correlated her codes on treatment of the elderly with codes on parental acceptance-rejection from the same sample. In the course of her work she asked several questions, including the following: In societies where children are accepted, are the elderly treated by adults with greater respect than in societies where children are rejected? In societies where children are accepted, is advice heeded and sought from the elderly more often than in societies where children are rejected? Do adults in societies where children are accepted have different views about death from the views maintained by adults in societies where children are rejected? For all three questions Birmingham found results consistent with PAR theory's general expectation that if parents reject their children, parents place their own dependent old age at risk for counterrejection.

Regarding the first question, Birmingham found a worldwide tendency for overall parental acceptance-rejection to be related significantly ($r = .25$, $p = .02$) to respect for the elderly. That is, insofar as parents are warm and loving toward their children, the offspring as adults tend to show respect for their aged parents. Parental hostility was related even more strongly but negatively to respect for the elderly ($r = -.30$, $p = .01$). That is, as parental hostility increases around the world, respect for the elderly decreases. Parental neglect is virtually the same ($r = -.33$, $p = .005$): As parental neglect of children increases, respect for the elderly decreases.

What about seeking advice from the elderly? Why are the aged sometimes sought out as a source of wisdom and experience, and sometimes their advice is mocked and discounted? Birmingham found here too that the quality of treatment of the elderly is related the world over to the quality of treatment of children. That is, insofar as parents accept their children, the advice of the aged tends to be sought and accepted ($r = .56$, $p = .0005$). And, as before, parental hostility is related negatively to attitudes toward advice of the elderly ($r = -.44$, $p = .008$); parental neglect, too, is related negatively to these attitudes ($r = -.54$, $p = .001$). That is, respect for advice of the elderly decreases insofar as parental hostility and neglect increase.

Death is recognized as a normal and natural part of life in most societies of the world, but in some places it is attributed to the working of evil forces, and must be combated at all costs. In other societies, death is preferred to a dependent old age: It is better to die than to be dependent on the people around you, especially your own children. Birmingham found that in societies where parents accept their children, old age and death are accepted as normal parts of life, but in societies where children are rejected, death often tends to be preferable to a dependent old age. Thus cross-cultural evidence supports the slightly revised dictum, "As you sow rejection onto your children, so shall you reap rejection in your own dependent old age."

This conclusion finds further support in the United States, where Rohner and Schrader (1982) studied the treatment of 27 elderly patients placed in nursing homes by their adult offspring. The authors asked whether or not adult offspring who recalled having been rejected in childhood behave less solicitously toward their now instrumentally dependent parents confined to nursing homes. Do these adult offspring visit their parents less often than those offspring who had been accepted? Do they write less often, call less often, and in other ways reveal less concern for these aged parents? The study was inconclusive because all but one of the adult offspring perceived themselves to have had at least "fair" relationships with their parents. Nonetheless, comparing those adults who reported having had only "fair" relationships with those reporting having had "good" relationships with their parents, the authors found that perceived acceptance-rejection made a difference. In general, those adults who had "good" relationships with their parents in childhood visited their parents in nursing homes more frequently than the others. They visited their parents several times a month, whereas those with only "fair" relationships said they visited their parents, on the average, about once a month. The authors suspect the estimate of the latter group may be overly optimistic, however, because when they asked the adult offspring when they last visited their parents, the offspring acknowledged that it had been about three to six months, on the average. One can speculate that adult offspring who had "poor" relationships with their parents (that is, those who felt positively rejected) would visit even less frequently, perhaps accounting for many of the elderly in nursing homes nationally who are said to be abandoned by their children (see Smith and Bengtson, 1979).

NOTES

1. The phrase "long-term effects" is ambiguous. Some researchers, for example, regard three months as long-term, but in PAR theory I am interested in sequellae of acceptance-rejection spanning five to ten or more years, or even spanning the course of a lifetime.

2. These children might be compared at around age 9 or 10 years, let's say, with a second group of children who had been rejected continuously from birth onward, and with a third group who had been continuously accepted—and perhaps a fourth group who were accepted as infants and rejected as children. From PAR theory one would

predict that after nine or ten years the first group of children—those who had been rejected in infancy and subsequently accepted as children—would not be measurably different from children who had been continuously accepted, but both groups would be different in ways predicted by the theory from children in the second and fourth groups who had been rejected after age 2 or later, regardless of what their infancy had been like in terms of the warmth dimension.

3. The conclusion is partly inferential because actual longitudinal data in the sample societies are unavailable. The inference is made in these small, stable, often tribal-organized societies that the adults were, in most cases, treated approximately the same way as they now treat their own children. Hence the current personality characteristics of adults probably reflect to a significant degree the continuity over time of personality characteristics developed in childhood, as a result—at least in part—of varying degrees of parental acceptance and rejection. This inference can be made only insofar as the sample societies were stable in their child training practices across two generations. Examination of historical documents pertaining to the sample ethnographies showed—where relevant information was available—that the great majority of sample societies had indeed been stable in this respect.

7

Coping with Perceived Rejection

REJECTION, CREATIVITY, AND COMPETENCE

This chapter addresses a topic alluded to several times throughout this book, specifically, the fact that some children and adults seem to deal with parental rejection and maltreatment more effectively than others. I also want to underscore the possibility that not all effects of rejection are necessarily negative. This statement is, of course, controversial, but as one looks at biographies of eminent personalities in history one discovers a surprising number of people who came from troubled, rejecting backgrounds. Louis Armstrong, Emily Bronte, Anton Chekhov, Maxim Gorky, Henrik Ibsen, John Stuart Mill, Edgar Allen Poe (Goertzel and Goertzel, 1962), George Bernard Shaw (Howe, 1982), and Mark Twain (Sears, 1979) are just a few of many well-known personalities who experienced rejection in childhood. And then there are infamous people such as Adolf Hitler, who reached the highest level of international notoriety despite being abused as a child and emotionally crippled as an adult (Miller, 1983). Did people such as these achieve political, scientific, artistic, literary, or humanistic accomplishments *because* of their life experiences, which included rejection, or *despite* them? Is it possible that in the process of working through or psychologically dealing with the experiences of rejection they were able to produce something truly unusual, innovative, and creative?

Some of these people are what I call "instrumental" copers (versus "affective" copers). That is, parental rejection does not seem to have impaired them significantly in the task-oriented, competence aspects of their lives, but the same cannot necessarily be said about them emotionally, in the sense of positive mental health. Hitler, for example, seemed to be an instrumental coper to a large degree, but biographies (for example, Miller, 1983) depict him as a desperately crippled human being emotionally.

The speculation that some incidents of special creativity are tied to the experience of parental rejection is supported in the research of Siegelman (1973), who studied the correlates of creativity among 144 male and 274 female college students. Using the Parent-Child Relations Questionnaire, Short Form 1 (Roe and Siegelman, 1963; Siegelman, 1965a) to assess students' perceptions of childhood acceptance-rejection, and the Sixteen Personality Factor Questionnaire (Cattell et al., 1957) to measure personality factors associated with creativity (see Cattell and Butcher, 1968), Siegelman found that students with personality traits frequently associated with creativity (including "reserved," "intelligent," "serious," "adventurous," "sensitive," "self-sufficient," and "independent") tended to describe both parents as more rejecting than loving while they were growing up.[1] Potentially less creative students more often described parents as loving. I should emphasize that these were not students who had actually created something novel. They were merely regarded as *potentially* creative by Cattell and Eber's (1968) measure of personality factors associated with creative scientists, artists, teachers, administrators, researchers, and writers. I should also note that the magnitude of correlations between perceived rejection and the personality factors associated with creativity was generally low, accounting for a maximum of 6% of the variance. Nonetheless, Siegelman's results are consistent with prior work done by Arasteh (1968) and Domino (1969), who reported little warmth between creative individuals and their parents.

These results seem to be consistent with a separate tradition of research linking loss and bereavement with unusual achievement or genius. Wolfenstein (1969), for example, developed the hypothesis that individuals' reactions to the rage of being abandoned through death can lead some persons to either outstanding accomplishments or outstanding antisocial behavior. Subsequently, in an empirical study of 699 eminent persons in history, Eisenstadt (1978) found that sampled "geniuses" in history had experienced orphanhood in youth significantly more often than noneminent controls. He sought to explain the relationship between childhood loss of parent and genius through a process of coping creatively with bereavement; that is, in coping with bereavement some individuals develop personality characteristics needed for long-term creative effort.

The possible tie between parental rejection and subsequent achievement finds further suggestive evidence in an anecdote related to me a few years ago by a psychologist whose job it was to try to determine what makes successful senior-level executives in giant corporations such as the Ford Motor Company and Xerox Corporation.[2] His task was to try to create an instrument that would predict who would be successful at the highest levels of management in these giant interlocking corporations. In the process of doing his work he looked at the people already in these positions. What were they like? Based on his first tentative impressions, he described what sounded very much like adults who had been rejected as children. That is, he described men who were emotionally unresponsive, cold, calculating (though rejected persons are not necessarily calculating), and perhaps defensively independent, and who had problems coping with hostility, especially their own. These executives did not, however, seem to have problems with impaired self-esteem and self-adequacy. The psychologist was unable at that time to comment on their emotional stability or worldview. These tentative conclusions seemed to suggest that if parents aspire for their children to reach the highest levels in the multinational corporate structure they must, among other things, reject them in the proper way and to the proper extent. Neither of us felt ready to accept this conclusion at face value, but it did dramatize the point—along with the other information already presented here—that adults from rejecting backgrounds may achieve instrumental success in business, the creative arts, the sciences, politics, and most other domains of human endeavor.

This optimistic portrayal of rejected, creative achievers is tempered by opposing data. Richardson (1965), for example, found that first-year college women who scored high on tests of creative thinking tended to perceive their parents as significantly more loving and less rejecting than did first-year college women who scored low on such tests. Moreover, Esty (1968) reported that college student leaders (versus nonleaders) came from families in which parents were perceived as more loving and less neglecting, rejecting, and overprotecting than nonleader controls. In addition, it is also the case that rejected children tend to do more poorly in school than accepted children (Barwick and Arbuckle, 1962; Covington, 1966; Faizel, 1968; Hahn, 1980; Starkey, 1980) and to perform less well on IQ and achievement tests (Chan, 1981; Manley, 1977; Starkey, 1980). So, overall, they are less likely than accepted children to reach the educational level required for certain kinds of major accomplishments.

AFFECTIVE COPING

Parental rejection does not seem to interfere with instrumental or task competence or occupational performance (instrumental coping) to the same extent as it impairs social-emotional development and functioning (affective coping). Solid evidence on the affective coping process is yet to be marshaled, but it may be that approximately 80% of rejected children respond the way PAR theory predicts.[3] That is, they succumb, in varying degrees, to the expectable effects of rejection described earlier. Perhaps 20% of these rejected children, however, manage to cope more effectively with perceived rejection than do most children. These children are represented graphically in Figure 7. As portrayed there, (affective) "copers" are children who perceive themselves to be rejected, but who nonetheless have basically positive mental health, as defined by PART's personality theory. (Hereafter in this chapter, when I refer to "coping" I mean "affective" coping.) They are children who seem to work well, play well, and love well. I want to emphasize, however, that these children are not "invulnerable" (see Skolnick, 1978): They are not protected from rejection by any impregnable suit of armor, as some popular writers suggest (for example, Hoover, 1976). I have no doubt that all rejected children hurt, but some manage to deal *more effectively* with the hurt than others. That is, they are better copers. In effect, I expect most copers to be intermediate in mental health status between the most accepted children and the most rejected children—but to be discernibly closer to accepted than to rejected children.

I am reluctant to attach the term "noncopers" to those rejected children who respond the way PAR theory predicts most rejected children will respond. These children—like most people—try to cope with life as best they can, but they do not seem to have the same internal or external resources to make the effort as successful. I call these children "troubled." Troubled children fall in the imaginary top-right quadrant of Figure 7 (where rejected children have negative mental health status).

Children can be disturbed for many reasons, only a few of which have to do with the perception of parental rejection. A family breaking up through divorce, for example, can be devastating for children, even though both parents work hard to reassure their children they are loved.[4] Disturbed children such as these fall in the upper-left quadrant of Figure 7 (where children have negative mental health despite being

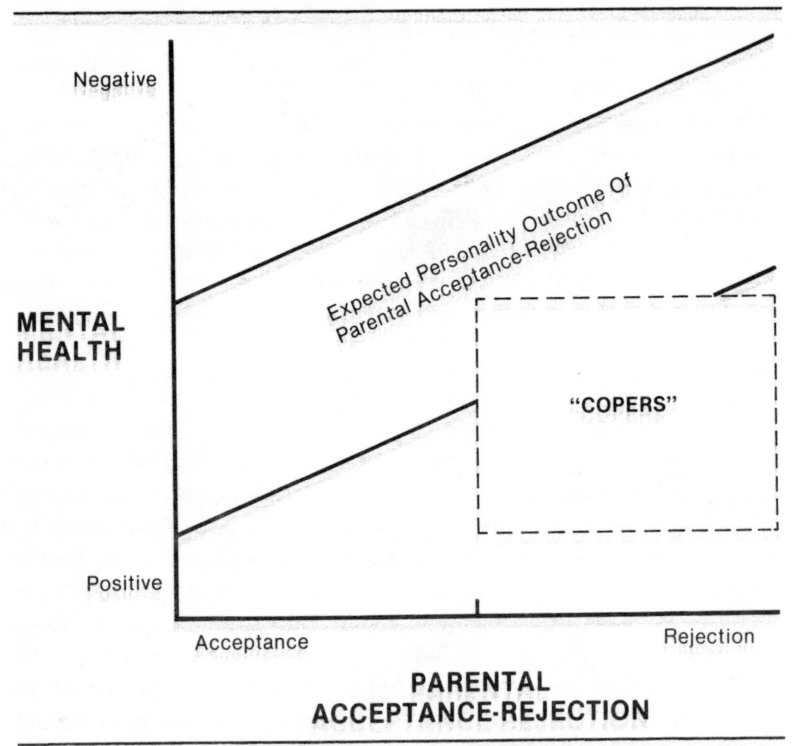

Figure 7 Copers in Relation to PART's Personality Theory

loved and accepted). I shall not deal with these children here because they are not directly pertinent to the major interests of PAR theory at this time.

FACTORS ASSOCIATED WITH AFFECTIVE COPING

Occasionally I am asked whether copers really exist or whether these exceptions to PART's personality theory are just a reflection of faulty theory or imprecise measurement. Do some children truly have the capacity to withstand day-to-day rejection without succumbing the way PAR theory predicts most rejected children will? Drawing influence from the phylogenetic model, I expect that such children do indeed exist, and that they are theoretically describable departures from PART.[5] If the phylogenetic model (with its emphasis on individuals' mental activity) is leading in the right direction, important questions then become:

What forms of mental activity allow some children to cope with rejection better than others? And, what additional self, other, and situational factors are involved?

At present, PART's "coping theory" is in a nascent state because little is known about factors that allow children to cope with perceived rejection. It is possible, however, that at least three social-cognitive factors, among other things, help rejected children cope: "sense of self," "self-determination," and the capacity to "depersonalize." With a qualification discussed later, I expect "copers" to differ from "troubled" children in all three of these social-cognitive factors.

Sense of Self

"Sense of self" refers to children's relative awareness of their own individual personhood, internally (that is, distinguishing self from nonself, psychologically, as well as differentiating certain aspects of self from other aspects of self) as well as externally (that is, distinguishing self from nonself as a physical organism). Children's understanding and evaluation of themselves and others is a progressively developing skill from infancy through adolescence (Flavell, 1974; Hill and Palmquist, 1978; Livesley and Bromley, 1973; Mahler and McDevitt, 1980; Montemayor and Eisen, 1977; Mullener and Laird, 1971). According to Maccoby (1983: 291-292), the development of a sense of self progresses in the following way:

> Initially, children's self-definitions are based on external characteristics—how they look, where they live, what activities they engage in. Later—after about the age of six or seven—they begin to define themselves in terms of psychological traits. With increasing age, group membership takes a more important place in self-definition.

Piaget (Piaget and Inhelder, 1969) characterizes much of this progression as decentration or, alternatively stated, by decreasing egocentrism. Piaget (1954) describes the process of decentration as the key progression occurring in the development of children's social cognition. For him, the initial state seems to be one of relative nondifferentiation of self and of external world. For example, the infant seems to lack much sense of body identity in that his foot or hand at first seem to be viewed as being external to "himself." Every now and then, this "thing" (his big toe) becomes visible to the infant lying in the crib waving his legs. The infant puts the "thing" in his mouth and gums it.

He discovers that he has a sensation in both his mouth *and* elsewhere (at the end of his foot). *This* thing (the toe) is not the same as *that* thing (a rattle). He gums *that* thing and nothing happens except for the sensation in his mouth. But when he gums *this* thing (his toe) it "feels back," as it were. Perhaps through a multitude of experiences such as this—in which the infant acts upon his environment—he comes to develop a sense of physical self and self-boundaries.

In the course of normal development children seem to gain, over time, an increasing awareness of themselves and of the world around them. They continuously develop a conception of self and others, and of their social relationships, so that at any given age some children have a more clearly differentiated sense of self than do other children. They are more aware of themselves physically and psychologically as entities that are distinguishable from all other things that are not self. These individuated children (Mahler, 1968; Mahler et al., 1975) have more awareness of a separate identity: "I am me." In developing the capacity for an articulated and differentiated sense of self the individuated child does not confuse "mother" or mother's feelings with "me" or my feelings. According to Piaget (1954), there can be no dissociation between self and other without a prior concept of self, no narcissism without Narcissus. Thus the idea of less egocentrism implies an ego from which to decenter, and decentration involves the development of a sense of self. Decentration assumes the prerequisite development of some conception of self in relation to the rest of the world, both in terms of physical and logical-mathematical reality and in terms of social reality—the rules and structures that contribute to the social nexus in which the child lives.

The development of a clearly differentiated internal, private, psychological "self" (versus a sense of physical self) is of predominant concern in PAR theory. The growing ability to understand what another person thinks, feels, sees, and intends, and the ability to differentiate these clearly from what oneself thinks, feels, sees, and intends are clearly developmental phenomena (Shantz, 1975; Flavell, 1974) that change progressively with age, and they reveal an increasingly complex, abstract, and clearly structured sense of self.[6] Because a sense of self is probably one of the factors allowing children to rely on themselves as a primary referent in psychological functioning, coping theory postulates that children with a more clearly differentiated sense of self are less affected by negative messages from a rejecting parent than are children with a less clearly differentiated sense of self. For example, when a rejecting parent exclaims, "You rotten little bastard!" the differentiated child is able to distinguish, "Is that *my* message to myself?" or "Is that not *my* message to myself?"

The ability to sort out these levels of messages realistically is expected in PART's coping theory to be an important asset, giving some children greater capacity to deal with a maltreating family environment. Theoretically, it seems likely, then, that a clearly differentiated sense of self may provide children with the possibility of relying to a significant degree on internal referents in psychological functioning; stated another way, the differentiated child seems able to function psychologically with greater degrees of separateness from others, for example, from the rejecting parent(s). On the other hand, children who have trouble maintaining their own sense of individuality, and who have difficulty recognizing the individuality of other family members—as sometimes happens in schizophrenic families (Singer et al., 1978)—are probably children who experience great difficulty coping with parental rejection.

Self-Determination

One important element in the development of children's sense of self is the development of a sense of having personal control over important life events (Maccoby, 1980). Like sense of self, self-determination (Smith, 1972, 1973) seems to be a developmental phenomenon that varies with age. Both across ages and within any given age group, children (and adults) vary in the degree to which they believe they have control over their lives or over significant events that happen to them (for example, see Heider, 1958; de Charms, 1968; Lefcourt, 1976). Children (and adults) vary in feelings about their personal efficacy (Douvan and Walker, 1956) for changing what happens in their lives (de Charms, 1979; Flavell, 1963; Lefcourt, 1983; Langer, 1983). Some believe they are instrumental in bringing about change. They believe they have at least some control over what happens to them through their own behavior or personal attributes. Others feel like pawns (de Charms, 1968); they feel they have no control over their lives. Things happen to them because of fate, chance, luck, or powerful others called "parents" (or, as one gets older, these powerful others can be teachers, spouses, employers, and the like).[7]

With respect to the coping process, children who feel more or less self-determined seem to believe they can influence, to a small degree at least, their rejecting parents' behavior, perhaps through altering their own behavior. The psychological world of children who believe they can do nothing to alter their parents' attitudes and behavior is dramatically different from the psychological world of children who think they can at least sometimes change things. The former are likely to experience a greater sense of hopelessness, helplessness, and futility, and they may be more likely to give up. This in turn may lead to depression (see Seligman, 1975). All these reactions reinforce the rejected child's already damaged sense of self-worth (personal value), self-adequacy (competence or mastery), perhaps worldview, and the other personality characteristics described earlier in personality theory. According to PART's coping theory, the child with a greater sense of self-determination should have an internal social-cognitive resource for avoiding, or at least minimizing, some of the more serious sequellae of rejection. According to Smith (1973), self-determined children are also more likely than others eventually to achieve self-actualization (Maslow, 1954). Empirical support for the significance of both self-determination and sense of self comes from a special panel under the auspices of the U.S. Office of Child Development, which reported that these two social-cognitive attributes are associated with social competence, and hence with coping in young children (Anderson and Messick, 1974).

Depersonalizing

Depersonalizing is the third social-cognitive attribute currently thought to be important in PART's coping theory. Like the other two, depersonalizing is no doubt a developmental progression in that probably all young children personalize to some degree. Gradually, many, but not all, develop the *capacity* (but maybe not always the actual *performance*) to *de*personalize. The ability to depersonalize is probably dependent on the prior developmental ability of interpersonal "perspective taking" (Selman, 1973), "decentering" (Piaget, 1970), or "role taking" (Baldwin, 1906; Mead, 1934)—the ability to see things as others see them (Shantz, 1975; Flavell, 1974). Very young children do not yet have this ability (Maccoby, 1980). Like the other social-cognitive factors discussed, depersonalizing is a dimension or continuum of behavior, not a static trait. That is, both children and adults vary in the extent to which they are capable of depersonalizing. At any given age, some children (and adults) are better able to depersonalize than others; some children (and adults) never achieve the ability.

"Personalizing" refers to the act of reflexively or automatically and egocentrically relating life events to oneself, of interpreting events primarily in terms of oneself, usually in a negative sense. People who are unable to *de*personalize tend to interpret interpersonal encounters, and even accidental events, as having special and direct reference to themselves. The phrase "She takes it personally" seems to summarize much of the meaning of personalizing. Recently, I observed an incident of personalizing in a local ice cream parlor. Several children were lined up waiting to be served. One child tripped on a carpet and fell into a 10- or 11-year-old boy in front of him. The second boy whipped around angrily, snarling, "Cut it out! Quit shoving!" This personalizer "knew" (erroneously) that the child behind him had shoved him deliberately. A child who has the capacity to depersonalize might have been irritated by such a bump, but normally would not egocentrically assume the shove was directed toward him or her personally. Thus children (and adults) who have the capacity to depersonalize can realistically distinguish events that are actually intended to refer to or be directed toward them from events that are not directed at them. They have the ability to adopt a nonpersonalistic stance when interpreting the behavior and motivation of others.[8]

According to PART's coping theory, the capacity to depersonalize provides another social-cognitive resource that allows children to process hurtful family interaction psychologically in a more benign way. It is very different, for example, for a child to interact with an indifferent or hostile parent if the child is able to infer that the parent's hostility is not meant for him or her personally than if the child personalizes all parental hostility regardless of its intended or true target. If children can understand why their parents feel or act the way they do, they may be better able to cope with rejection. The difference between a personalizer versus a depersonalizer is shown poignantly in the responses of two 10-year-olds to an interview question: "Why do you suppose your daddy moved out?" (The parents in each case had separated, and were in the process of getting a divorce.) The depersonalizer responded, "Because he and Mom don't like each other anymore. They don't get along." The personalizer, on the other hand, responded, "Daddy doesn't love *me* anymore because he moved out!"

All three of these social-cognitive factors seem to help provide psychological shields against the more corrosive effects of parental rejection. However, these attributes themselves are also apt to be affected by rejection. For example, drawing on a sample of 271 middle-class,

8- through 11-year-olds, Rohner et al. (1980) found that 11-year-olds who perceived themselves to be *rejected* (as measured by the Child PARQ) were not significantly more self-determined—as measured by "locus of control" (Nowicki and Strickland, 1973)—than 8-year-olds who also perceived themselves to be rejected; *accepted* 11-year-olds, on the other hand, were dramatically more self-determined on the average than accepted 8-year-olds. Additional evidence regarding the positive correlation between parental rejection and low self-determination, as measured by external locus of control, is found in Lefcourt (1976) and in Rohner (1979).

Efforts to explain the coping process become complicated to the degree that self-determination and the other social-cognitive attributes are themselves affected by rejection—insofar as rejection hinders the optimal development of these capabilities. Under these conditions the social-cognitive attributes cannot be used as wholly independent factors explaining portions of the coping process, and it becomes a complicated methodological problem to determine what *independent* effects these attributes have in helping rejected children minimize the erosion of their mental health. However, the fact that these social-cognitive attributes are affected by parental acceptance-rejection does not preclude the likelihood that the attributes do help children cope.

SOCIAL-SITUATIONAL AND OTHER (PERSON) FACTORS ASSOCIATED WITH COPING

"Context" variables and "other" (person) variables also seem to be implicated in the process of affective coping, along with the above-mentioned "self" or "cognitive" variables. That is, a full understanding of the coping process—as well as other features of behavior and development—is probably to be achieved only within the multivariate framework of a "person-in-context." This, of course, is a familiar idea, dating back at least to Lewin (1946), but it is also an idea espoused by many contemporary researchers, including Belsky (1980), Erchak (1981), Parke and Collmer (1975), Rutter (1978, 1979b), and many others. This multivariate approach is a reminder that the behavior of individuals is a function, in somewhat indeterminate ways, of multiple interactions among "self," "other," and "context" variables (Rohner and Rohner, 1978). Thus, in addition to knowing about social-cognitive factors in the child's "self"—and about such other personal characteristics as the child's age, sex, intelligence, temperament, and the like—one also needs to know who the significant "others" are in the environment, what the environment (context) itself is like, and how these various elements interact. For example, what form does the rejection take, how chronic and consistent is it, and by whom is it inflicted? Does the child live in an intact or broken family, a crowded or spacious household, with poor or affluent parents who are educated or uneducated (see, for example, Bilge and Kaufman, 1983)?

A specific research hypothesis coming from the multivariate approach states that the likelihood of children being able to cope effectively with rejection is enhanced if a warm, alternate caretaker is available to the rejected child. The presence of an accepting caregiver or other emotionally supportive person in a child's life seems to be an important "other" (person) factor moderating the outcome of rejection (see Cournoyer, n.d.). Substantial evidence supports this hypothesis. Garmezy's (1981: 248) research on the types of experiences that help children cope with stress, for example, suggests that "adaptive stressed children seemed to have enjoyed compensatory positive experiences outside the family, and a bond with some supportive surrogate figure(s)." In a similar vein, Rutter (1978, 1979a) reports that even in highly discordant and unhappy homes, a relationship with one of the parents marked by a high level of warmth and the absence of severe criticism appears to protect the child to a large degree. Rutter found that only 25% of the offspring in such homes manifested conduct disorders, whereas 75% of the children from similar but quarrelsome families without a supportive relationship manifested conduct problems. Many other studies reviewed by House (1983) and by House and Kahn (1985) document the importance of social support for both the quality and quantity of life.

There are any number of specific hypotheses such as the above-cited research hypothesis that can be derived from the multivariate approach. The bottom line, however, is that in order to predict coping effectively one must no doubt know about all three elements in the multivariate approach: (1) What is the child like? (2) What is (or are) the rejecting parent(s) like, and are there "significant others" in the child's life? And (3) in what context does all this occur? Where information about all three elements is available one can generally improve predictive and explanatory power substantially. At this time, very little empirical evidence exists on these matters as they relate to the affective coping process. (A modest study of the antecedents of child maltreatment discussed in Appendix A, however, shows the heuristic value of this approach.)

COPING WITH EXTREME REJECTION: A CASE STUDY OF "CLOSET CHILDREN"

Close confinement, including the phenomenon of "attic children" or "closet children" (children who are forced to live for months or years in total isolation within dark closets, attics, cellars, and the like), is a subissue within child maltreatment and rejection. The phenomenon has theoretical implications for cognitive, social, emotional, and language development of children in that the claim is sometimes made, for example, that children must acquire language between 2 years and puberty or they will be forever blocked in normal language competence (Lenneberg, 1967; Fromkin et al., 1974). The claim is also made that extreme deprivation produces irreversible cognitive deficits.[9]

Closet children are often used as test cases for "critical-period" hypotheses such as these. Following is a longitudinal study of "closet children" who were able to cope remarkably well with extreme and long-term deprivation/rejection. The case study casts significant doubts on many of these critical-period hypotheses, at least in their mechanical (or nonprobabilistic) form.

A Case Study of Coping

Two monozygotic twin boys—Peter and John—born in Czechoslovakia in 1960, were closeted and beaten daily for about five and a half years before being rescued. They are now young adults in their 20s. The growth and development of the twins has been followed continuously by Koluchova (1972, 1976, 1977) and others for a quarter century. Even though one cannot be certain what specific constellation of factors allowed these boys to cope with their profoundly handicapping early experiences (beyond the fact that they eventually fell into the hands of a warm and loving foster mother and other caring people who worked hard to help them overcome their handicaps), the boys did seem to overcome to a very large degree the most damaging consequences of their early victimization.

Peter and John's mother died shortly after the twins were born. Their father could not care for them for the first eleven months of their lives because his job required him to travel for the railway, so he put them in a children's home. During this time their physical and mental development was normal. The father than applied to have the boys taken to his sister's home, but shortly after that he remarried and put the boys back into the children's home until his own new household could be set up. The story really begins when Peter and John were about 18 months old, in the home of the father, new stepmother, two natural older sisters, a stepbrother, and a stepsister. Their new house was in a suburb of a small town in Czechoslovakia where nobody knew them. The stepmother hated Peter and John, though it is not clear why. She beat them regularly, often on the head, with a wooden kitchen spoon until it broke, and she often put a feather comforter over their heads to mute their terrified screams. The father knew what was going on, but he was afraid of his wife and felt unable to intervene on behalf of his sons. So the boys were left under the brutal tyranny of the stepmother, who so frightened the other children that they too avoided the boys, as they were told to do. The other children, especially the woman's own children, however, were reasonably well cared for. The two stepsons received the brunt of her ruthlessness. For about five and a half years the boys were locked in an unheated closet and often carried to a dark cellar, where they were beaten. They were forbidden to talk or play with anyone, and they were seriously malnourished. They were, in effect, put in utter social isolation, with only the most perfunctory of physical care and virtually no emotional care.

In August 1967, the boys' father brought one of the boys to a pediatrician, asking for a certificate to exempt him from being admitted to primary school. The 6-year-old boy looked very much like a 3-year-old: He hardly walked, and at first sight he appeared to be profoundly retarded. The doctor agreed to postpone school entry, but he was suspicious, and insisted that the twins be placed in a kindergarten and that the family be investigated by a social worker and a district nurse. The stepmother violently resented the intrusion, but knowing she was likely to be caught, tried to cover all signs of the maltreatment.

Over the course of the next three months it became clear that the boys had been criminally neglected and abused. The boys were removed from the family and placed at first in a home for preschool children. After discovering that they were not physically well, however, the authorities put Peter and John in an orthopedic hospital, where they were found to have acute rickets as well as other medical problems. They had to be brought to the hospital kindergarten in wheelchairs because they could barely walk, and, indeed, they could not walk at all when shoes were put on them for the first time. In the hospital, Peter and John were extremely timid and mistrustful, and they seemed to be so deeply retarded that they could not be tested psychologically. They were unable to respond to pictures, for example, because they had never seen any, so they could not interpret the third dimension portrayed in the two-dimensional space (see Hudson, 1967; Deregowski, 1980). They reacted with surprise and horror to television, to moving toys, and to traffic on the streets.

Gradually their shyness and terror dissipated, and they became more inquisitive about their environment. At this time they began to react positively and indiscriminately in their relations to adults, a not uncommon reaction with some maltreated and institutionalized children (Rutter, 1979; Tizzard and Tizard, 1971; Tizard and Rees, 1975; Tizard and Hodges, 1978). Their relationships with other children, however, were uncontrolled and immature for their age. They were highly distractable, and had no social skills or speech. In fact, they communicated with each other more by using gestures characteristic of very young children than by speech. They tried to imitate adult speech, but they could repeat only two or three poorly articulated words at a time. Their IQs, as well as anyone could judge, were at the level of imbecility. (In December 1967, at 7 years, 3 months of age, the boys had measured mental ages around the 3-year-old level.) But their overall behavior, and especially their accelerated progress while in the hospital, made some professionals feel their profound developmental deficits were the result of their social, emotional, and physical deprivation, and not of organic retardation. Other experts, however, were doubtful about their educability.

After a period of hospitalization Peter and John were returned to the children's home, where they continued to make good progress, and they began to interact more effectively with other children. Their relationships with adults and children improved steadily, and they began to acquire many of the skills appropriate to preschoolers. They learned to interpret pictures, they were able to walk, and they learned to run, jump, and ride a scooter. Their gross motor coordination improved dramatically, though their fine motor coordination was still problematic, and they were still unable to concentrate for long. After about six months in the children's hospital their measured mental ages rose to about 4 years of age.

In the fall of 1968 the boys were admitted to a school for the mentally retarded. Doubt still lingered about whether or not they were truly mentally retarded, but in any case they could not be put in a public school. They could, however, be tested on the Wechsler Intelligence Scale for Children (WISC). Peter scored 80 on the test and John scored 72. (A score of 100, plus or minus 10 points, is considered "average" intelligence.)

The following July, in 1969, the boys—now nearly 9 years old—were placed in a foster family of two unmarried, middle-aged sisters, one of whom had already adopted a baby girl some years earlier. The second sister became foster mother of the boys. To some this may not seem like an ideal family setting in the usual sense, but it was apparently very good for the boys, who, over time, established a deep emotional bond with their foster mother. The boys were removed permanently from their own parents (who were found guilty of criminal neglect), and began to thrive in their new family. By the fall of 1969 the boys were admitted to the first grade in a school for mentally retarded children. They soon adapted to the school and substantially outstripped their classmates, so with trepidation the authorities put the boys into second grade in a normal school at the beginning of the next year. Here the boys continued to do reasonably well. They were then age 10, and were working with normal 7- and 8-year-olds.

At the beginning of the 1971-1972 school year, the twins, now 11-year-olds, attended the third grade. Their speech was entirely adequate for their age, both in form and content. (This fact raises doubts about arguments regarding the irreversibility of speech deficits.) In school and in a children's collective the boys were agile, cheerful, and popular, and, according to Koluchova (1976), they showed no signs of eccentricity or social maladjustment. They were the best pupils in the arithmetic class. Peter's IQ had now risen to 95, and John's had risen to 93—both in the "normal" IQ range.

Gradually, the boys became aware of their late start in school, and began to feel self-conscious about being so much older than their classmates. So, during the fourth grade the boys worked hard to master fifth-grade material, which they were able to do with the support and encouragement of their teachers and foster mother. Midyear, Peter and John were moved from the fourth grade directly into the sixth grade. They were then with children more nearly their own age, though most classmates were still a year and a half younger than the twins. The boys' self-confidence was reinforced by this move, even though their performance fell into the average range. Both of them enjoyed school. They loved to read, they rode bicycles well, they could swim and ski, they played the piano well, and they had creative technical talent.

In the 1974-1975 school year the boys attended, at age 14, the seventh grade. By this time their IQs, as measured by the WISC, had risen to 100 for Peter and 101 for John. By 1977, when the twins were 17 years old, they had completed with average grades the basic nine years of required schooling in Czechoslovakia, and they were admitted to an exacting vocational school of precision mechanics. Their WISC scores in 1977 rose still further, to range between 105 and 110.

Physically the twins were nearly identical in looks and behavior at that time. In fact, only family and close friends could tell them apart. They were about 5′10″ tall, with spindly legs, and each weighed about 123 pounds. According to Koluchova (1977), puberty for the boys was delayed about a year in comparison with the average youth in Czechoslovakia, and even though they were 17 years old their interests were on a level more typical of Czech youths of around 15 or 16. They were interested mainly in riding bicycles, swimming, outdoor games, and playing the piano, which they did well. The read a lot, and played chess well. Finally, even though they did not like to talk about their prior experiences, they did continue to express certain fears from time to time, especially with respect to darkness.

I heard about the twins for the last time in the fall of 1984 (Z. Matějček, personal communication, September 25, 1984). They were then 24 years old, and had successfully completed apprenticeships in calculator repairs. Both men were employed in a large machine factory, and both had enrolled in a technical school for further study. Being somewhat more skilled manually than Peter, John specialized in the repair of electric office equipment; Peter was somewhat better than John at intellectual tasks, and this was reflected in the fact that he specialized in electronic office equipment. Both men were due to fulfill their military obligation sometime during 1985, but in the meantime they continued to live with their foster mother, with whom they maintained a close relationship. They were both successful socially, including in heterosexual relations. In fact, Peter was engaged to be married sometime in 1985 to a nurse who worked at a local hospital; John had just recently gone through an unsuccessful love affair, and had no romantic involvements at that time. The IQ score of both young men had risen to about 115, and both men had grown substantially: Peter was then about 6′1″ and weighed 145 pounds; John was about 6′ tall and weighed 139 pounds.

The intellectual and language gains made over the span of 24 years by these severely rejected and maltreated twins is remarkable. At age 7 they were without speech and virtually untestable, but judged to be in the IQ range of imbeciles—perhaps with IQs of 40 or so. They made the greatest IQ gains between their ninth and tenth years, after moving to the home of a warm, loving foster mother, and after attending their first year in school. From that point onward they made steady progress, becoming bright, competent, socially successful adults. This case study shows that cognitive and language deficits resulting from severe, early deprivation can, contrary to the opinion of some experts, be remedied.

Unfortunately, from the perspective of coping theory, Koluchova does not provide sufficient detail to make more than tentative speculations about specific factors associated with the ability of these boys to cope so well—in the long run—with their early deprivation experiences. (Indeed, one cannot rule out, from Koluchova's reporting, the possibility that the young men may still have lingering emotional problems.) The fact that two of them—monozygotic twins at that—suffered the maltreatment together may have a bearing on their coping success. That is, unlike some other classic cases of closet children who did not fare as well—such as Anna, Isabelle, and, more recently, Genie (Curtis, 1977)—these twins had each other for at least minimal human comfort and contact during the period of their extreme deprivation. Of course, their adoption into a warm, caring foster home must also have had great impact in their successful development. In this respect this case of extreme deprivation seems to reinforce PAR theory's assumptions about the potential remediating effects of affective and instrumental intervention by warm, supportive "others" in helping children cope with and even overcome many of the most damaging effects of extreme rejection.

NOTES

1. Cattell and Butcher (1968) intend the term "independence" to refer to aggressive and self-directing behavior. Independence thus does not have the same meaning here as defined in PAR theory.

2. This anecdote results from a fortuitous but passing encounter at an annual meeting of the American Psychological Association. After the psychologist departed, I realized that I had not made note of his name and address to follow up on his final results.

3. This conclusion derives from the observation that in study after study—in the United States and internationally—approximately 80% of the children whose scores fall at or above the midpoint of 150 on the Child PARQ (revealing the children's perception of being rejected) also have scores that fall above the midpoint of 105 on the Child PAQ (revealing a more negative than positive mental health status of children).

4. Some children of divorce, of course, feel rejected by one or both parents (that is, they experience undifferentiated rejection) even though both parents try very hard to reassure the child that he or she is indeed loved.

5. This conclusion is consistent with the findings of Clarke and Clarke (1976: 268), who write that there is, apparently, "virtually no psychosocial adversity to which some children have not been subjected, yet later recovered, granted a radical change of circumstances." Rutter (1978: 57) concurs with this assessment: "Even with the worst circumstance that human beings can devise, only a proportion of the children succumb, and ameliorating factors can do much to aid normal development." Much of the current literature on children's coping with stress (though not specifically with parental rejection) is ably reviewed and analyzed in Garmezy and Rutter (1983).

6. PAR theory's conception of the process of self-differentiation (sense of self) seems similar to Werner's (1948; Langer, 1970) organismic theory, which postulates that all development is a process of transition from global, undifferentiated states to states of greater differentiation, specification, and hierarchic integration. Development shifts from egocentrism to "perspectivism," in Werner's scheme.

7. The concept of "self-determination" has been used and analyzed widely in psychology, and it has appeared under at least nine different but often highly interrelated labels, including "personal causation" (de Charms, 1968, 1979), "personal efficacy" (Douvan and Walker, 1956), "personal control" (Gurin et al., 1978), "locus of causality" (Heider, 1958), "perceived control" (Langer, 1983), "internal versus external locus of control" (Rotter, 1966; Lefcourt, 1976, 1983), and "primary versus secondary control" (Weisz et al., 1984). Piaget's 1930 concept of "psychological causation" antedates all the above usages (Flavell, 1963).

8. Personalizing may be a normal (nonpathological) expression of the clinical phenomenon labeled "ideas of reference," in which the individual interprets casual, routine, or trivial occurrences as having highly charged and personal reference to him- or herself. Sometimes, "ideas of reference" reach a sufficient intensity to warrant the clinical diagnosis of "delusion," but this behavior is well beyond any proper connotation of personalizing.

9. See Kagan (1976), Kagan and Klein (1973), Clarke and Clarke (1976), and Rutter (1972, 1979a) for critical discussions of this claim.

8

Parental Acceptance-Rejection, Expressive Behaviors, and Expressive Systems

This chapter returns directly to PAR theory's sociocultural systems model. It focuses especially on the relations between parental acceptance-rejection and the one remaining element so far not discussed in the model, namely, institutionalized expressive systems and behaviors. The more extensively the correlates of parental acceptance-rejection in the sociocultural model are examined, the more one discovers how widely the effects of parental acceptance and rejection permeate the entirety of sociocultural systems. These effects not only deal with maintenance systems, and with personality dispositions of children and adults highlighted up to this point, but bear on the total functioning of societies, including expressive domains such as occupational choices, religious beliefs, and artistic preferences. Apropos of this, this chapter begins with individuals' self-selected "career" choices expressing personality and life-history factors relevant to parental acceptance-rejection.

PARENTAL ACCEPTANCE-REJECTION AND CAREER CHOICES

Green Berets and Vietnam War Resisters

For ideological, personal, and other reasons during the Vietnam war era some young men refused induction into the armed services. Some of these war resisters fled to Canada and other countries, and some stayed in the United States to protest. Many served prison sentences for their anti-war activities and sentiments. Contrasting sharply with this group was a group of men who not only enlisted for military duty, but sought active combat in Vietnam of the kind that implied the greatest personal danger. These were the Green Berets, a Special Forces Detachment of the U.S. Army. In order to become Green Berets, the soldiers had to pass a series of psychological tests and successfully complete a rigorous obstacle course. Green Berets were highly dedicated and highly trained pro-war, volunteer professional soldiers especially trained for combat duty. Why would some men be disposed toward avoiding the military confrontation in Vietnam and others seek it out? What factors in the life histories and personalities of the two groups helped make involvement in one collective activity more personally appealing than the other (Devereux, 1961; Spiro, 1961)? From the work of Mantell (1974), it seems that quite different life trajectories are associated with each group becoming involved respectively in pro-war and anti-war careers.

Interviewing respondents from five to fifteen hours each, Mantell collected a life history from each of 25 war resisters and 25 Green Berets. He also administered two major personality inventories, the Edwards Personal Preference Schedule (Edwards, 1959) and the Minnesota Multiphasic Personality Inventory (see Dahlstrom and Welsh, 1962). To gather information on classes of behavior such as "fascism," "dogmatism," "political-economic conservatism," "traditional family ideology," and personal "rigidity," he borrowed from other standardized questionnaires and constructed his own questionnaire items. The war resisters were recruited through anti-war groups in New York City. Some were younger staff members of the War Resisters League, some were fieldworkers in the League, some were persons who had sought counseling at the League's central office, and some were persons awaiting sentencing to federal jail terms for draft evasion. The Green Berets were also soldiers on active duty temporarily stationed in Germany. Of the 25 soldiers, 20 had already gone through one or more combat tours in Vietnam.

Who were these young men who chose such different "careers"? The majority of Green Berets in Mantell's sample came from working-class backgrounds, but the war resisters came from both working-class and middle-class backgrounds. The actual family experiences of the two groups, however, contrasted dramatically. One or both parents of the Green Berets tended to be strict, authoritarian, emotionally cold and isolated, unresponsive, mechanical, formal, rigid, and dominating (Mantell, 1974). In general, neither parent showed respect for the son's rights and individuality. As individuals, the parents themselves tended to be intolerant, nonintellectual, tense, and sometimes violent. Nonetheless, these families were—outwardly at least—also stable, self-sufficient, and psychologically cohesive. Parents imposed strict rules on their children, and each person in the family had his or her prescribed tasks. Punishment took the form of threats, blows, and other forms of intimidation. Parents of Green Berets provided little opportunity for the expression of individual feelings or opinions. Usually, only one opinion was expressed, and that was voiced as an absolute edict by the dominant parent.

The family life of the Green Berets was governed by demands for conformity; deviation from the rules often brought swift and severe disciplinary action. Emotional sensitivity and expressions of affection were regarded as unmanly, and signs of weakness. The youths, especially in the eyes of their fathers, were supposed to be emotionally "tough." Even though the majority of the Green Berets did not feel their parents rejected them per se, or that their parents were actively hostile toward them, most of the men did report that one or both parents were almost always irritable. In addition, 80% claimed to have never experienced emotional closeness with either parent; only 40% reported any parental affection, but this affection came from both parents in only 12% of the cases.

As adolescents, Green Berets tended to be passive toward their parents, and had little conflict with them. They also appear to have stayed away from home as much as possible. To all outward appearances, adolescence seems to have been a reasonably happy, successful, and active period for Green Berets. They were busy with work and play, and they were socially active and popular with many friends and girlfriends. They were average to good students, they held many prestigious positions in school athletic and other organizations, and they pursued intensely a variety of hobbies, such as hunting, fishing, and mechanics. This public behavior contrasted sharply, however, with the youths' private activities. As described by Mantell (1974: 83):

> Most of them were involved in petty acts of juvenile delinquency, led a sexual life which would not have met with public approval, engaged in daring and adventuresome acts for thrills, were exposed to violent death as the passive witnesses of suicides, drownings, traffic accidents, and as

> active hunters, and were also involved in numerous fights. In a sense, the Green Berets led double lives. They were outward conformers who were able to break easily with the standards prevailing in their communities. At the same time, they remained sensitive to social and legal sanctions, and altered undesirable behavior once they were detected and punishment became a real threat.

These life experiences, and the personality and behavioral dispositions that resulted from them, seem to have made involvement in the Special Forces an attractive choice for the Green Berets. For most of them, killing men and sometimes women and children became routine and caused no discomfort.[1] Indeed, the most frequent response to killing unarmed persons (men, women, or children) was "no feeling at all" (Mantell, 1974: 156). Most of the Green Berets in the sample viewed themselves as professional soldiers and would have been willing to work as mercenaries. "With few exceptions the Green Berets made little attempt to disguise the fact that they saw themselves as hired guns, paid killers who were not particularly concerned with the employers or their victims" (Mantell, 1974: 175).

Most of these men were uninformed and disinterested in the social or political issues surrounding the Vietnam conflict. None had joined the Special Forces because of personal commitment to political, social, or religious ideals. Mostly they were seeking adventure and excitement, and, according to Mantell, in one way or another all of them were running away from their previous lives. Describing the Green Berets in staccato language, Mantell (1974: 177-178) summarized much of the foregoing when he wrote:

> The Special Forces soldier had been accustomed since early childhood to very hard, severe, and arbitrary discipline . . . in the form of whippings, intimidation, and beatings. . . . There was little or no warmth in their families. . . . Punishments took violent forms. . . . There were weapons in the homes. . . . They've been accustomed to the use of weapons since early childhood. . . . They hunted and used the weapons to kill. . . . They did not have strong ties to anything beyond the rest of the family. . . . The families were isolated units. . . . There were no positive expressive emotional ties within the family. . . . They began their sexual experience at a remarkably early age. . . . Average for first intercourse would be about fifteen and a half. . . . Although they had intercourse frequently throughout adolescence they did not have emotional ties to these girls. . . . They don't report having had deep friendships with any-

> one. . . . They enjoy the service. . . . They have respect for law enforcement agencies and clearly know what can happen to them if they do something criminal. . . . They've killed many people, men, women, and children in Vietnam and have no guilt feelings or nightmares.

Childhood and adolescence were markedly different for the war resisters, who were raised by parents one, or more often both, of whom tended to be warm, affectionate, nonaggressive, friendly, gentle, calm, easygoing, and relaxed. Parental control in most of these families was fairly permissive, nonauthoritarian, flexible, and rational. Physical violence or the threat of it occurred in about half the families, but it played a subordinate role. Parents of war resisters did not demand compliance from their sons as did parents of Green Berets. Rather, they attempted to justify their actions and views in a rational way. These parents praised, reasoned with, and rewarded their sons as ways of encouraging compliance; they seldom used physical punishment or its threat—though most war resisters recalled vaguely having been spanked when they were small children. The overall relationship between parents and children was characterized by mutual respect for each others' rights and individuality. It was also characterized by patience, helpfulness, understanding, acceptance, and freedom of movement and expression. As a result of these experiences war resisters felt deep affection for their parents, and most felt their parents were happy with each other. The marriages, like the families themselves, were marked by mutual respect and companionship. But of course they had their tensions too, at least occasionally. Open hostility was chronic within only two families, however.

Adolescence for the war resisters seemed to have been a busy time, marked by intellectual and social growth. Nearly every war resister gained social distinction through athletic, artistic, or academic achievement. Most of them had regular chores to do at home, and the majority held part-time jobs to earn pocket money and to save for their college education. (All but two war resisters went to college, but a few dropped out after their freshman years.) In addition to their high school and work activities, all the war resisters pursued leisure-time hobbies. For them, individualism took precedence over conformism. This individualism, however, sometimes brought them into conflict on matters of principle, politics, and policies with teachers, other students, or community groups. During adolescence, the war resisters experienced a period of intense and often painful self-discovery. They developed feelings of humanitarian obligation both to themselves and to the world around them, and they eventually developed a sense of independence, individuality, and self-importance. But the process of self-discovery was also characterized by repeated episodes of self-criticism, doubt, guilty conscience, and intellectual and emotional turmoil, including deep religious preoccupation. Nonviolence, a belief in the equal worth of all humans, and a sense of responsibility to speak up for one's beliefs culminated in the decision to refuse military service in the Vietnam war.[2] Even though the war resisters were ready to engage in heated verbal disputes, few ever resorted to intimidation or physical violence, nor were they involved in acts of delinquency.

These profiles of Green Berets and war resisters show that the two groups of men were self-recruited from very different backgrounds—backgrounds that are pertinent to parental acceptance-rejection theory. Even though few of them reported themselves to have been categorically rejected as children, a significantly greater number of Green Berets than war resisters lived with parental hostility ($\chi^2 = 4.51$, $p < .05$), indifference ($\chi^2 = 8.32$, $p < .01$), lack of affection ($\chi^2 = 6.75$, $p < .01$), and overall rejection ($\chi^2 = 6.93$, $p < .01$). Moreover, all Green Berets came from strict, authoritarian families, whereas 64% of the war resisters came from more permissive families ($\chi^2 = 22.48$, $p < .001$).

Mantell does not provide information on all the personality dispositions of interest to PAR theory, but where data are available results are consistent with expectations for these dispositions. Specifically, war resisters as a group showed greater needs than Green Berets on the Edwards Personal Preference Schedule (EPPS) to help others ("nurturance" on the EPPS, which was very low for Green Berets and one of the highest scores for war resisters) and to have many friends ("affiliation" on the EPPS, also high for the war resisters and low for the Green Berets). These personality dispositions seem to suggest a greater emotional responsiveness on the part of the war resisters than on that of the Green Berets. This interpretation is enhanced by the life histories, which show that the war resisters had the capacity for deep emotional relationships. For the Green Berets, on the other hand, other people—especially women—were primarily objects of expedience. In fact the Green Berets had no close, intimate relationships with men *or* women.

The Green Berets scored higher on the EPPS "aggressiveness" scale than did the war resisters, indicating a greater need for verbal aggression. Aggression and violence of all kinds, however, were a normal and routine part of the Green Berets' everyday professional lives.

The EPPS showed that the war resisters had stronger needs than Green Berets to be helped by others ("succorance" on the EPPS). Behaviors called "succorance" on the EPPS are one expression of "dependence" in PAR theory. Of the fifteen psychological needs assessed on the EPPS, the Green Berets scored lowest on this one. This fact, taken in conjunction with the Green Berets' greater emotional unresponsiveness and their tendency toward aggression, suggests a kind of defensive independence described earlier in this book. This interpretation is supported by life-history data, where the Green Berets made it clear that they considered it a sign of weakness to reach out emotionally to others. They prided themselves on being emotionally "tough."

Also consistent with the postulates of PAR theory is the fact that the war resisters' scores were higher than those of the Green Berets on a Minnesota Multiphasic Personality Inventory scale assessing "positive self-regard" (that is, self-esteem and self-adequacy, or simply "self-evaluation" in PART). It is not possible from the psychological tests or life history material presented by Mantell to assess differences between war resisters and Green Berets on the two remaining personality characteristics important in PAR theory, namely, emotional stability and worldview.

Overall, the major postulates of PAR theory seem to be supported by this evidence. That is, in relation to war resisters, the Green Berets experienced greater parental hostility, indifference, lack of affection, and overall rejection. And, as expected in PAR theory, they developed most, if not all, of the expected personality dispositions to a greater degree than did the war resisters. For the purposes of this chapter, however, a more important matter is the nonrandom expressive self-selection of men from systematically different backgrounds and personalities into systematically different "career" choices. It seems doubtful that any of the men recognized explicitly the power of his own life history and of his own internal psychological dispositions in motivating him to seek greater satisfaction in one life course versus the other.

Gormly (1983) provides experimental support for this general argument that persons with specific personality dispositions tend to select social settings where behaviors congruent with those dispositions tend to occur. More specifically, in a sample of 62 college males he found that insofar as men were rated by peers as being high on the personality traits of "energetic" and "sociable" the men also tended to self-select themselves into energetic activities ($r = .62$, $p < .001$) and into sociable events ($r = .53$, $p < .001$), respectively. An independent body of research in the United States, a body of work influenced heavily by Roe's (1956, 1957) "theory" regarding the relationship between children's socialization experiences and adults' occupational preferences, confirms the fact that socialization experiences of children and adults may also be associated with their occupational preferences. Specifically, these particular studies (Green and Parker, 1965; Porter, 1967; Schneider, 1968; Walters and Stinnett, 1971) show that children, adolescents, and adults who experienced warm, accepting, and satisfying parent-child relationships tend to make person-oriented occupational choices, whereas persons who are raised by cold, rejecting parents tend to select non-person-oriented occupations.

Caribbean Fishermen and Cane Cutters

Working on the West Indies island of St. Kitts, Aronoff (1967) provided additional insight into the question of why some people choose one form of occupation and others choose a different form when both are equally accessible and no clear material benefits accrue more to one job than to the other. (For all practical purposes, men on St. Kitts could work either as cane cutters on the sugar cane plantations or they could become fishermen.)

St. Kitts is a small, semitropical, volcanic island on which sugar cane is intensively cultivated. In fact, at the time of Aronoff's work, 97% of the island's arable land was devoted to sugar cane production, and almost all of the land was held by large plantation owners. Because laborers could not own land, most were dependent on the sugar estates for their entire income, which was seasonal. Most of the men began working on the estates when they were about 16 years old. After a period of doing poorly paid odd jobs, the youths were eventually allowed to gravitate toward one of the main adult occupations, most often cane cutting. Cutting was done in gangs of nine to eleven men in a wedge-shaped formation. Each cutter stood two rows apart from his neighbor and worked with a steady rhythm. With his machete, he cut the stalk near the base, stripped off the leaves, cut the stalk in two, and tossed the pieces onto a pile to be picked up later.

Cane cutting is arduous, dull, monotonous teamwork requiring little initiative and leaving little room for individual achievement. Heading each gang was a head cutter, whose job it was to set the work pace.

Head cutters were often bitterly accused of whimsical, arbitrary behavior, of satisfying their own needs at the expense of the other men. Cutters directed a continual stream of angry complaints and hostile abuse against the head cutter, but they felt hopeless about being able to bring about effective change. The gangs tended to be fragmented: Each cutter was concerned mainly with his dyadic relation with the head cutter, but not much with other cutters. In fact, relationships among cutters within a gang tended to be marked by distrust and suspicion—although one could also observe pleasant banter, storytelling, and singing throughout the day, all of which made the boring, exhausting job more bearable. According to Aronoff (1967: 95) the motivational system of most cane cutters was dominated by "the desire for a safe, stable, and highly organized world." On the estate, they felt they could achieve security and escape job requirements demanding a sense of competence and initiative. Such job requirements were thrown into the hands of the head cutters, who had to organize the group, provide the energy for its continuation, and assume the entire range of responsibilities required for its functioning.

Whereas cane cutters began work in midadolescence, men did not begin working as fishermen until they were about 30 years old. Younger men normally worked first for some years on a sugar estate during crop time, and fished when cane reaping was completed. Pot fishing, the most common form of fishing in the town of Dieppe Bay studied by Aronoff, required money to be put aside from one's weekly cane cutting salary until a substantial amount was saved to purchase fish pots or buy supplies to build one's own fish pots.[3] The most common crew structure—and the one that functioned most effectively in Dieppe Bay—involved two or occasionally three full-time fishermen. Each fisherman owned fifteen to thirty pots or fish traps, which were set out on the sea bottom at strategic locations. Periodically the pots were raised and emptied. Fishing was a fairly skilled occupation requiring a psychological sense of competence, self-direction, initiative, and responsibility, all characteristics lacking in most cane cutters. It was also an occupation involving a fair amount of risk and expense: boats, pots, and nets needed repair and maintenance, and could be lost at sea. Even maintaining one's equipment flawlessly, however, did not assure a steady or guaranteed income given that fish sometimes did not enter the pots, or pots were sometimes lost in heavy seas. Every time a man cut a stalk of cane he knew he had earned a definite amount of money. Fishermen had no such certainty even though they expended the same effort every time they went out. Occasionally they brought in enormous hauls, but overall fishing was neither more nor less financially lucrative than cane cutting.

Unlike the cane cutters, who were suspicious and feared the intentions of men they worked with, fishermen tended to see each other as essentially good, competent, and sociable. Fishermen also felt in control of their lives. They were able to respond to the personal qualities of their fellows, and could evaluate each other on this basis rather than on the basis of power and relative position, as was typical among the cane cutters.

What life experiences were associated with the selection of such different occupational choices, and what personality dispositions seemed to be linked with each? Drawing on a sample of fifteen cane cutters and fourteen fishermen in Dieppe Bay, Aronoff addressed these questions. Through interviews he collected life-history information from the men, and he assessed their personality sructures by using sentence-completion tests and projective questions.

Childhood Experiences of Fishermen and Cane Cutters. Aronoff found that the men who chose to become and *remain* cane cutters had very different early family experiences from the men who eventually became fishermen.[4] Cane cutters experienced significantly ($\chi^2 = 4.99$, $p < .025$) more family instability, parental deprivation, and rejection in childhood up to age 12 than did fishermen. That is, the cane cutters lost or were left by their mothers and fathers much more often and at an earlier age than the fishermen, and cane cutters had a greater number of siblings who died while the cane cutters were still children. Overall, the cane cutters were deprived of basic love relationships to a significantly greater extent than fishermen. After loss of the parent—especially if that parent was the mother, with whom children of Dieppe Bay tended to have the greatest bond of attachment—the boy was often cared for by his maternal grandmother, often an old, inflexible, and cranky woman who subsisted on a meager income now made more meager by this intruder. If the boy was given to the care of an aunt, who usually had a large family of her own, he was often put into a "Cinderella" role, in which he was given all the household chores and suffered the persecution of his aunt's own children. Rarely did the father himself care for his children. And rarely did surrogate parents care for the boys with the same affection and concern as did their own mothers. These were shattering experiences for the boys, many of whom also had to assume financial responsibility for themselves as well as contribute to their new households at a fairly young age.

The father's role in the lives of cane cutter boys was marginal, distant, and uninvolved. Mainly, he was an economic provider, but not a companion or source of emotional support. Beyond his financial support, the father's most important responsibility was to discipline the boy and teach him manners. Fathers of cane cutters were not only distant from their children, but disengaged in relationships with their wives and consorts; there was generally little interaction or affection between spouses. Their relationship was mainly quid pro quo: He provided money, she provided meals and sexual gratification.

The cane cutters' relationships as children with their mothers were very different from their relationships with their fathers. In Dieppe Bay the mother-child bond was of the greatest importance: Children and adults universally expressed deep, sentimental attachment to their mothers, who were normally expected to be their children's major caretakers. Mothers provided a rich source of warmth, security, and protection for their children. Half the cane cutters, however, had lost their mothers before the boys were 14 years old (and half had lost their fathers before the boys were 2 years old). The picture is very different for fishermen. As children nearly 80% of the fishermen still lived with their mothers by age 14 (though nearly half had lost their fathers by then). They were also spared the unhappy Cinderella experiences lived through by so many cane cutters, and thus they found significantly greater gratification of their needs for warmth and affection from both their mothers and father.

Personality Profiles of Fishermen and Cane Cutters. These different sets of socialization experiences are associated with the formation of distinctively different personality profiles in cane cutters and fishermen. Men who remained cane cutters were, according to Aronoff, dominated by a desire for a secure, stable, organized, and predictable world—a world well provided by cane cutting. On the estate the cane cutters felt they could achieve security and escape job requirements that demanded a sense of competence and initiative. Beyond these characteristics the cane cutters also displayed personality dispositions immediately related to their rejection experiences in childhood. One of their cardinal attributes was emotional unresponsiveness. Apparently, rejection and parental loss in childhood led cane cutters to the conclusions that people were untrustworthy, and in order to protect themselves they closed themselves off from further bonds with other people; they were afraid to "let people in." Moreover, cane cutters were suspicious of people and the world in general (negative worldview). Neither individuals nor the larger world could be trusted, and cane cutters had no confidence in themselves to do anything about it (negative self-adequacy). These feelings led cane cutters to make a number of self-deprecating remarks (negative self-esteem), and were associated with problems in handling their own and others' hostility and aggression. Aronoff did not provide enough information to draw a conclusion about the two remaining personality dispositions of concern to PART's personality theory (namely, dependence and emotional stability), but he did address several issues pertinent to the theory when he wrote, "The basic principles which organize the cane cutters' family life are the need for security, the need to be taken care of and the incapacity to become deeply involved in the lives of other people—whether wife, children, or friends. Their childhood experiences had left them hostile to the world and fearful of the consequence of establishing personal attachments" (Aronoff, 1967: 201).

Personality profiles of men who become fishermen bear only a distant similarity to the one just drawn for cane cutters. According to Aronoff, fishermen—unlike cane cutters—were independent, self-motivated, and felt in control of their lives. They were prepared psychologically to meet the demands and responsibilities of fishing. Beyond these attributes, fishermen also displayed behavioral dispositions associated with their more or less accepted childhood. They were, for example, able to enter into committed, intimate relationships with the women in their lives, and with their children (emotional responsiveness). They felt good about themselves (positive self-esteem) and about their own capabilities (positive self-adequacy), and they seemed to feel that other people and the world were essentially good and trustworthy (positive worldview). Fishermen seemed not to be as angry or aggressive—overtly or covertly—as cane cutters. From evidence provided by Aronoff one can probably also conclude that fishermen did not respond to minor obstacles and daily frustrations with the same degree of irritation or upset as cane cutters. That is, they seemed to be more emotionally stable.

Aronoff does not provide evidence needed to make clear inferences about the level of dependence of fishermen. Overall, however, there is little doubt that the fishermen and cane cutters in Dieppe Bay operated at different levels of psychological functioning associated with significantly different socialization experiences. Because of these life differences, I believe, cane cutters found it less threatening than fishermen—or, stated positively, cane cutters found it more psychologically attractive—to confine themselves to the tedium of the cane field rather than cope with unknown and uncontrollable vagaries of the sea.[5] Thus once again life experiences seem to be associated with expressive self-recruitment into different collective activities.

PARENTAL ACCEPTANCE-REJECTION AND RELIGIOUS BELIEFS

Up to this point I have written about the relationship between parental acceptance-rejection and expressive *behaviors* of individuals in the domain of occupational self-recruitment. Now I shift emphasis slightly to focus on the relation between parental acceptance-rejection and institutionalized expressive *belief* systems—especially religious belief systems. Following this I return to a discussion of expressive (religious) *behavior* of individuals in the United States.

In virtually every society of the world, people have something that can be called a religious system, if one is willing to define the concept of religion broadly enough. Moreover, the world of religion, the supernatural, is usually personalistic (Spiro, 1966). That is, people have feelings about whether the supernatural (God, the gods, the spirit world, and the like) is essentially benevolent or malevolent—whether it is kind, loving, supportive, warm, generous, protective, or in some other way "positive," or whether it is hostile, treacherous, unpredictable, destructive, or in some other way "negative."[6] Why is the supernatural viewed in some societies as essentially benevolent, whereas in others it is taken as being malevolent? This question has been asked many times throughout history, but from the perspective of parental acceptance-rejection theory I believe that much of one's view of the supernatural is the symbolic extension of a negative worldview resulting from parental rejection. In effect, rejected children, having experienced so much psychological hurt at the hands of their parents, are insecure, anxious, angry, feel that emotional involvement with others is dangerous, and come to expect little more from life itself. The very nature of life and of the world is apt to be seen as threatening, dangerous, and untrustworthy. This perception is derived from the fact that children's interpretations about the world are based on their own experiences they know or believe others to have had. An individual's worldview extends this interpretation about the empirical world to an interpretation about the very *essence* of life and the universe. It is a very simple extension to attribute these unhappy characteristics to God, the supernatural, and the unknown.

The logic of the argument outlined above leads me to expect that the supernatural is likely to be viewed as more malevolent in societies where children are rejected than in societies where they are accepted. More specifically, as suggested in Figure 8, I expect to find few if any cases of belief in a benevolent supernatural in societies where most children are rejected. On the other hand, I expect people in the majority of, but by no means all, societies where most children are accepted to believe in an essentially benevolent supernatural. The upper-left-hand cell of Figure 8 is not likely to be empty, however, because people can believe in a malevolent god or supernatural for many reasons. Parental rejection is only one such reason. Rejection by itself is thought to be potent enough to induce many people to start believing in a malevolent supernatural, but for people who are raised with warmth, love, and affection, other things can sometimes intrude into their lives, leading them to doubt the supernatural and to make negative attributions.

Let us look at evidence bearing on these expectations. A subsample of 34 societies from the Love sample included 18 cases where children were accepted. Of these eighteen societies, 13 believed in benevolent supernaturals; 5 did not. This is consistent with the prediction made in Figure 8 for accepting societies. All but 1 of the 16 societies in this sample where children were rejected had malevolent deities. Again, this is consistent with the expectations drawn in Figure 8. A chi-square test of the relationship between parental acceptance and beliefs in a benevolent supernatural versus parental rejection and beliefs in a malevolent supernatural is significant ($X^2 = 15.3$, $p = .0005$).

It is worth looking at the single "exception" to the general expectation that the "parental rejection/benevolent supernatural" cell in Figure 8 would be empty. This cell had one case in it, a Muslim community in Egypt (Ammar, 1954). Even though the children in that community tended to be rejected, according to the ethnographer who did the fieldwork, the ethnographer also reported an essentially benevolent supernatural. Closer inspection revealed that the ethnographer tended to draw

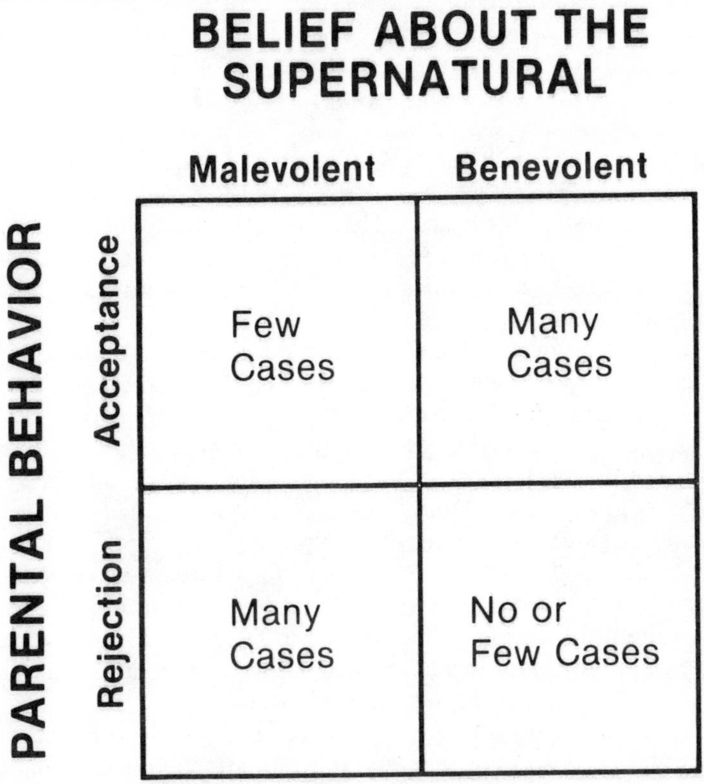

BELIEF ABOUT THE SUPERNATURAL

PARENTAL BEHAVIOR		Malevolent	Benevolent
	Acceptance	Few Cases	Many Cases
	Rejection	Many Cases	No or Few Cases

Figure 8 **Expected Relationship Between Parental Acceptance-Rejection and Belief in a Benevolent Versus Malevolent Supernatural**

heavily in his description from the Koran, which preaches that there is but one God, Allah, and Mohammed is his prophet. Like God of the New Testament, Allah is portrayed more or less as one of love, compassion, and concern. In effect, the ethnographer drew heavily from the great religious tradition of Islam, which rose above and masked—in the holocultural coding process at least—the local religious beliefs of the townspeople themselves. Malevolent spirits and other ominous supernatural forms were downplayed by the ethnographer in the description of the religious system of these people.

Following the convergence-of-methodologies approach argued for in anthroponomical research, it is useful to follow up on these holocultural studies with an intracultural study in the United States on the relation between parenting and religious beliefs. Drawing from a national probability sample of 1121 adolescents, Potvin (1977) surveyed males and females between the ages of 13 and 18. Included in his sample were Protestants, Catholics, and Jews. Potvin used a questionnaire format, measuring both parental affection and parental control. Unfortunately, he did not get information about the youths' perception of parental hostility or neglect. He asked questions about mothers' behavior toward the youths versus fathers' behavior, but found that the correlation between mothers' and fathers' behavior was so high that he combined them.

Several interesting trends emerged from this work. For example, 45% of those youths who believed in God believed that God is both loving and punishing; 19% believed that God is loving but not punishing; 2% said that God is not loving, He is only punishing; and 3% said that God is not loving, but neither is He punishing.[7] Nearly one-third of the adolescents in America today, however, do not believe in God. They either doubt God's existence or positively disbelieve in a personal God. More to the point, however, Potvin found support for and extended the conclusions reached cross-culturally: Adolescents in America who came from affectionate families tended to believe in a personal and loving God; those adolescents who came from families in which there was little affection tended to be nonbelievers.

Parental affection, then, distinguished significantly between two groups, believers and nonbelievers. Parental affection also predicted belief in a loving God. But what distinguished a loving and *punishing* God from a loving and *nonpunishing* God? Here Potvin found that parental control was critical. Those youths who came from controlling families tended to believe in a punishing God: The more control they experienced, the more punishing God was viewed as being. Overall, however, as one might expect, the best predictors of a belief in a personal God were the religious practices of the family, and the number of years the youths spent studying religion. Socialization experiences of warmth and control were second-order predictors. They were important for determining youths' individualized views about God, for example, whether God is loving or nonloving, punishing or nonpunishing. In effect, then, institutionalized religious doctrine may tell us whether God exists and, to some degree, whether God is loving or punishing. But our own life experiences of parental warmth and control influence whether or not we *believe* the church doctrine.

PARENTAL ACCEPTANCE-REJECTION AND ARTISTIC PREFERENCES

I now review the relationship between parental acceptance-rejection and one final expressive domain—artistic productions and preferences. This issue represents a rare and intriguing paradox in anthroponomical research. That is, both intracultural and cross-cultural research on a single expressive issue yield highly significant but diametrically opposed results.

Drawing from a world sample of 75 societies, Barry (1957) related levels of artistic complexity to measures of "severity of socialization." He found a strong worldwide correlation ($r = .71, p < .01$) between the severity of socialization experienced by children in the sample societies and complexity of artistic designs typically produced in those societies. Societies above the world median on complexity of design tended to be above average in severity of socialization. Drawing stimulus from Barry's work, I later found that artistic productions in societies where children are rejected tend to be more complex than in societies where they are accepted (Fisher's exact, $p = .03$) (Rohner, 1975).[8] Thus it appears that a stable worldwide relationship exists between stressful family experiences in childhood and institutionalized expressive (artistic) productions in adulthood. These results are consistent with a large body of holocultural literature showing that different classes of expressive behavior are positively related to specific socialization experiences in childhood (see Levinson and Malone, 1980).

In an effort to assess the validity and generalizability of Barry's and my own earlier holocultural findings—and in keeping with the logic of anthroponomical research—we (Rohner and Frampton, 1982) did an intracultural study within the United States. In this study we focused on the relation between adults' current artistic *preferences* and their retrospective recall of the acceptance-rejection experienced in childhood.[9] Artistic preference was measured in terms of individuals' liking for two sets of photographs graded on level of complexity, following Barry's (1957) measures of artistic complexity. Thus in this research we asked whether or not a relationship exists between the degree to which people recall themselves to have been accepted as children and their current preferences for graphic art varying in complexity of design.

There were 25 respondents ranging in age from 17 to 77 years who participated in the research. All but one came from a middle-class background, and none had any special training or experience with graphic art. All respondents completed the Adult PARQ and ranked two sets of photographs of modern, abstract painting. Each set of photos contained five pictures that varied in overall complexity of design, from simple to complex. After determining that respondents' artistic preference scores on the two sets were strongly correlated ($r = .87$, $p < .001$), the two scores were summed. The mean of these scores constituted the overall artistic preference score used in this study.

Total PARQ scores correlated robustly ($r = -.52$, $p < .007$) with artistic preference scores, but the sign of the correlation coefficient shows that perceived parental acceptance in childhood is associated with preference for *more* complex art—rather than the less complex art associated with parental acceptance in holocultural research. Numerous efforts were made to explain this paradox. For example, we looked to see if there were sex, age, or education differences in subjects' responses to the PARQ and to the photos, but there were none. We also looked to see if different forms of acceptance-rejection were related to respondents' artistic preferences, and they were. Of the four PARQ scales (warmth/affection, hostility/aggression, indifference/neglect, and undifferentiated rejection) only perceived warmth/affection was correlated significantly by itself with artistic preferences ($r = -.57$, $p < .004$). Perceived maternal hostility, neglect, and undifferentiated rejection were not by themselves related to artistic preference, but they were all correlated in the same negative direction as warmth.

Numerous inquiries such as these failed to explain the paradox, but they did raise another fruitful issue. As noted earlier, different expressions of acceptance-rejection sometimes seem to have different effects on subsequent behavior. That is apparently true too of the relation between parental warmth (versus other forms of acceptance-rejection) and artistic preferences. A similar conclusion was reached in a more recent study of the relation between acceptance-rejection (as measured by the Adult PARQ) and expressive interest in spectator sports (as measured by a sports-interest rating scale) among 42 middle-class adults. In that study, Cournoyer and Rohner (1982) found that as perceived neglect (but not other forms of acceptance-rejection) increased, interest *decreased* in spectator sports such as football, baseball, boxing, ice hockey, bowling, golf, and wrestling. No cross-cultural evidence yet bears on this issue.

NOTES

1. This conclusion is supported by the Green Berets' scores on the Minnesota Multiphasic Personality Inventory, which shows the absence of guilt, serious conflict, or depression.

2. Not all war resisters refused military service for reasons of "principle." At least three refused mainly because of expedience and other personal considerations—although all voiced opposition to the war in Vietnam.

3. Other forms of fishing not requiring this investment were available to the men of Dieppe Bay, but pot fishing was most common and is emphasized here.

4. Almost all the men were cane cutters at one time or another. The issue here is, Who remained cane cutters and who eventually became fishermen?

5. One might counter the "expressive behaviors" hypothesis argued here with the much simpler hypothesis that the two groups of men learned and entered the same occupations as their fathers. Aronoff's data refute this latter hypothesis, however.

6. Some religious systems are very complicated and difficult to place on a single dimension of benevolent-malevolent—for example, Hinduism, with its pantheon of multifaceted gods. Nonetheless it is usually possible for people to make overall judgments about their beliefs in the supernatural, especially about their personalistic deities, spirits, and the like.

7. There were so few cases of youths believing that God is nonloving and nonpunishing, or that God is nonloving but punishing, that I shall concentrate only on the other categories.

8. In a modest follow-up study, Adamopoulos and Bontempo (1984) provided suggestive evidence that the relationship between parental rejection and artistic complexity is also affected by independence training of children.

9. Because there is no single, dominant art tradition in the United States, we could not measure institutional artistic *productions.* As a substitute we used a measure of individualized artistic *preferences.*

9

Epilogue: Looking Back and Looking Ahead

As I look back upon this book and review between a single set of covers the distillation of more than 25 years of work—of a long series of promising leads that paid off, interspersed with disappointing false starts and dead ends—I am impressed by how much PAR theory researchers have learned, but how little we ultimately know. In this final chapter, I will summarize the conceptual foundations of the theory along with the most important lessons learned in constructing and testing the theory, and I will point out methodological deficiencies, unanswered questions, and remaining problematics to be dealt with in the future.

PART'S CONCEPTUAL AND METHODOLOGICAL FOUNDATIONS REVIEWED

It may not be essential to adopt all postulates and assumptions guiding the development of PAR theory, but it is important to recognize that the theory has been, in fact, constructed within a specific epistemological framework. A brief review of the conceptual and methodological foundations on which PART is grounded might be useful here. In this regard, I find it convenient to organize PAR theory's most salient assumptions and postulates within the context of the hierarchical framework of concepts shown in Figure 9.

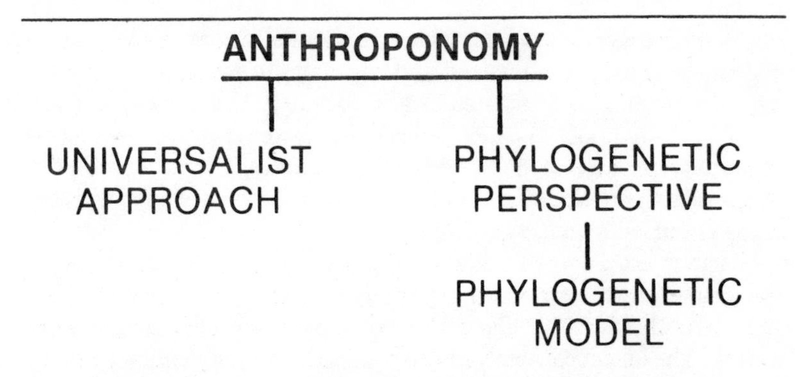

Figure 9 Hierarchical Structure of PART's Principal Organizing Concepts

Anthroponomy and the Universalist Approach

As shown in Figure 9, the apical organizing construct guiding the development and testing of PART is "anthroponomy"—the science that searches for cross-culturally valid principles of human behavior, principles that can be shown empirically to generalize to all sociocultural groups, races, and languages, or to specified subsets of these. PART is one of several programs of research and theory development committed to the search for anthroponomical principles, in this case to principles that relate to the antecedents, consequences, and correlates of parental acceptance and rejection. If one is serious about trying to establish valid panhuman principles of behavior (which, of course, many behavioral scientists are not, at least in their own work), then a relevant question becomes: How should one go about achieving that goal? The universalist approach shown in Figure 9 is an answer to that methodological-conceptual question. For reasons described in Chapter 2, the universalist approach argues for a convergence-of-methodologies and convergence-of-procedures approach in the context of cross-cultural comparative research as well as intracultural research. PART researchers' responses to the rigorous demands of the universalist approach have been to employ three paradigms (methodologies) of research: holocultural research, community study research, and psychological research. Nested within the community study and psychological research paradigms is a convergence-of-procedures approach utilizing, when possible, self-report questionnaires, interviews, and behavior observations. Moreover, PART research draws from the sociocultural systems model, which provides a way of thinking about the antecedents, consequences, and correlates of parental acceptance-rejection within both individuals and societies. The model itself provides a multivariate *systems* perspective on these issues, just as the "multivariate approach" described in Chapter 7 (and amplified in Appendix A) provides a multivariate perspective for enhancing predictions about *individual* functioning.

Various programs of anthroponomical research used by other behavioral scientists rely on other paradigms and procedures, but all test their hypotheses within the context of cross-cultural comparative research. The extent to which anthroponomists actually employ a multimethod research strategy is variable. This is true too in PART research. That is, even though PART research has utilized for many years a multimethodology strategy, much less of the work has relied on either convergence-of-procedures (especially interviews or behavior observations) or the multivariate approach, which asks researchers to look simultaneously at the joint and unique effects of Self, Other, and Context variables. This is recognized as a limitation of the work actually accomplished, but not as a limitation of the theory per se or its epistemological foundations.

Implications of the Phylogenetic Perspective and the Phylogenetic Model

Whereas the left side of Figure 9 concentrates on methodological-conceptual issues, the right side focuses on conceptual-theoretical issues relevant to anthroponomy in general and to PAR theory in particular. For PAR theory, two basic epistemological assumptions derive from the phylogenetic perspective. First, humans everywhere have a phylogenetically acquired need for positive response from people most important to them. For children, these people are usually called "parents." Second, children have a phylogenetically acquired tendency to respond in consistent ways—specified at least in part in PART's personality theory—when they do not get this positive response. It is probably not possible to test the first assumption empirically, but the second and perhaps more important assumption is the very issue that much of PAR theory has addressed empirically for more than a quarter of a century.

From the phylogenetic model in Figure 9 comes several additional expectations, assumptions, and postulates guiding PAR theory. One of these is that because of individual differences in cognition or mental activity specified in the phylogenetic model (along with variations brought about by individual differences in biology and experience denoted in the model), some individuals do not respond fully to the effects of rejection as postulated in PART's personality theory. This assumption leads to PART's coping theory, detailed at length in Chapter 7. Moreover, through the line of reasoning suggested in Chapter 1 about individual differences in mental activity (and in biology and experience), a by-product of the phylogenetic model is PART's belief in the partial *indeterminacy* of human behavior. Belief in this indeterminacy leads PAR theorists to reject the concept of invariants or constants in human behavior and development, and to assert the "probability model" in its place. Thus universals sought in anthroponomy (and in PAR theory) are generally *probabilistic* universals, not exceptionless uniformities.

Finally, I assume, along with many others, that mental activity coordinates all human experience. That is, experience is given meaning through the mental activity of the individual; experience is thus susceptible to many interpretations. This individual variance in the interpretation of experience contributes to PART's belief in the partial indeterminacy of human behavior, and it contributes importantly to PART's greater emphasis on a phenomenological rather than a behaviorist perspective.

STRUCTURE OF PAR THEORY

Elements in Figure 9 constitute the philosophy-of-science base on which much of PAR theory is grounded. From these elements and their implications come PART's four major issues, addressed in the introduction and reviewed in question form below. These four issues in turn have structured PAR theory over time into its three principal theoretical components. More specifically, PAR theory asks the question: (1) Is it true that children and adults everywhere—regardless of cultural, racial, linguistic, ethnic, or other differences—respond in the same way when they perceive themselves to be rejected by their parents? This question has led over the years to the development of PART's personality theory. In addition, the question is asked: (2) What gives some children the resilience to withstand the corrosive drizzle of day-to-day rejection without developing the same mental health problems experienced by most rejected children? This question has led over time to the development of PART's coping theory. The last two questions are embedded in PART's sociocultural systems model and theory: (3) Why do some parents accept their children and others reject them? That is, what are the significant psychological, environmental, and maintenance systems antecedents or causes of parental acceptance-rejection? Finally, (4) What else in a sociocultural system is related to the experience of parental acceptance-rejection? This question pertains mainly to the expressive correlates of parental acceptance-rejection.

WHERE TO FROM HERE: LOOKING AHEAD

PAR theory researchers have made a solid beginning in addressing these issues, but many, many questions remain unanswered and certain methodological problems need remedying in each of the three theoretical components of PAR theory. I address some of the most salient of these issues in the following sections.

Problems and Prospects in Personality Theory

Personality theory is the best developed and most advanced of PART's three theoretical components. By my own standards of science I am personally willing to affirm—from evidence compiled over the past 25 years—the strong likelihood that children and adults the world over do indeed tend to respond to perceived rejection as PART's personality theory postulates. In effect, I am willing to elevate the principal postulates of personality theory to the level of anthroponomical principles. Behavioral scientists using different standards of science may not be willing to accept this likelihood, however.

In accepting the major postulates of personality theory, I do not wish to minimize the limitations of individual studies on which this conclusion is based. That is, for example, some of these studies drew from small samples, and the majority paid scant attention to multivariate analyses of data. All of the studies were no doubt flawed in some way. Nonetheless, as I argue in Chapter 2, it seems reasonable to infer that if a single set of conclusions emerges across a variety of imperfect studies, employing a variety of imperfect procedures and methodologies in a variety of cultural, racial, ethnic, and other groups widely distributed over the face of the earth, the conclusions must be robust, and they are quite likely accurate and widely generalizable.

A second conclusion about which I believe one may be reasonably confident—based on two worldwide holocultural samples and numerous intracultural studies in cross-cultural settings as well as in the United States—is that, on the average (but with some notable exceptions), children around the world experience far more acceptance than rejection. Similarly, adults around the world seem to have been accepted as children far more often than they were rejected. These conclusions are reassuring in view of the much-publicized horrors that appear to have been perpetrated against children historically (see, for example, DeMause 1975, 1982) as well as currently in the United States and internationally.

Results such as these appear to be fairly firm and cross-culturally generalizable, but, as indicated above, many questions in PAR theory remain unexplored, and some issues already addressed have proven to be problematic. For example, most PART research concentrates on children's and adults' evaluations of *overall* acceptance or rejection experienced at home. So far, only minimum effort has been given to examining the differential effects of discrete forms of rejection such as parental aggression versus coldness (that is, low warmth), or perceived indifference versus undifferentiated rejection. Very often the different forms of rejection seem not to have significantly different effects. But, as shown in Chapter 5, parental coldness, for example, correlates differently with child dependence than do other forms of parental rejection. Moreover, as noted in Chapter 8, only perceived warmth/affection correlated significantly by itself with artistic preference among a sample of Americans. Also as reported in Chapter 8, perceived neglect, but not other forms of rejection, is associated with lowered interest in spectator sports. This question regarding the differential effects of various forms of acceptance-rejection is especially salient in Chapter 5, where an attempt was made to identify a hierarchy of most- to least-damaging forms of parenting.

Even though little is known about the differential effects of various forms of rejection, virtually nothing is yet known about the effects of consistent versus inconsistent acceptance-rejection, and no research has yet asked important questions about the effects of long-term, chronic rejection versus short-term rejection. Obviously, no research has yet put all these issues together in a single multivariate model. The interaction of form, severity, consistency, and duration of acceptance and rejection must, however, make a substantial difference in the outcome of the acceptance-rejection process. A long-term longitudinal research design is required for the effective study of the unique and joint effects of and interactions among complex factors such as these. This points to another currently unmet need within PART research, that is, the need for longitudinal research, which helps to eliminate plausible rival hypotheses regarding time order and causal directionality among classes of correlated variables.

Longitudinal research is critical for addressing issues raised in Chapter 6 about parental acceptance-rejection in life-span perspective. For example, does parental rejection have significant long-term effects if it occurs during the first year of life only—as many psychodynamic theorists claim—or does it have long-term effects only if it begins for the first time in childhood (for example, at around 18-24 months or later), as PAR theory postulates? This question is important because the "primacy of infancy" postulate is central to much of psychodynamic theory and by implication in psychodynamic therapy and treatment programs. If that assumption proves to be wrong, then parts of psychodynamic theory and associated therapy and treatment programs will stand in need of significant revision. This issue is embedded in two larger but unresolved questions asked at the beginning of Chapter 6: (1) What effects does parental rejection seem to have when it is experienced for the first time at different stages of life—infancy, childhood, adolescence, adulthood, and old age? (2) Is there a period in human development when humans are especially vulnerable or susceptible to effects of rejection?

Related to these issues is the question of whether other forms of loss or disruption—real or anticipated—of a primary relationship (such as may occur because of death, divorce, extended parent-chld separation, or the breakup of a love affair or friendship) may have effects similar to those of parental rejection. That is, are rejectionlike effects similar to those postulated in personality theory likely to appear at any time in life when a primary relationship is disrupted or terminated?

What are the true anthroponomical effects of rejection and perhaps other forms of loss, real or threatened? In Chapter 4, more than two dozen behavioral, personality, and developmental issues are cited that have been implicated as consequences of parental rejection. Only a few of these have yet been studied systematically from the perspective of PART's personality theory. The seven personality dispositions described in personality theory are almost certainly not the only reliably emergent social-emotional consequences of parental rejection, however. Future developments in PAR theory are likely to identify and incorporate other such dispositions. But even among the currently existent traits in personality theory, one disposition—dependence—continues to be problematic, as described at length in Chapter 5. Moreover, the precise shape of the dependence/independence curve illustrated in Figure 6 (in Chapter 5) has yet to be established with confidence. Especially uncertain are the conditions under which—as well as the point (or range) on the warmth dimension where—normal dependence among rejected persons generally begins to shift toward defensive independence.

Finally, I should emphasize that even though parental acceptance-rejection is related significantly in study after study to all personality dispositions cited in personality theory (except dependence as measured by the PAQ), the magnitude of the correlations is often modest, indicating that the warmth dimension by itself does not account for the majority of the variance in the psychosocial functioning of individuals. Undoubtedly, the predictive power of personality theory—as well as the other theoretical components of PAR theory—will be enhanced substantially when the influences of other forms of parenting (especially parental control or permissiveness-strictness and parental discipline or punishment) are also taken into account.

Problems and Prospects in Coping Theory

Coping theory is the least well developed of PART's major theoretical components, but from the perspective of social policy implications it may ultimately prove to be most important. Personality theory tells us what is likely to happen to children who perceive themselves to be rejected or accepted, and sociocultural systems theory (and model) helps us understand the major conditions under which parents are likely to accept or reject their children—and to tell us about some of the expressive, personality, and other correlates of parental acceptance and rejection. Knowing how children are likely to respond and what some of the significant conditions are under which parents are apt to accept or reject has important policy and practice implications, of course, but it seems unlikely that Americans currently are willing to take the steps required to bring about massive social, political, and economic changes needed to minimize rejection and maltreatment of children.

Thus it may not be possible now to eradicate conditions that promote parental rejection, but it may be possible to help many rejected children deal more effectively than before with the pain of parental rejection. That is, after identifying significant self, other (person), and context factors that help "copers" deal with the rejection process, it may be possible to intervene with these factors on behalf of children who do not cope as well—and thereby not only improve the psychosocial functioning and happiness of these individuals, but also reduce the probability that the effects of rejection will extend onto multiple offspring in the succeeding generation. If, for example, a sense of self-determination eventually emerges as a significant social-cognitive attribute helping copers deal with rejection, as postulated in coping theory, then it might be possible to help children who cope less well develop a greater sense of self-determination—thereby providing them with a psychological resource for dealing better with the hurt of rejection. The same can perhaps be done for noncopers if other social-cognitive attributes such as sense of self and the capacity to depersonalize emerge as significant coping factors. Few tasks seem more worthwhile than ones such as these, which try to bring well-grounded research data closer to the applied needs of practitioners providing services to people in need.

Coping theory has a long way to go before this vision is implemented effectively. Indeed, at this point, coping theory offers far more questions than answers. For example, what other social-cognitive factors, aside from those currently incorporated into the theory, are associated with the coping process? Moreover, some social-cognitive factors seem themselves often to be affected by rejection. The fact that one's level of social-cognitive development is influenced by rejection produces the complicated methodological and conceptual problem of identifying the independent effects of social-cognitive attributes on coping per se.

What additional self, other, and context variables aside from those now postulated in coping theory help children deal with parental rejection? And how do these factors interact with each other to produce distinctive coping outcomes? At a different level of abstraction an important question emerges: What is the relationship between the normal social-cognitive process of personalizing and the clinical process of "ideas of reference"? Are delusional "ideas of reference" merely an elaboration and intensification of personalizing, or are the processes qualitatively different phenomena?

Finally, limited empirical and anecdotal evidence suggests the challenging possibility that for some people parental rejection may be associated with creativity and unusual personal achievement. A serious need in coping theory research is to explore this possibility. To what extent have these eminent persons attained their stature *because* of earlier parental rejection or *despite* it? This question touches directly on the distinction between affective coping and instrumental coping, two concepts that themselves need further elucidation and construct validation. Perhaps the largest single issue in this context is the need to confirm unequivocally the existence of true *affective* copers. Is it really true that seriously rejected children are able to maintain positive mental health as defined in PART's personality theory? It appears so, of course, but this point needs careful documentation and elucidation.

Problems and Prospects in Sociocultural Systems Theory/Model

The sociocultural systems model and its implied theory are important for magnifying PART's perspective beyond the individual to total sociocultural systems or societies. Although the model reminds one that human behavior is affected by complex multivariate, interactive, changing, and often reflexive classes of variables (such as the seven classes of elements specified in the model), the current state of behavioral science methodology is not yet sufficiently developed to allow one to study all these variables simultaneously as they relate to the antecedents, consequences, and correlates of parental acceptance and rejection.

Although complex multivariate analyses of relationships implied within the sociocultural systems model must await future development, many bivariate and simpler multivariate relationships are fairly well established. I shall let one simple bivariate relationship implied in the model illustrate the several relationships that could be mentioned, and I shall let this one example illustrate potential policy and practice implications of the model. I refer here to cross-cultural and intracultural evidence from a variety of methodological sources affirming the fact that social isolation of a parent within a single-parent household is one significant risk factor in a long list of social-situational and maintenance systems factors associated worldwide with potential parental rejection and child abuse. (See Appendix A for a discussion of social isolation in the context of child abuse and neglect in the United States.)

As discussed earlier in this book, a great amount of evidence in the United States and internationally supports the conclusion that a parent who is home alone in continuous social isolation with one or more young children is likely to experience considerable psychological stress, including loneliness, tension, boredom, often irritability, and sometimes depression—a constellation of psychological dispositions that places children at risk for rejection and other forms of maltreatment. Tens of thousands of young, unemployed mothers in this country are in just this position. A variety of interventions, however, can reduce the risk of these parents intentionally and unintentionally maltreating their children. For example, it is often possible to bring another supportive adult into the home from time to time, such as may happen in "parent aide" programs or in various "grandparent" programs. It is also often possible to get the potentially rejecting or abusive parent involved in an outside support group such as Parents Anonymous. Still a third class of possibilities is to get the children out of the house for periods of time through day care, or sometimes through Big Brother or Big Sister programs. The point here, for policymakers and practitioners, is to find ways to help parents escape social isolation, and thereby eliminate a critical context known to be associated worldwide with parental rejection and child maltreatment.

In addition to issues of sweeping importance such as these, the sociocultural systems model and theory contain several more delimited problematics. For example, as reported in Chapter 8, parental acceptance-rejection seems to be linked with people's self-recruitment into different occupations, but little is yet known about the psychosocial mechanisms actually associated with this process. Also, are one's occupation or other task choices related significantly to affective/instrumental coping processes? Relationships such as these may be direct (for example, parental acceptance-rejection may be linked directly in some ways to occupational self-recruitment), but other relationships in the model are almost certainly indirect, mediated relationships. For example, earlier I reported a weak correlation between parental acceptance-rejection and climate. I doubt, however, that climate often has a true, independent effect on variations in parental acceptance-rejection. But it may have an effect as mediated through sociocultural beliefs and behaviors cross-culturally about body (especially skin-to-skin) contact between parents and children. That is, as I speculated in Chapter 3, variations in skin-to-skin touching between parents and children may be related directly both to parental acceptance-rejection and to climate. This speculation is yet to be tested, but it punctuates the point that more work is needed on the way in which climate and other features of the natural environment—and indeed other elements in the model—may indirectly shape or influence styles of parenting in the United States and cross-culturally. The study of issues such as these and, ultimately, the evaluation of the overall adequacy of PAR theory are tasks for the future.

Appendix A: Child Abuse and Neglect and Parental Rejection

This appendix provides a brief overview of some of the major issues in the field of child abuse and neglect, and their relation to parental rejection. These issues are closely related but on a slight tangent to the major purpose of this book, and are, for that reason, presented as an appendix. Many readers, however, would quite rightly fault the book if I failed to mention child abuse and neglect at some point in the context of PAR theory.

RELATIONSHIP BETWEEN CHILD ABUSE AND NEGLECT AND PARENTAL REJECTION

Parental acceptance-rejection, or the warmth dimension of parenting, is a higher-order construct than child abuse and neglect. That is, abuse and neglect are often specialized forms of rejection, but the notion of child abuse and neglect does not exhaust the definition of rejection. In fact, there is a problematic relationship between child abuse and rejection in that most children who perceive themselves to be rejected are not legally reported (or maybe even reportable) as abused, and many children who are reported as abused do not perceive themselves to be rejected (Herzberger et al., 1981). From a research point of view one difficulty with the issue of child abuse and neglect (hereafter, for brevity, often referred to by the acronym CAN) is that it is defined largely by state statute (Wolfe, 1985), and, by and large, state statutes are poorly operationalized for research purposes. Statutes defining CAN include behaviors that may be useful for legal purposes, and statutes may provide courts with some degree of satisfaction in handling abuse cases, but from a research point of view it is nearly impossible to talk about the effective causes or consequences of "child abuse and neglect"—at least in a generic sense—because so many unrelated and poorly defined forms of behavior are included in the statutes. Moreover, CAN is defined somewhat differently from state to state, and especially from nation to nation in terms of local values or norms (see, for example, Kahn and Kamerman, 1980; Kamerman, 1975; Gelles and Cornell, 1983, 1985). Even more troublesome is the fact that within any given country definitions shift among various professions, such as law, nursing, social work, sociology, pediatrics, and law enforcement (Giovannoni and Becerra, 1979; Aber and Zigler, 1981; Lena and Warkov, 1978). Unlike CAN, parental acceptance-rejection is defined in more universalist conceptual and operational terms, and is therefore amenable to standardized empirical scrutiny from one community or nation to another.

The Venn diagram in Figure A.1 shows those portions of child abuse and neglect—as they have been defined customarily in past decades—that lie on the periphery of rejection. In the past several years legislators nationally have broadened their conception of CAN, and accordingly the abuse and neglect circles in the diagram have shifted noticeably into the "rejection" range—although there are still forms of abusive behavior (as defined by legal statutes) that do not necessarily imply rejection. Certain types of "sexual abuse" (for example, some child pornography) is a case in point.

An illustration may help clarify the distinction between rejection and abuse. Several years ago an unusual incident of apparent violence occurred against a child in Britain. An attractive girl of about 12 had been attending school near London for several years. When she returned to school in the fall, her face was covered with a pattern of ropelike scars standing out on her chin and cheeks, crossing her forehead, and extending down her nose. The teacher sent the child to the headmaster, who called the authorities. School officials were shocked to learn that the child's mother had slashed her face repeatedly and then ground ash into the open wounds. Every few days throughout the summer the girl's mother broke open the wounds to put in more ash, and then pat it down to stop the bleeding. The authorities charged the mother with child abuse, and the courts were about to remove the child from her family when an anthropologist at a nearby university became aware of the incident. It sounded familiar to him. Upon inquiry, he found the family

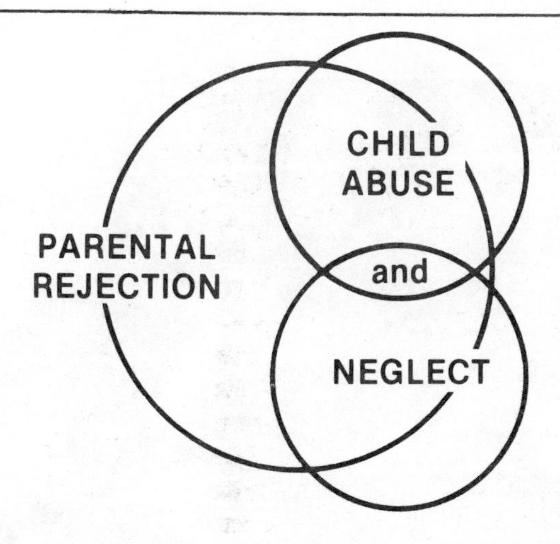

Figure A.1 Relationship Between Parental Rejection and Child Abuse and Neglect

was from East Africa and then, for him, all the pieces fell in place. Rather than being maliciously abusive toward her child, the immigrant mother had been acting responsibly, according to the customs of her people in East Africa. The daughter had menstruated for the first time during the summer, and according to tribal custom she was now marriageable, but in order to attract a suitable husband she must be properly adorned with facial scars similar to those, apparently, of the woman shown in Photo A.1. (People the world over routinely adorn and beautify themselves and their offspring through scarification; tatooing; body and facial painting; stretching their earlobes; inserting nose plugs, lip plugs, and earrings; reshaping skulls; and so forth.) The mother was acting responsibly according to her cultural norms to make her daughter maximally eligible for marriage. Both mother and daughter believed that no bachelor would take an interest in the daughter if the mother had not done this, and both were pleased with the outcome of the mother's work.

Here then is a case reported as massive abuse by legal authorities in which in fact no abuse and certainly no rejection was intended; quite the contrary. The mother had the greatest love and concern for her daughter, and the accusation and public outcry that the mother had viciously abused her daughter were devastating for both mother and daughter.

Photo A.1 Decorative Facial Tatoos on an East African (Fulani) Woman (photo courtesy of James C. Faris)

A second illustration attracting recent national attention shows how some forms of parenting may indeed be considered abusive by probably all definitions of child abuse in this country, but not rejecting as construed in PAR theory: On January 29, 1985, ten days after learning that her husband had been having an affair for three years with another woman, Fumiko Kimura—a lonely and despondent 32-year-old Japanese-American mother—waded over her head into the Pacific Ocean with her 6-month-old daughter and 4-year-old son. She held her two children under water and she herself began swallowing large amounts of water in an attempt to commit suicide. Two college students rescued the threesome (Bradlee, 1985). Mrs. Kimura survived; her two children did not. Subsequently, she was charged with first-degree murder "with special circumstances," a charge applied to California to murders committed during rape or robbery, or under certain other special circumstances (Pound, 1985).

The case has special interest in this context because it highlights an important distinction between child abuse and parental rejection as understood in PAR theory. Mrs. Kimura acted in a recognized and tacitly condoned way by time-honored Japanese custom, but in a way that is also illegal in Japan and the United States. Her act of *oyaku-shinju* ("parent-child suicide") is said to happen almost daily in Japan (Bradlee, 1985) when individuals experience serious "loss of face" (or under other exceptional circumstances), as did Mrs. Kimura, who felt guilty about failing her husband as a wife, "thereby causing him to have the affair" (Bradlee, 1985: 2). It is important to emphasize that Mrs. Kimura loved her children passionately. She devoted her life to her children and to her husband (Bradlee, 1985), but she apparently felt that suicide—an honorable way of dying in Japan—was the only honorable way for her to deal with her sense of failure as a wife, mother, and person. And, according to Mamoru Iga, a Japanese-American sociologist, it is more acceptable in Japan for a mother to take her children with her in suicide than to leave them behind, because Japanese children are regarded as property—almost appendages—of their mothers, and there is substantial prejudice against children without parents (Bradlee, 1985).

This case provides a clear-cut illustration of child abuse (physical assault) as defined later, but it seems just as clear that it is not a case of rejection in the sense of maternal hostility, indifference, or lack of affection toward children. Mrs. Kimura's behavior finds its counterpart in the widespread distribution of infanticide; the destruction of newborns cross-culturally is unrelated to parental acceptance or rejection of the surviving offspring (Rohner, 1975).

Similar issues surround the problem of distinguishing statutory neglect (versus the child's perception of neglect, discussed below) from rejection, as shown in Figure A.1. The problem of neglect in CAN is raised frequently when, for example, parents refuse to provide medical treatment for seriously ailing children (Streiker, 1984). Sometimes these are true cases of neglect, but not infrequently the incidents are brought to public attention because the parents believe in religious, ethical, or cultural systems that prohibit the use of "modern" medicine. Such parents get locked into the legalistic power structure that defines them as being bad and culpable, when in fact they are often deeply concerned (that is, nonrejecting) about their child. But they feel obligated to honor a divergent value system. Deep moral, ethical, and legal questions are raised by cases such as these in which the family system is confronted with questions about "parents' rights" versus "children's rights."

DEFINITION AND TYPES OF ABUSE AND NEGLECT

Up to this point I have talked about child abuse and neglect without defining the terms. There are no fully agreed-upon definitions, but most specialists in the United States include in the concept of "abuse" the idea of nonaccidental injury of a child perpetrated by a parent or other responsible caretaker. "Neglect" typically refers to the harming of a child through either the lack of proper care or the lack of adequate supervision. Child abuse and neglect take many different forms. A federally sponsored, national study of child abuse and neglect (hereafter referred to as the National Incidence Study), in fact, catalogued 21 different forms of child maltreatment (U.S. Department of Health and Human Services, 1981). The 21 types of abuse and neglect were grouped into 6 major categories: physical assault, sexual exploitation, emotional abuse, physical neglect, educational neglect, and emotional neglect. All forms of abuse (versus neglect) in this study involved nonaccidental physical, mental, or emotional injury or impairment of moderate or greater severity. The injuries were the foreseeable results of purposive acts committed by parent(s) or other adult caretakers, or were the results of acts committed by noncaretakers but knowingly permitted by the parent or parent substitute. The various neglect (versus abuse) categories included extreme parental (or caretaker) inattention to the child's basic needs for care, protection, or control.

The term "physical assault" in the National Incidence Study was used more or less synonymously with the commonly used term "battering." Sexual exploitation included penile penetration (oral, anal, or genital, homosexual or heterosexual) and other forms of molestation with or without genital contact. The category also included the promoting of prostitution. "Emotional abuse" included verbal or emotional assault, close confinement (such as tying children's arms or legs together, or confining them to a closet, attic, or other enclosure for long periods, as described in Chapter 5), and other forms of emotional abuse such as threatening physical or sexual assault, and withholding food or sleep. "Physical neglect" encompassed a variety of situations, including the following: abandonment; refusing custody of a child; refusing to allow or provide recommended care for a professionally diagnosed injury, illness, or other health condition; failure to seek competent medical attention for a serious injury, illness, or other health conditions; and inadequate physical supervision, such as leaving a young child physically unsupervised for long periods. Chronic truancy knowingly permitted by the parent(s) was the most common form of educational neglect, but this category also included regularly keeping school-age children at home to work for pay, to care for siblings, and for other such reasons. Emotional neglect included three subcategories: inadequate nurturance (that is, extreme parent/guardian inattention to a child's needs for affection, attention, or emotional support); encouraging or permitting seriously maladaptive behavior such as severe assaultiveness, chronic delinquency, or debilitating drug or alcohol abuse; and an "other" category that included refusal to permit recommended treatment for a child's diagnosed emotional condition, or failure to seek professional assistance for a severely debilitating emotional condition.

INCIDENCE AND EFFECTS OF ABUSE, NEGLECT, AND REJECTION

Over a million children each year are reported to be abused, battered, and neglected by their parents in the United States. Perhaps more children die each year at the hands of their parents than from any single disease (Apthorp, 1970; Connecticut Child Welfare Association, 1974).

In fact, a few years ago, Douglas Besharov, then director of the National Center of Child Abuse and Neglect, said that if child abuse were a communicable disease—like polio, mumps, or measles—America would be in the midst of a national epidemic (*Washington Post,* 1975). Since the time of that statement the annual incidence of reported abuse and neglect in America has nearly doubled. No one really knows how many American children are maltreated, but the estimate sometimes made—and it is really a best-guess estimate—is somewhere between 2 and 4 million children each year. It is possible, though, that five or ten times as many children may be rejected, abused, neglected, and maltreated as are actually reported. An emotionally distraught mother, for example, may slap her baby because the infant has been crying fretfully for two days. The force of the blow is more than the mother intends, and the baby falls from the high chair, hits its head against the corner of the table, and gets a concussion. In the emergency room the mother explains, "My baby fell from the high chair reaching for a glass of juice." Her explanation seems plausible. The attending physician believes it and the incident goes unreported. Interviews with pediatricians suggest that incidents such as these are commonplace (Ness, 1971).

Many fewer cases of emotional maltreatment (that is, emotional abuse and emotional neglect; 13%) are reported nationally than physical abuse (27%) or physical and educational neglect (61%) (American Humane Association, 1981a). Physical abuse (that is, assault) as well as physical and educational neglect, unlike many instances of emotional maltreatment, involve events that can be seen. Incidents of battering, malnourishing, or truancy leave physical traces that child protective service agencies, the police, and the courts can work with, and because agencies and courts are better able to deal with events or incidents than with processes (which is what emotional maltreatment typically is), it is likely that emotional maltreatment is seriously underreported nationally. This conclusion is supported by results from the useful but somewhat flawed (Finkelhor and Hotaling, 1984) National Incidence Study, which was based on a national probability sample of 652,000 maltreated children in 26 counties across the nation. Investigators in the National Incidence Study drew on reports by professionals and agencies as well as official state and local Child Protective Services (CPS) agencies. The authors of this study reported that emotional abuse and emotional neglect accounted for 30% of all maltreated children (versus the 13% officially reported nationally). In fact, emotional abuse by itself (21% of all cases) was the third most common form of child maltreatment, following only physical assault (32% of all cases) and educational neglect (28% of all cases). The relative incidence of other forms of child maltreatment, in rank order—following emotional abuse—were physical neglect (17% of all cases), emotional neglect (9% of all cases), and sexual exploitation (7% of all cases).[1]

The "process" of emotional maltreatment or rejection may not leave visible marks, but it can be more damaging developmentally than single "events" of physical abuse of physical neglect. Ultimately, fractures heal and bruises fade (see Elmer, 1977), but the emotional wounds created by long-term rejection do not disappear easily. Indeed, the National Incidence Study found that of the six major classes of maltreatment, children who experience emotional neglect developed the most serious impairments. Of these children, 74% experience serious injury or impairment such as attempted suicide, severe failure-to-thrive, and drug overdoses. These results are especially noteworthy in PAR theory because extreme inattention to children's needs for affection, attention, and emotional support was the most frequent single expression of emotional neglect. And these behaviors, unlike some other forms of CAN, are clearly expressions of rejection.[2] Only 9% of the physically abused children in the National Incidence Study experienced serious injury, but overall (across all forms of maltreatment), 20% of the children in the National Incidence Study suffered seriously. All suffered at least moderately.

SOCIOCULTURAL DISTRIBUTION OF ABUSE, NEGLECT, AND REJECTION

It is not just Americans who abuse, neglect, and reject their children. Every industrialized nation of the world seems to have serious problems of abuse, neglect, and rejection (that is, child maltreatment). This has become evident from publications stemming from several international conferences on child abuse and neglect (see also Gelles and Cornell, 1985). It is also becoming increasingly clear that Third World countries have significant problems of abuse and neglect (Korbin, 1981), but less is known about them because their record-keeping and reporting procedures tend to be poorly developed. Moreover, behavior that would be called abusive, neglecting, or rejecting in the United States is regarded as proper and responsible parenting in many nations (Rohner, 1975).

Many Americans hold a popular but incorrect image that CAN is primarily a working-class or lower-class phenomenon. That image was especially strong until national statistics started pouring in over the past few years as mandated by improved legislation in virtually all states. It is now known that child maltreatment—abuse, neglect, and rejection—occurs in all social strata in America, and probably within all ethnic groups. For several reasons, however, abuse and neglect (but probably not parental rejection, at least as operationalized on the PARQ) do seem to occur more often in working-class America than in middle-class America. First, more working-class Americans than middle-class Americans believe in parents' rights to use physical coercion or physical punishment. Middle-class Americans tend to believe more in psychological techniques of control (Brofenbrenner, 1958; Maccoby, 1980; Waters and Crandall, 1964), and are somewhat more apt to use techniques of love withdrawal, sending children to their rooms, persuasion, and distraction than working-class Americans, who tend more toward spanking and other forms of physical coercion. An angry parent who uses physical coercion as a means of discipline runs the risk of having the physical force get out of control, perhaps ending in an episode of battering—a ruptured spleen, a fracture, a hematoma, or some other medical problem that is ultimately reported to a protective services agency as a case of abuse (these parents may not typically reject their children, however). Moreover, working-class families are exposed to more environmental stresses of all kinds—economic, medical, social, and the like—than are middle-class families, and they have fewer material and sometimes fewer inner psychological resources for managing stress (Kohn, 1973). So it is perhaps no surprise that, according to the American Humane Association (1981), nearly half the families reported for child maltreatment in America are lower-class families on public assistance.

The authors of the National Incidence Study supported this conclusion when they reported that families earning less than $7,000 a year have an estimated incidence rate ten times higher than families earning $25,000 or more. Basically, there appears to be an inverse relationship between annual income and the incidence of child maltreatment. This conclusion was confirmed in a national survey of family violence by Straus et al. (1980; Gelles, 1980). One should be cautious, however, when interpreting these figures because mandated reporters may be less inclined to report more affluent middle-class families than lower-income families. Also, because of their greater affluence, middle-class families on the average have more privacy than working-class families. They are, for example, more likely to own their own homes, and it is hard to know what goes on behind closed doors when families are separated by half an acre. Neighbors in a tenement apartment, on the other hand, are likely to hear the yelling when a parent hits a child. In other words, official reporting may be somewhat biased in favor of middle-class families.

HISTORICAL PERSPECTIVE ON ABUSE, NEGLECT, AND REJECTION

Child maltreatment—abuse, neglect, and sometimes rejection—has a very long history in the Western world, going back at least 2,000 years (Despert, 1970; Sommerville, 1982). Roman civil war, for example, recognized the right of fathers to kill their offspring (*patria potestas*): "At Rome the rights of the father of a family over his children were unlimited. The newborn child was laid at his feet. If he wished to recognize it, he stooped and took it in his arms. If he turned away from it, the child was carried out of the house and exposed in the street. When it did not die of hunger and cold, it belonged to any one who was willing to burden himself with it, and became his slave. The father always held over his son the right of life and death" (Pellison, 1897: 19). This absolute right of fathers was no mere localized Roman custom, but was advocated by classical Greeks, too, including such historical figures as Plato and Aristotle. Aristotle, for example, commented on the father-son relationship, saying, "The justice of a master or a father is quite a different thing from that of a citizen, for a slave is property, and there can be no injustice to one's property" (Russell, 1945: 174).

I do not want to create the impression that the early Greeks and Romans uniformly maltreated their children. Undoubtedly, few of them exercised the absolute "father right," and in any case other writers of the early centuries advocated a much milder treatment of children. Plutarch, the second-century Greek biographer and moralist, for example, wrote that fathers "should freely exercise indulgence, remembering that the boy is to be won...by 'exhortation and rational motive, and on no account to be forced thereto by whipping' " (Pellison, 1897: 20-21). And the philosopher Favorinus wrote, "Is it not being only half a mother, to reject one's child just after having given it life?" (Pellison, 1897: 20).

One of the more dramatic episodes of child maltreatment in history was initiated in the thirteenth century by King Fredrick II, Emperor of the Holy Roman Empire (Ross and McLaughlin, 1949). He wanted to find out what *the* original human language was, what language children would speak if they were uninfluenced by their caretakers. Would they speak Hebrew? Greek? Latin? Arabic? Or the language of their parents? In order to find out he isolated a group of infants, and told the foster mothers and nurses attending them not to talk to them, not to prattle to them, or make vocal sounds of any kind—but merely to care for their physical needs. His experiment was a failure, however, because all the infants died. Apparently, "they could not live without the petting and joyful faces and loving words of their foster mothers" (quoted in Ross and McLaughlin, 1949: 336).

Courts in America did not recognize that parents might go too far with their children until very late in the nineteenth century. The first successful trial of a case of child abuse was in New York City in 1874, and related to a 9-year-old illegitimate girl, Mary Ellen Wilson (Rubin, 1982). Etta Wheeler, a church worker visiting an elderly woman in a tenement house, heard about Mary Ellen, who was beaten daily, stabbed with scissors, and tied to a bed. Mary Ellen was also seriously malnourished, and showed other signs of physical abuse and neglect. Wheeler tried to intervene on Mary Ellen's behalf. She went to protective agencies, including the police, the district attorney, and the New York Department of Charities, but they could do nothing. All attempts at invervention on Mary Ellen's behalf proved fruitless until, in desperation, the church worker went to Henry Bergh, a member of the American Society for the Prevention of Cruelty to Animals. Wheeler pointed out that animals were legally protected from the kind of violence Mary Ellen was experiencing, and that Mary Ellen too was part of the animal kingdom. Therefore, it ought to be possible for the SPCA to intervene, which it did. They argued that this child deserved at least as much protection as a common dog, and on those grounds they won the first court case in America of protecting a child against abuse and neglect. Mary Ellen was removed from the abusive woman, Mary Connolly, to whom she had been indentured. Mrs. Connolly was subsequently sentenced to a year in prison, and Mary Ellen was given a new home. It is an odd commentary on American life that it took the Society for the Prevention of Cruelty to Animals to defend successfully the first officially recognized maltreated child.

It was not until the 1960s that the significance of willfully or nonaccidentally inflicted physical injury on children received widespread public recognition in the United States. Prior to that time radiologists had observed repeatedly a phenomenon that they called "unrecognized trauma." They found that children brought to hospitals for X-rays of fractures often had several fractures in various stages of healing. Reports given by parents about these fractures did not always make sense. So, in 1960, C. Henry Kempe, a former physician at the University of Colorado Medical School, and his associates undertook a nationwide survey of young children who had received serious physical abuse. In 1961 he and his associates held a symposium in Chicago on the "battered child syndrome." This marked the first professional recognition of child abuse by the medical world, in this case by pediatricians. In 1962 Kempe et al.'s landmark article "The Battered-Child Syndrome" appeared in print. They wrote, "The battered-child syndrome, a clinical condition in young children who had received serious physical abuse, is a frequent cause of permanent injury or death. The syndrome should be considered in any child exhibiting evidence of fracture of any bone, subdural hematoma, failure to thrive, soft tissue swellings, or skin bruising, in any child who dies suddenly or where the degree and type of injury is at variance with the history given regarding the occurrence of the trauma" (Kempe et al., 1962: 17).

Taking interest in the work of Kempe and associates, the press brought national attention to the issue. Americans were outraged that violence against children seemed to be so common, but in those days no one had any idea of the true magnitude of the problem. Hardly had the ink dried in Kempe et al.'s 1962 article when Fontana and his associates (1963) enlarged the issue from simple "battering" to a more generic "maltreatment syndrome," including willful neglect as well as physical injury by caretakers.

Most states in the early 1960s had legislation that protected children in certain respects from serious neglect, truancy, and so forth, but did not have child abuse legislation per se. Between 1963 and 1967—largely in response to publicity given to the work of Kempe, Fontana, and others—every state enacted legislation requiring certain categories of persons to report suspected CAN to appropriate law enforcement or welfare authorities (Gil, 1970). Legislation also offered protection from retaliation to those who reported in good faith. Because of continually improving legislation and reporting procedures nationally, the reported incidence of CAN has grown nearly 200 times beyond what the earliest records in the 1960s seemed to suggest. In one state, Connecticut, for example, the first official reports in 1967 showed 67 cases of abuse and neglect. Fifteen years later the incidence of reported maltreatment had grown to more than 12,000 cases per year, and this incidence rate now seems to be holding steady. Some states report three to four times as many cases.

SEX AND AGE TRENDS IN ABUSE, NEGLECT, AND REJECTION

There seems to be little sex discrimination in the maltreatment of children. That is, boys and girls are, overall, abused, neglected, and rejected in about equal proportions, though specific forms of maltreatment are associated more with one sex than the other. This is especially true of sexual maltreatment, which females—particularly 9- through 17-year-olds—experience much more frequently than boys, but the same aged girls experience the deprivation of necessities less often than boys (American Humane Association, 1981b). Also, according to national data compiled by the American Humane Association, maltreatment is distributed across all ages, birth through 18 years. However, infants under 1 year of age and adolescents 16 years and older seem to experience maltreatment less often than other age groups (American Humane Association, 1981a). As indicated earlier in this book, children between 7 and 13 years of age in the United States perceive themselves to be rejected in approximately equal numbers.

The National Incidence Study reported somewhat different age trends. In that study maltreatment was found to increase directly with increasing age. That is, infants and young children up to 6 years were abused and neglected least often, middle-aged children, from 6 through 14, were intermediate in the maltreatment experienced, and 15- through 17-year-olds experienced the most maltreatment (U.S. Department of Health and Human Services, 1981). Why such a discrepancy exists in the results of two national studies is not immediately clear. Both studies agree, however, that infants and very young children are maltreated less often than older children. In fact, according to the National Incidence Study, nearly twice as many middle-aged children and nearly three times as many adolescents over 15 years old are abused or neglected as young children.[3] More of this maltreatment takes the form of neglect than abuse. In fact, about twice as many children in the United States are neglected as are abused.

PERPETRATORS OF CHILD MALTREATMENT

Who does the maltreating? About 96% of all reported cases of abuse and neglect are perpetrated by the child's parent(s). Of these, nearly two-thirds are mothers and one-third are fathers (American Humane Association, 1981a). It is not that mothers are more disposed toward abuse than fathers in any endogenous sense, but because mothers spend so much more time with children than fathers they are also exposed to the stresses of child rearing to a much greater extent—and they react to those stresses with increased incidents of maltreatment.

Nearly half the households where children are reported to be maltreated in America are headed by a young, single, unemployed, female caretaker who is usually poor (American Humane Association, 1981a, 1981b). This interacting constellation of factors—young, single, unemployed, and poor—is, of course, a very great source of stress.

A MULTIVARIATE APPROACH TO RESEARCHING CHILD ABUSE AND NEGLECT

Research on child abuse and neglect has tended to draw from one of four perspectives. One, the psychiatric or psychopathological perspective (for example, see Spinetta and Rigler, 1972; Gelles, 1973; Gelles and Straus, 1979), places emphasis on the personality and behavioral characteristics of individual abusers, and often looks for potential pathology in the abuser. The second perspective does not have a simple label, but looks to the effects of abuse on the child, and has a spinoff that to a lesser extent also looks at children's role in stimulating or "provoking" their own abuse (for example, see Gelles, 1973; Straus et al., 1980). It highlights the role of social-environmental stress as a significant factor in child abuse. It often emphasizes patterns of faulty interaction within the family—ineffective parenting skills, for example (Parke and Collmer, 1975). The fourth perspective might be termed the "sociocultural perspective" (Gelles, 1980). It provides a macro-level analysis of CAN in that it looks at cultural and subcultural attitudes and norms regarding family interaction, and at institutional arrangements that seem to promote or allow child maltreatment. Each of these four perspectives provides a different way of interpreting child abuse and neglect. Each also tends to imply a different form of prevention or treatment, and each tends to be associated with different professional disciplines.

Increasingly, sentiment is growing among experts that child abuse and neglect as well as the more general issue of parental rejection are "multidetermined" phenomena (for example, see Belsky, 1980; Erchak, 1981; Garbarino, 1977, 1979; Garbarino and Gilliam, 1980; Gelles and Cornell, 1985; Gelles and Straus, 1979; Parke and Collmer, 1975; Straus, 1980; Wolfe, 1985). Any one of these single-causation models by itself is deficient. That is, rarely does any single factor or class of factors predict abuse or rejection well. Although we know that parents in extreme social isolation are more prone toward rejection and abuse than parents who are surrounded by support networks—family, friends, institutional networks within the community—we also know that this social-situational factor by itself is a fallible predictor of abuse and rejection, although it may be significantly correlated with abuse. In addition to social-situational and cultural factors such as these, one also needs information about the parent from the "psychiatric" perspective and about the child who is ultimately the target of abuse.

These four perspectives are embedded in the multivariate approach, which, as indicated earlier, asserts that behavior of the individual is a function (in an unspecified way) of multiple interactions among Self, Other, and Context variables. In the context of child maltreatment and acceptance-rejection the multivariate approach implies that if professionals want to maximize their ability to predict maltreatment they must know about the personal characteristics, beliefs, and behavior of the abusive or rejecting parent (Self), as these factors interact with the personal characteristics and behavior of the targeted child (Other), and as both are in turn influenced by and interact with context or social-situational and cultural factors (Context).

More specifically, in order to identify children at risk for maltreatment it is useful to know about the parents' own childhood histories of warmth or abuse, their personality dispositions, parenting beliefs and expectations, attitudes toward the child, and the like. In addition, one should try to determine how the personal characteristics of the parent(s) interact with the personal and behavioral characteristics of the child, and how all these factors are affected by such social-situational and cultural factors as household composition (for example, whether the family is intact or broken, crowded, and so on), employment status, family social class and ethnic identity, community norms regarding family violence, parents' role gratifications or frustrations, conflict between spouses, and other such context factors that might accentuate or relieve stress. The negative amplitude of any of the elements (that is, Self, Other, or Context) in the multivariate approach may or may not produce maltreatment or rejection. For instance, a normal, healthy mother (positive Self) with a healthy, normally easy-to-be-with child (positive Other) may be unexpectedly and traumatically abandoned by her husband (negative Context). Will the mother react with an episode of out-of-character abuse against the child who reminds her of her husband? Maybe or maybe not. Knowing this one fact by itself about the family situation is insufficient for predicting maltreatment of this child. However, as I shall point out later, the presence of other stress factors in the family, especially if these factors include all three elements (that is, Self, Other, and Context), sharply increase the probability of some form of family disruption or violence.

Rutter (1979) made a similar observation with respect to the etiology of psychiatric disorders in children. He observed that maladaptive behavior is associated with the number of stresses to which children are subjected. He and his associates found that a single stress, even if chronic, did not necessarily increase a child's risk for psychiatric disorder significantly over those children who had not been exposed to any of the risk factors studied. Two or three stresses operating concurrently, however, resulted in a fourfold increase in psychiatric disorder. The presence of four or more simultaneous risk factors (of the six they studied, listed below) produced a tenfold increase in the rate of disorder. The six family variables Rutter and associates found to be associated with psychiatric disorder in children were as follows: "(1) severe marital discord; (2) low social status; (3) overcrowding or large family size; (4) paternal criminality; (5) maternal psychiatric disorder; (6) admission into the care of local authority" (Rutter, 1979: 52). Elsewhere, Rutter (1978: 50) reported that the effect of combining the chronic stresses cited above was more than simply additive; it was interactive: "The risk which attended several concurrent stresses was much more than the sum of the effects considered individually." This is the same argument made for the etiology of child maltreatment and rejection, as amplified in the following research illustration.

AN EMPIRICAL STUDY OF CHILD ABUSE AND NEGLECT USING A MULTIVARIATE APPROACH

A few years ago I was involved in a small study that looked at the single-perspective approaches and then tried to combine these single perspectives into a multivariate framework (Rohner and Rohner, 1979a). Fourteen abusive families were matched with eleven nonabusive famlies in terms of age of parents and of children, ethnicity of the families, number of children in the families, and total number of people living together within households (as a measure of crowding). Sample children were all between the ages of 7 and 11 years, and in every case but one the mother was the major caretaker.

Information was solicited from every family about the parent(s) (S), the child (O), and the situation (C). For example, using the Parental Acceptance-Rejection Questionnaire (PARQ), we elicited the mothers' perceptions of the warmth and affection, hostility/aggression, indifference/neglect, and undifferentiated rejection they expressed toward their children, and that they saw themselves as having experienced in their own childhood. Moreover, mothers' perceptions of both their own and their childrens' personality dispositions were elicited as assessed by the Personality Assessment Questionnaire (PAQ). In addition, the Child versions of the PARQ and PAQ were administered, thereby eliciting the same information from the children's own viewpoint. Social-situational information about each family was also collected, including the occupational status of each adult, their educational achievement, income, and information about certain kinds of family stresses such as marital conflict and divorce or separation. Finally, information about the parents' attitudes and expectations toward the children and the homemaking role was collected.

In all, thirty individual "risk factors" were identified. These risk factors could be grouped into three categories consistent with the three major components of the multivariate approach, as shown in Table A.1. Looking at the risk factors one at a time, and comparing abusive with nonabusive families, one can see that only 10% of the factors (that is, only three factors) in the sample distinguished abusive from nonabusive families: Only "inconsistent discipline," "parents themselves being abused by children," and the presence of a child with a "physical and/or intellectual problem" distinguished abusive from nonabusive parents in the sample. In many respects the nonabusive families did

TABLE A.1
Frequency of Risk Factors Associated with Abusive and Nonabusive Families

	Risk Factors	*Family Type* *Abusive (N = 14)*	*Nonabusive (N = 11)*
Self (Parent's Characteristics)			
1	Hostile/aggressive	3	3
2	Dependent	7	5
3	Negative self-esteem	3	1
4	Negative self-adequacy	5	0
5	Emotionally unresponsive	5	3
6	Emotionally unstable	6	3
7	Negative worldview	4	2
8	Parent(s) with psychiatric problems	2	0
9	Belief that physical punishment all right	8	4
10	Unrealistic expectations for child	1	1
11	Child expected to satisfy parent's needs	2	0
12	Child seen as "bad"	4	0
13	Inconsistent discipline	7*	1*
14	Pregnancy unwanted	0	0
15	Parents themselves abused as children	9*	2*
Other (Child's Characteristics)			
16	Hostile/aggressive	9	4
17	Dependent	13	7
18	Negative self-esteem	5	3
19	Negative self-adequacy	4	5
20	Emotionally unresponsive	11	9
21	Emotionally unstable	12	8
22	Negative worldview	4	0
23	Physical and/or intellectual problems	6*	0*
24	Premature, low-birth-weight infant	0	0
Context (Situational Factors)			
25	Large family, crowding	($\bar{X}$ = 6.5)[a]	($\bar{X}$ = 5.6)
26	Broken family	7	4
27	Social isolation of parent(s)	1	0
28	Presence of unemployed spouse	0	1
29	Marital conflict, family violence	4	1
30	Home frustration of parent	0	0

a. Numbers in parentheses refer to the mean number of persons in the household.
$*p < .05$.

not look very different from abusive families. For example, even though one or both parents had been abused as children in 64% of the abusive families, one or both parents had been abused as children in 18% of the nonabusive families; 50% of the parents in abusive families were inconsistent in their rule enforcement, but so were 18% of the parents in nonabusive families. Only with respect to physical/intellectual handicaps were the two types of families dramatically different in this sample. That is, 43% of the abusive families had children with excessively high activity levels or with some academic or other school-related problem. None of the nonabuse parents in this sample had such children.

Considering the entire list of risk factors collectively from the perspective of the multivariate approach, the picture changes substantially. Cumulatively the overall number of risk factors experienced by abusive families is significantly ($p < .001$) higher than the number experienced by nonabusive families: On the average, abusive families experienced slightly more than ten risk factors ($\overline{X}$ = 10.4, SD = 2.5), and the nonabusive families experienced only about six factors ($\overline{X}$ = 6.3, SD = 2.6). From these data it is clear that, on the average, abusive families experienced significantly greater numbers of stresses in their lives than nonabusive families. But one should also observe that most nonabusive families also experienced stress. So the simple presence of stress per se is not the critical factor distinguishing abusive from nonabusive families. Rather, it appears that the cumulative effect of multiple stresses is a better predictor of intrafamilial violence, especially if those stresses occur across all three components in the multivariate approach—self, other, and context. This speculation is reinforced in this study in that 64% of the abusive parents had one or more problems in each of the three domains, but only three out of the eleven (24%) of the nonabusive parents had problems in each domain. And these three families may well have been candidates for future abuse or other maladaptive behavior.

In their national study of family violence, Straus et al. (1980) came to similar conclusions regarding the social-situational causes of child abuse as well as spouse abuse. More specifically, regarding husband-wife violence (spouse abuse), the authors found in their national probability sample of 2,143 families that low scores on the 25-item Spouse Abuse 'Prediction' Checklist had small effects on the rate of marital violence, but the effects doubled, and doubled again, as checklist scores rose. As summarized by the authors, "Couples with up to three of the checklist characteristics have violence rates under two percent. But with four of the characteristics, the rate rises to five percent. With six it more than doubles, and so on'' (Straus et al., 1980: 205).[4]

A similar trend was found regarding the authors' 16-item Child Abuse 'Prediction' Checklist. Scores in the national sample on this checklist ranged from 0 to 16. The average American family had between five and six checklist characteristics.[5] As with ''predictors'' of spouse abuse, the authors found that the higher parents' scores were on the Child Abuse 'Prediction' Checklist, the greater the rate of actual child abuse in families. More specifically, ''children whose parents had none of these characteristics, or only a few, were completely free of child abuse. On the other hand, one out of every hundred children whose parents had three of these characteristics was abused severely enough to be included in the Child Abuse 'Prediction' Index. Thereafter, the rate of child abuse climbs steadily. One-third of the children whose parents had ten or more of these characteristics were abused during the year'' (Straus et al., 1980: 211-212). It should be noted here that the work of these authors concentrated almost entirely on social-situational factors associated with family violence; the work did not include all classes of factors described in the multivariate approach mentioned above.

NOTES

1. The percentages add up to more than 100% because some children were included in more than one category.
2. In this regard, an important research question for the future asks whether or not child abuse and neglect have any consistent effects on the social-emotional development of children if they are not perceived (by the child) as forms of rejection.
3. This conclusion seems to be contradicted directly in Straus et al.'s (1980), national survey of family violence. As reported by Gelles (1980: 90), ''Our survey found that children who were most vulnerable to physical abuse were the youngest (3 to 5 years of age) and the oldest (15 to 17 years of age).
4. Straus et al.'s (1980) Spouse Abuse 'Prediction' Checklist includes items such as ''husband employed part time or unemployed,'' ''family income under $6,000,'' ''wife dominant in family decisions,'' and ''husband worried about economic security.''
5. Straus et al.'s (1980) Child Abuse 'Prediction' Checklist includes items such as ''was verbally aggressive to the child (insulted, smashed things, etc.),'' ''above-average conflict between husband and wife,'' ''grew up in family where mother hit father,'' and ''husband dissatisfied with standard of living.''

Appendix B: Child PARQ, Child PAQ, and Background Data Schedule

This appendix contains the child version of the Parental Acceptance-Rejection Questionnaire (PARQ) and the child version of the Personality Assessment Questionnaire (PAQ), along with scoring sheets for both instruments. Detailed descriptions of these questionnaires, their validity and reliability, instructions for scoring, and like matters are included in the *Handbook for the Study of Parental Acceptance and Rejection* (Rohner, 1984a). The appendix also includes the Background Data Schedule, described briefly in Chapter 2 and discussed in detail in the *Handbook* (Rohner, 1984a). This version of the schedule is appropriate for use in most of North America and Europe. Often it must be adapted to some degree for use in other sociocultural systems.

CHILD PARQ:
PARENTAL ACCEPTANCE-REJECTION QUESTIONNAIRE

_______________________	_______________________
Name (or I.D. number)	Date

Here are some statements about the way mothers act toward their children. I want you to think about how each one of these fits the way your mother treats you.

Four lines are drawn after each sentence. If the statement is basically true about the way your mother treats you then ask yourself, "Is it almost *always* true?" or "Is it only *sometimes* true?" If you think your mother almost always treats you that way, put an X on the line ALMOST ALWAYS TRUE; if the statement is sometimes true about the way your mother treats you then mark SOMETIMES TRUE. If you feel the statement is *basically* untrue about the way your mother treats you then ask yourself, "Is it *rarely* true?"; "Is it almost *never* true?" If it is rarely true about the way your mother treats you put an X on the line RARELY TRUE; if you feel the statement is almost never true then mark ALMOST NEVER TRUE.

Remember, there is no right or wrong answer to any statement, so be as honest as you can. Answer each statement the way you feel your mother really is rather than the way you might like her to be. For example, if your mother almost always hugs and kisses you when you are good, you should mark the item as follows:

	TRUE OF MY MOTHER		NOT TRUE OF MY MOTHER	
	Almost Always True	Sometimes True	Rarely True	Almost Never True
1. My mother hugs and kisses me when I am good..................	X	______	______	______

_______________________ _______________________

Relationship of Referent to Respondent (if not Mother) Questionnaire Administered By

Okay, now let's try three more to make sure you know how to answer these questions.

	TRUE OF MY MOTHER		NOT TRUE OF MY MOTHER	
	Almost Always True	Sometimes True	Rarely True	Almost Never True
My Mother				
1. thinks it is my own fault if I get into trouble...............	______	______	______	______
2. likes for me to bring friends home...........	______	______	______	______
3. spends as much time with me as she can......	______	______	______	______

NOW GO TO NEXT PAGE AND BEGIN

Remember, there are no right or wrong answers, so answer each sentence the way you really feel.

	TRUE OF MY MOTHER		NOT TRUE OF MY MOTHER	
My Mother	Almost Always True	Sometimes True	Rarely True	Almost Never True
1. says nice things about me				
2. nags or scolds me when I am bad				
3. totally ignores me				
4. does not really love me				
5. talks to me about our plans and listens to what I have to say				
6. complains about me to others when I do not listen to her				
7. takes an active interest in me				
8. encourages me to bring my friends home, and tries to make things pleasant for them				
9. ridicules and makes fun of me				
10. ignores me as long as I do not do anything to bother me				
11. yells at me when she is angry				
12. makes it easy for me to tell her things that are important				
13. treats me harshly				
14. enjoys having me around her				
15. makes me feel proud when I do well				
16. hits me, even when I do not deserve it				
17. forgets things she is supposed to do for me				
18. sees me as a big brother				

My Mother	TRUE OF MY MOTHER		NOT TRUE OF MY MOTHER	
	Almost Always True	Sometimes True	Rarely True	Almost Never True
19. praises me to others				
20. punishes me severely when she is angry				
21. makes sure I have the right kind of food to eat				
22. talks to me in a warm and loving way				
23. gets angry at me easily				
24. is too busy to answer my questions				
25. seems to dislike me				
26. says nice things to me when I deserve them				
27. gets mad quickly and picks on me				
28. is concerned who my friends are				
29. is really interested in what I do				
30. says many unkind things to me				
31. ignores me when I ask for help				
32. thinks it is my own fault when I am having trouble				
33. makes me feel wanted and needed				
34. tells me that I get on her nerves				
35. pays a lot of attention to me				
36. tells me how proud she is of me when I am good				
37. goes out of her way to hurt my feelings				
38. forgets important things I think she should remember				
39. makes me feel I am not loved any more if I misbehave				
40. makes me feel what I do is important				

	TRUE OF MY MOTHER		NOT TRUE OF MY MOTHER	
My Mother	Almost Always True	Sometimes True	Rarely True	Almost Never True
41. frightens or threatens me when I do something wrong				
42. likes to spend time with me				
43. tries to help me when I am scared or upset				
44. shames me in front of my playmates when I misbehave				
45. tries to stay away from me				
46. complains about me				
47. cares about what I think and likes me to talk about it				
48. feels other children are better than I am no matter what I do				
49. cares about what I would like when she makes plans				
50. lets me do things I think are important, even if it is inconvenient for her				
51. thinks other children behave better than I do				
52. makes other people take care of me (for example a neighbor or relative)				
53. lets me know I am not wanted				
54. is interested in the things I do				
55. tries to make me feel better when I am hurt or sick				
56. tells me how ashamed she is when I misbehave				
57. lets me know she loves me				

	TRUE OF MY MOTHER		NOT TRUE OF MY MOTHER	
	Almost Always True	Sometimes True	Rarely True	Almost Never True
My Mother				
58. treats me gently and with kindness..........	________	________	________	________
59. makes me feel ashamed or guilty when I misbehave............	________	________	________	________
60. tries to make me happy..	________	________	________	________

Mother, Child, and Adult PARQ Scoring Sheet

Name (I.D.)__________

Date __________

Warmth/Aff	Agg/Host	Neg/Indif	Rej (undif)	
1 ____	2 ____	3 ____	4 ____	
5 ____	6 ____	7* ____		
8 ____	9 ____	10 ____	11 ____	
12 ____	13 ____	14* ____		
15 ____	16 ____	17 ____	18 ____	
19 ____	20 ____	21* ____		
22 ____	23 ____	24 ____	25 ____	
26 ____	27 ____	28* ____		
29 ____	30 ____	31 ____	32 ____	
33 ____	34 ____	35* ____		
36 ____	37 ____	38 ____	39 ____	
40 ____	41 ____	42* ____		
43 ____	44 ____	45 ____	46 ____	
47 ____	48 ____	49* ____		
50 ____	51 ____	52 ____	53 ____	
54 ____				
55 ____			56 ____	
57 ____				
58 ____			59 ____	
60 ____				
____	____	____	____	____
Σ W/A	Σ A/H	Σ N/I	Σ R(u)	Total PARQ** Score
(61-62)	(63-64)	(65-66)	(67-68)	(69-71)

NOTE: If more than one version of the PARQ is used, circle on each scoring sheet whether responses there refer to the Mother, Child, or Adult PARQ.
*Reverse scoring required.
**Total PARQ = sum of all four scales, with entire warmth scale reverse scored. (To reverse score the warmth scale, subtract the warmth scale score from 100.)

CHILD PAQ:
PERSONALITY ASSESSMENT QUESTIONNAIRE

______________________________ ______________________
Name (or I.D. number) Date

Here are some sentences that tell how different people feel about themselves. Read each sentence and think how well it describes you. Work as fast as you can; give your first thought about each item and move on to the next one.

Four lines are drawn after each statement. If you feel the statement is *mostly true* about you then ask yourself, "Is it almost *always* true?" or "Is it only *sometimes* true?" If you think the statement is almost always true put an X on the line ALMOST ALWAYS TRUE; if you feel the statement is only sometimes true, mark SOMETIMES TRUE. If you feel the statement is MOSTLY UNTRUE about you then ask yourself, "Is it *rarely* true?" or "Is it almost *never* true?" If it is rarely true, then put an X on the line RARELY TRUE; if you feel the statement is almost never true, mark ALMOST NEVER TRUE.

Remember, there is no right or wrong answer to any statement, so be as honest as you can, and answer each statement the way you think you really are rather than the way you would like to be. For example, if you almost always feel good about yourself then put an X on the line below the words "Almost Always True."

	TRUE OF ME		NOT TRUE OF ME	
	Almost Always True	Sometimes True	Rarely True	Almost Never True
1. I feel good about myself	X			

NOW TURN TO THE NEXT PAGE

____
Questionnaire Administered By

Okay, now let's try three more to make sure you know how to answer these questions.

	TRUE OF ME		NOT TRUE OF ME	
	Almost Always True	Sometimes True	Rarely True	Almost Never True
2. I like my friends to cheer me up when I am unhappy...........				
3. I get mad when I cannot do something I want.....				
4. I am in a bad mood.....				

NOW GO TO NEXT PAGE AND BEGIN

Remember, there are no right or wrong answers, so answer each sentence the way you really feel.

	TRUE OF ME		NOT TRUE OF ME	
	Almost Always True	Sometimes True	Rarely True	Almost Never True
1. I think about fighting or being mean..........				
2. I like my mother to feel sorry for me when I feel sick..............				
3. I like myself...........				
4. I feel I can do the things I want as well as most people.........				
5. I have trouble showing people how I feel.......				
6. I feel bad or get angry when I try to do something and I cannot do it..				
7. I feel that life is nice.....				
8 I want to hit something or someone				
9. I like my parents to give me a lot of love				
10. I feel that I am no good and never will be any good..................				
11. I feel I cannot do anything well..................				
12. It is easy for me to be loving with my parents...				

	TRUE OF ME		NOT TRUE OF ME	
	Almost Always True	Sometimes True	Rarely True	Almost Never True
13. I am in a bad mood and grouchy without any good reasons..........	______	______	______	______
14. I see life as full of dangers............	______	______	______	______
15. I get so mad I throw and break things........	______	______	______	______
16. When I am unhappy I like to work out my problems by myself............	______	______	______	______
17. When I meet someone I do not know, I think he is better than I am.......	______	______	______	______
18. I can compete successfully for the things I want.....	______	______	______	______
19. I feel I have trouble making and keeping good friends...........	______	______	______	______
20. I get upset when things go wrong.............	______	______	______	______
21. I think the world is a good, happy place......	______	______	______	______
22. I make fun of people who do dumb things.........	______	______	______	______
23. I like my mother to give me a lot of attention	______	______	______	______
24. I think I am a good person and other people should think so too......	______	______	______	______
25. I think I am a failure....	______	______	______	______
26. It is easy for me to show my family that I love them..................	______	______	______	______
27. I am cheery and happy one minute and gloomy or unhappy the next.....	______	______	______	______
28. For me the world is an unhappy place........	______	______	______	______
29. I pout or sulk when I get mad...............	______	______	______	______
30. I like to be given encouragement when I am having trouble with something	______	______	______	______

	TRUE OF ME		NOT TRUE OF ME	
	Almost Always True	Sometimes True	Rarely True	Almost Never True
31. I feel pretty good about myself				
32. I feel I cannot do many of the things I try to do				
33. It is hard for me when I try to show the way I really feel to someone I like				
34. It is unusual for me to get angry or upset				
35. I see the world as a dangerous place				
36. I have trouble controlling my temper				
37. I like my parents to make a fuss over me when I am hurt or sick				
38. I get unhappy with myself				
39. I feel I am a success in the things I do				
40. It is easy for me to show my friends that I really like them				
41. I get upset easily when I meet hard problems				
42. Life for me is a good thing				

Mother and Child PAQ Scoring Sheet

Name (ID) ____________________

Date ____________________

Hostility/ Aggression	Dependency	Negative Self-Esteem	Negative Self-Adequacy	Emotional Unresponsiveness	Emotional Instability	Negative Worldview
1 ______	2 ______	3* ______	4* ______	5 ______	6 ______	7* ______
8 ______	9 ______	10 ______	11 ______	12* ______	13 ______	14 ______
15 ______	16* ______	17 ______	18* ______	19 ______	20 ______	21* ______
22 ______	23 ______	24* ______	25 ______	26* ______	27 ______	28 ______
29 ______	30 ______	31* ______	32 ______	33 ______	34* ______	35 ______
36 ______	37 ______	38 ______	39* ______	40* ______	41 ______	42* ______
______	______	______	______	______	______	______
Σ Hostility/ Aggression (43-44)	Σ Dependency (45-46)	Σ Negative Self-Esteem (47-48)	Σ Negative Self-Adequacy (49-50)	Σ Emotional Unresponsiveness (51-52)	Σ Emotional Instability (53-54)	Σ Negative Worldview (55-56)

____

Total PAQ Score (57-59)

NOTE: If both versions of the PAQ are used, circle at the top of each scoring sheet whether responses there pertain to the mother or child PAQ.
*Reverse scoring required.

BACKGROUND DATA SCHEDULE

Name of respondent ______________________ Date __________
last first initial

A. *CHILD DATA*. This section refers to the child participating in the research.

1. *Name:* (or ID number of child)______________________

2. *Sex:* ______1. Male ______2. Female

3. *Birth date:* Month______ Day______ Year______

4. *Age.* How old was (s)he on his/her last birthday?______________

5. *Education.* What grade in school is (s)he in now? (If not in school, what grade was (s)he in when (s)he last attended school?

______1. First	______ 7. Seventh	13. Other (specify)
______2. Second	______ 8. Eighth	______________
______3. Third	______ 9. Ninth	______________
______4. Fourth	______10. Tenth	
______5. Fifth	______11. Eleventh	
______6. Sixth	______12. Twelfth	

B. *MOTHER DATA*. This section refers to (and is usually completed by) the mother or major female caretaker (if any) of the child described in section A above.

6. *What is your relationship to the child?*

______1. Mother

______2. Other______________________(please specify)

7. *Birth date:* Month______ Day______ Year______

8. *Age:* How old were you on your last birthday?______________

9. *Ethnicity:* Are you a member of a minority (i.e., national or ethnic) group?

______1. No

______2. Yes (e.g., Black, Italian, Polish, Puerto Rican, etc.)

____
name of minority group

10. *Language:* What is the major language you speak at home?

______1. English

______2. Other______________________(please specify)

11. *Religion:* What is your religious preference?

    ______1. Protestant

    ______2. Catholic

    ______3. Jewish

    ______4. None

    ______5. Other______________________(please specify)

12. *Education:* What is the highest grade you *completed* in school?

    ______1. Less than high school (grade 12)

    ______2. High school (or passed high school equivalency test)

    ______3. High school, plus business or trade school diploma or equivalent

    ______4. One to four years of college, but did not graduate

    ______5. Graduated from college with B.S., B.A., or equivalent degree

    ______6. Postgraduate professional degree (e.g., M.A., M.S.W., D.D.S., L.L.D., Ph.D., M.D.)

13. *Employment:* Are you now employed?

    ______1. Unemployed; not looking for work (including retired, sick, disabled, on strike, etc.)

    ______2. Unemployed; looking for work

    ______3. Employed part-time

    ______4. Employed full-time

    ______5. Other______________________(Please specify)

14. *Occupation:* What is (was) your usual or main occupation (including housewife)?

    i. Occupation name or title______________(please specify)
    (Please give the most specific title appropriate)

    ii. What are (were) your main duties______________

    ____
    (please be specific)

15. *Household composition:* List below all persons now living in your household and indicate their relationship to you. (Include persons who usually live with you but who are now absent.)

	Name	Age at Last Birthday	Sex	Relationship to You
i.				
ii.				
iii.				
iv.				
v.				
vi.				

16. *Marital status:* Check all the following that are true.

    ______1. Married and living with husband

    ______2. Not married but living with someone (consensual union)

    ______3. Separated (i.e., married but not living with husband)

    ______4. Divorced

    ______5. Widowed

    ______6. Never married (including annulments)

17. *Children:* How many children do you have?______________

18. *Birth order:* Putting all your children in order from oldest (first born) to youngest (last born), where does child described in this research fall (e.g., only child, first born, second born, etc.)?______________

19. *Family stress:* Have you or your husband (or the "man of the house," if any) experienced any of the following problems during the past year?

    i. Death or desertion by someone you (or he) really cared for (e.g., spouse, close friend, relative)?

    ______1. No

    ______2. Yes

    ii. Divorce?

    ______1. No

    ______2. Yes

    iii. Serious physical or mental illness?

    ______1. No

    ______2. Yes

iv. Long-term unemployment?

______1. No

______2. Yes

v. Serious family conflict (e.g., marital conflict)

______1. No

______2. Yes

vi. Other serious problems?

______1. No

______2. Yes________________________(please specify)

20. *Recreational preferences:*

i. When you have free time, how often do you visit with friends or relatives (other than members of your own household)?

______1. Rarely or never

______2. Sometimes, but not often

______3. Often (or, "As often as I can")

ii. How often do you get outside your home, e.g., to visit friends, attend sports events, go to a movie, have dinner out, etc?

______1. Rarely or never

______2. Sometimes, but not often

______3. Often (or, "As often as I can")

C. *FATHER DATA:* This section is to be completed with reference to the child's father (or whoever the most significant male is in the child's life).

21. *What is his relationship to the child?*

______1. Father

______2. Other____________________________(please specify)

22. *Does the child's father (or "significant male") normally live in the same household with the child?*

______1. No

______2. Yes

23. *Birth date of father (or "significant male"):*

Month______ Day______ Year______

24. *Age:* How old was he on his last birthday?___________

25. *Ethnicity:* Is he a member of a minority (i.e., national or ethnic) group?

______1. No

______2. Yes (e.g., Black, Italian, Polish, Puerto Rican, etc.)

____
name of minority group

26. *Language:* What is the major language he speaks at home?

______1. English

______2. Other______________________________(please specify)

27. *Religion:* What is his religious preference?

______1. Protestant

______2. Catholic

______3. Jewish

______4. None

______5. Other______________________________(please specify)

28. *Education:* What is the highest grade he *completed* in school?

______1. Less than high school (grade 12)

______2. High school (or passed high school equivalency test)

______3. High school, plus business or trade school diploma or equivalent

______4. One to four years of college, but did not graduate

______5. Graduated from college with B.A., B.S., or equivalent degree

______6. Postgraduate professional degree (e.g., M.A., M.S.W., D.D.S., L.L.D., Ph.D., M.D.)

29. *Employment:* Is he now employed?

______1. Unemployed; not looking for work (including retired, sick, disabled, on strike, etc.)

______2. Unemployed; looking for work

______3. Employed part-time

______4. Employed full-time

______5. Other______________________________(please specify)

30. *Occupation:* What is (was) his usual or main occupation?

    i. Occupation name or title:____________________________
    (please give most specific title appropriate)

    ii. What are (were) his main duties?________________________

    ____

References

Aber, J. Lawrence, III, and Edward Zigler (1981). "Developmental considerations in the definition of child maltreatment," in Ross Rizley and Dante Chicchetti (eds.) Developmental Perspectives on Child Maltreatment. San Francisco: Jossey-Bass.

Adamopoulos, John and Robert N. Bontempo (1984) "A note on the relationship between socialization practices and artistic preference." Cross-Cultural Psychology Bulletin 18: 4-7.

Adler, Alfred (1927) The Practice and Theory of Individual Psychology. New York: Harcourt.

———(1963) The Problem Child: The Life Style of the Difficult Child as Analyzed in Specific Cases. New York: Capricorn.

Ahlstrom, W. M. and R. J. Havighurst (1971) 400 Losers. San Francisco: Jossey-Bass.

Ainsworth, Mary N.S. (1973) "Development of infant-mother attachment," pp. 1-84 in B. Caldwell and H. Ricciuti (eds.) Review of Child Development Research (Vol. 3). Chicago: University of Chicago Press.

American Humane Association (1981a) National Analysis of Official Child Neglect and Abuse Reporting, 1980. Denver: Author.

———(1981b) The National Study on Child Neglect and Abuse Reporting. Denver: Author.

Ammar, Hamed (1954) Growing Up in an Egyptian Village. London: Routledge & Kegan Paul.

Anderson, S. and S. Messick (1974) "Social competency in young children." Developmental Psychology 10: 282-293.

Apthorp, J. S. (1970) "Can we prevent child beating?" Family Weekly (February 8): 20.

Arasteh, J. D. (1968) "Creativity and related processes in the young child." Journal of Genetic Psychology 112: 77-108.

Aronoff, Joel (1967) Psychological Needs and Cultural Systems: A Case Study. Princeton, NJ: D. Van Nostrand.

Ausubel, David, E. E. Balthazar, I. Rosenthal, L. S. Blackman, S. H. Schpoont, and J. Welkowitz (1954) "Perceived parent attitudes as determinants of children's ego structure." Child Development 25: 173-183.

Averill, James R. (1968) "Grief: its nature and significance." Psychological Bulletin 70: 721-748.

———(1983) "Studies on anger and aggression: implications for theories of emotion." American Psychologist 38 (November): 1145-1160.

Ayres, Barbara (1954) "A cross-cultural study of factors relating to pregnancy taboos." Ph.D dissertation, Radcliffe College.

Bachman, Jerald G. (1970) "The impact of family background and intelligence on tenth-grade boys," in Jerald G. Bachman et al., Youth in Transition (Vol. 2). Ann Arbor: University of Michigan, Institute for Social Research.

Baer, D. J. and J. J. Corrado (1974) "Heroin addicts relationships with parents during childhood and early adolescent years." Journal of Genetic Psychology 124: 99-103.

Baldwin, Alfred L., Jean Kalhorn, and Fay H. Breese (1945) "Patterns of parent behavior." Psychological Monographs 58, 3.

———(1949) "The appraisal of parent behavior." Psychological Monographs 63 (4, Whole No. 229).

Baldwin, J. M. (1906) Social and Ethical Interpretations of Mental Development. New York: Macmillan.

Bandura, Albert and Richard Walters (1963) Social Learning and Personality Development. New York: Holt, Rinehart & Winston.

Barry, Herbert, III (1957) "Relationships between child training and the pictorial arts." Journal of Abnormal and Social Psychology 54: 380-383.

———(1980) "Studies using the standard cross-cultural sample," Herbert Barry III and Alice Schlegel (eds.) Cross-Cultural Samples and Codes. Pittsburgh: University of Pittsburgh Press.

———Irvin L. Child, and Margaret K. Bacon (1959) "Relation of child training to subsistence economy." American Anthropologist 61: 51-63.

Barry, Herbert, III, and Alice Shlegel [eds.] (1980) Cross-Cultural Samples and Codes. Pittsburgh: University of Pittsburgh Press.

Barwick, Janice M. and Dugald S. Arbuckle (1962) "A study of the relationship between parental acceptance and the academic achievement of adolescents." Journal Educational Research 56: 148-151.

Bates, J. E. (1980) "The concept of difficult temperament." Merrill-Palmer Quarterly 26: 299-319.

Bateson, Gregory and Margaret Mead (1942) Balinese Character (Special Publication, Vol. 2). New York: Academy of Sciences.

Bayley, Nancy and Earl S. Schaefer (1960) "Maternal behavior and personality development data from the Berkeley growth study." Psychiatric Research Reports 13: 155-173.

Beaglehole, Ernest and James Ritchie (1961) "Basic personality in a New Zealand Maori community," in Bert Kaplan (ed.) Studying Personality Cross-Culturally. Evanston, IL: Row, Peterson.

Becker, Howard S. (1963) Outsiders. New York: Free Press.

Becker, Wesley C. (1960) "The relationship of factors in parental ratings of self and each other to the behavior of kindergarten children as rated by mothers, fathers and teachers." Journal of Consulting Psychology 24: 507-527.

———(1964) "Consequences of different kinds of parental discipline," pp. 169-208 in Martin L. Hoffman and Lois W. Hoffman (eds.) Review of Child Development Research. New York: Russell Sage Foundation.

Bell, Richard Q. (1968) "A reinterpretation of the direction of effects in studies of socialization." Psychological Review 75: 81-95.

———and Lawrence V. Harper (1980) Child Effects on Adults. Lincoln: University of Nebraska Press.

Beller, Emanuel K. (1955) "Dependency and independence in young children." Journal of Genetic Psychology 87: 25-35.

Belsky, Jay (1980) "Child maltreatment: an ecological integration." American Psychologist 35: 320-335.

——— and Russell A. Isabella (1985) "Marital and parent-child relationships in family of origin and marital changes following the birth of a baby: a retrospective analysis." Child Development 56: 342-349.

Bender, L. and H. Yarnell (1941) "An observation nursery." American Journal of Psychiatry 97: 1158-1174.

Benedict, Ruth (1934) "Anthropology and the abnormal." Journal of General Psychology 10: 59-80.

Berlin, Brent (1970) "A universalistic-evolutionary approach in ethnographic semantics," pp. 1-18 in Ann Fischer (ed.) "Current directions in anthropology (Part 2)." Bulletin of the AAA 3, 3 (Special Issue).

———Dennis E. Breedlove, and Peter H. Raven (1973) "General principles of classification and nomenclature in folk biology." American Anthropologist 75: 214-242.

Berlin, Brent and Paul Kay (1969) Basic Color Terms: Their Universality and Evolution. Berkeley: University of California Press.

Berman, S. (1959) "Antisocial character disorder: its etiology and relationship to delinquency." American Journal of Orthopsychiatry 29: 612-621.

Berry, John W. (1976) Human Ecology and Cognitive Style. Beverly Hills. CA: Sage.

———(1980) "Introduction to methodology," pp. 1-28 in H. C. Triandis and John W. Berry (eds.) Handbook of Cross-Cultural Psychology (Vol. 2). Boston: Allyn & Bacon.

Bilbro, Thomas, Michael Boni, Barbara Johnson, and Steven Roe (1979) "The Relationship of parental acceptance-rejection to the development of moral reasoning." University of Connecticut, Center for the Study of Parental Acceptance and Rejection. (unpublished)

Bilgé, Barbara and Gladis Kaufman (1983) "Children of divorce and one-parent families: cross-cultural perspectives." Family Relations: Journal of Applied Family and Child Studies 32: 59-71.

Birmingham, Moira T. (1982) "Treatment accorded the elderly and the young: a holocultural study." University of Connecticut, Center for the Study of Parental Acceptance and Rejection. (unpublished)

Blalock, Hubert M., Jr. (1979) Social Statistics. New York: McGraw-Hill.

Block, Jack and Norma Haan (1972) Lives Through Time. Berkeley, CA: Bancroft.

Bowlby, John (1940) "The influence of early environment in the development of neurosis and neurotic character." International Journal of Psychoanalysis 21: 154-178.

———(1944) "Forty-four juvenile thieves: their characters and home life." International Journal of Psychoanalysis 25: 107-128.

———(1951) Maternal Care and Mental Health. Geneva: World Health Organization.

———(1969) Attachment and Loss (Vol. 1): Attachment. New York: Basic Books.

———(1973) Attachment and Loss (Vol. 2): Separation, Anxiety and Anger. New York: Basic Books.

Bradlee, Ben, Jr. (1985) "Two deaths and a clash of cultures." Boston Globe (March 21): 2.

Brislin, Richard (1970) "Back-translation for cross-cultural research." Journal of Cross-Cultural Psychology, 1: 185-216.

———[ed.] (1976) Translation: Application and Research. New York: Wiley/Halsted.

———Walter J. Lonner, and Robert M. Thorndike (1973) Cross-Cultural Research Methods. New York: Wiley-Interscience.

Bronfenbrenner, Urie (1958) "Socialization and social class through time and space," pp. 400-425. in E. E. Maccoby et al. (eds.) Readings in Social Psychology. New York: Holt, Rinehart & Winston.

———(1961) "Toward a theoretical model for the analysis of parent-child relationships in a social context," in J. D. Glidewell (ed.) Parental Attitudes and Child Behavior. Springfield, IL: Charles C Thomas.

Brunswik, Egon (1955) "Representative design and Probabilistic theory in a functional psychology." Psychological Review 62: 193-217.

Burlingham, D. T. and A. Freud (1944) Infants Without Families. New York: International University Press.

Buss, Arnold H. and Robert Plomin (1975) A Temperament Theory of Personality. New York: John Wiley.

Buss, David M. (1984) "Evolutionary biology and personality pathology: toward a conception of human nature and individual differences." American Psychologist 39: 1135-1147.

Cameronchild, Jessica (1978) "An autobiography of violence." Child Abuse and Neglect 2: 139-149.

Campbell, Donald T. and Donald W. Fiske (1959) "Convergent and discriminant validation by the multitrait-multimethod matrix." Psychological Bulletin 56: 81-105.

Campbell, Donald T. and Julian C. Stanley (1963) Experimental and Quasi Experimental Designs for Research. Chicago: Rand McNally.

Campo, Anthony T. (1985) "Predicting substance abuse: an explanatory model of the relationship between parental acceptance-rejection and substance abuse." Ph.D. dissertation, University of Connecticut, Storrs.

Cattell, R. B. and H. J. Butcher (1968) The Prediction of Achievement and Creativity. Indianapolis: Bobbs-Merrill.

Cattell, R. B. and H. W. Eber (1968) Handbook for the Sixteen Personality Factor Questionnaire. Champaign, IL: Institute for Personality and Ability Testing.

Cattell, R. B., D. R. Saunders, and G. Stice (1957) Handbook for the Sixteen Personality Factor Questionnaire. Champaign, IL: Institute for Personality and Ability Testing.

Champney, Horace (1941) "The measurement of parent behavior." Child Development 12: 131-166.

Chan, Jimmy (1981) "Correlates of parent-child interaction and certain psychological variables among adolescents in Hong Kong," in J.L.M. Dawson et al. (eds.) Perspectives in Asian Psychology. Lisse: Swets & Zeitlinger.

Chomsky, Noam (1965) Aspects of the Theory of Syntax. Cambridge: MIT Press.

———(1966) "Topics in the theory of generative grammar," pp. 1-60 in T. Sebeok (ed.) Trends in Linguistics (Vol. 3). The Hague: Mouton.

Clarke, Ann M. and A.D.B. Clarke, (1976) Early Experience: Myth and Evidence. New York: Free Press.

Clausen, John A. (1972) "The life course of individuals," pp. 457-514 in M. W. Riley et al. (eds.) Aging in Society (Vol. 3): A Sociology of Age Stratification. New York: Russell Sage Foundation.

Cline, V. B., J. M. Richards, Jr., and W. E. Needham (1963) "A factor analytic study of the father form of Parent Attitude Research Instrument." Psychological Record 13: 65-72.

Cohen, Donald J. and Bennet A. Shaywitz [eds.] (1982) Neurobiological Research on Autism. Autism and Developmental Disorders 12, 2 (Special Issue).

Cole, Dorothy (1933) "Treatment of child guidance treatment cases characterized by parental attitudes of moderate rejection or marked ambivalence." Smith College, Studies in Social Work.

Coleman, James C. (1956) Abnormal Psychology and Modern Life. New York: Scott, Foresman.

Colletta, Nancy D. (1981) "Social support and the risks of maternal rejection by adolescent mothers." Journal of Psychology 109: 191-197.

Colwell, James M. (1961) "Relation of controlling and hostile attitude of mothers to certain personality traits in children." Dissertation Abstracts 22: 1241.

Comrie, Bernard (1981) Language Universals and Linguistic Typology. Chicago: University of Chicago Press.

Conger, John J. (1977) "Parent-child relationships, social change and adolescent vulnerability." Journal of Pediatric Psychology 2: 93-97.

———and W. C. Miller (1966) Personality, Social Class, and Delinquency. New York: John Wiley.

Connecticut Child Welfare Association, Inc. (1974) The Care-Line (first annual report). Hartford, CT: Author.

Cooley, Charles H. (1902) Human Nature and the Social Order. New York: Scribner's.

Costa, Joseph J. (1984) Abuse of the Elderly: A Guide to Resources and Services. Lexington, MA: D. C. Heath.

Cournoyer, David (1985) "Reanalysis of data pertaining to Table 6, "most damaging to least damaging parenting styles.' " University of Connecticut, Center for the Study of Parental Acceptance and Rejection. (unpublished)

———(n.d.) "That unloved feeling: coping with perceived parental rejection." Ph.D. dissertation in progress, University of Connecticut, Storrs.

———and Ronald P. Rohner (1982) "Parental acceptance-rejection and interest in spectator sports in the U.S." University of Connecticut, Center for the Study of Parental Acceptance and Rejection. (unpublished)

Covington, Harold D. (1966) "A comparative study of chidlren's perceptions of parental acceptance and their educational success." Ph.D. dissertation, Ohio State University.

Curtiss, Susan (1977) Genie: A Psycholinguistic Study of a Modern-Day "Wild Child." New York: Academic Press.

Dahlstrom, W. G. and G. S. Welsh (1982) An MMPI Handbook. Minneapolis: University of Minnesota Press.

Dasen, Pierre and Alastair Heron (1981) "Cross-cultural tests of Piaget's theory," pp. 295-341 in Harry C. Triandis and Alastair Heron (eds.) Handbook of Cross-Cultural Psychology (Vol. 4): Developmental Psychology. Boston: Allyn & Bacon.

David, Henry P. and Zdenek Matějček (1981) "Children born to women denied abortion: an update." Family Planning Perspectives 13: 32-34.

Dawson, John L.M. (1971) "Theory and research in cross-cultural psychology." British Psychological Society Bulletin 24: 291-306.

de Charms, Richard (1968) Personal Causation. New York: Academic Press.

———(1979) "Personal causation and perceived control," in L. C. Perlmuter and R. A. Monty (eds.) Choice and Perceived Control. Hillsdale, NJ: Erlbaum.

DeMause, Lloyd (1975) "Our forebears made childhood a nightmare." Psychology Today (April): 85-88.

———(1982) Foundations of Psychohistory. New York: Creative Roots.

Deregowski, Jan B. (1980) "Perception," in H. C. Triandis and W. Lonner (eds.) Handbook of Cross-Cultural Psychology (Vol. 3): Basic Processes. Boston: Allyn & Bacon.

Despert, J. Louise (1970) The Emotionally Disturbed Child: An Inquiry into Family Patterns. Garden City, NY: Doubleday.

Devereux, George (1961) "Two types of modal personality models," in Bert Kaplan (ed.) Studying Personality Cross-Culturally. Evanston, IL: Row, Peterson.

DeVos, George A. and Arthur A. Hippler (1969) "Cultural psychology: comparative studies of human behavior," pp. 323-417 in Gardner Lindzey and Elliot Aronson (eds.) The Handbook of Social Psychology (Vol. 4). Reading, MA: Addison-Wesley.

Domino, G. (1969) "Maternal personality correlates of sons' creativity." Journal of Consulting and Clinical Psychology 33: 180-183.

Douvan, E. and A. M. Walker (1956) "The sense of effectiveness in public affairs." Psychological Monographs 70: 1-19.

Duncan, D. B. (1975) "t-tests and intervals for comparisons suggested by the data." Biometrics 31: 339-359.

Duncan, Pam (1971) "Parental attitudes and interactions in delinquency." Child Development 42: 1751-1765.

Dunn, Judith, C. Kendrick, and R. MacNamee (1981) "The reaction of first-born children to the birth of a sibling: mothers' reports." Journal of Child Psychiatry and Psychology 22: 1-18.

Edwards, A. (1959) Edwards Personal Preference Schedule. New York: Psychological Corporation.

Eisenstadt, J. Marvin (1978) "Parental loss and genius." American Psychologist (March): 221-223.

Ekman, Paul (1980) The Face of Man: Expressions of Universal Emotions, a New Guinea Village. New York: Garland STPM.

———(1982) Emotion in the Human Face. New York: Cambridge University Press.

Elder, Glen H. Jr. (1985) "Linking family hardship to children's lives." Child Development 56: 361-375.

Elmer, Elizabeth (1967) Children in Jeopardy. Pittsburgh: University of Pittsburgh Press.

———(1977) Fragile Families, Troubled Children: The Aftermath of Infant Trauma. Pittsburgh: University of Pittsburgh Press.

English, Horace and Ava C. English (1958) A Comprehensive Dictionary of Psychological and Psychoanalytical Terms. New York: Longmans, Green.

Erchak, Gary M. (1981) "The escalation and maintenance of child abuse: a cybernetic model." Child Abuse and Neglect 5: 153-157.

Erickson, Edwin E. (1977) "Cultural evolution." American Behavioral Scientist 20: 669-680.

Erickson, Erik (1950) Childhood and Society. New York: Norton.

———(1968) Identity: Youth and Crisis. New York: Norton.

Esty, Johnathan F. (1968) "Early and current parent-child relations perceived by college student leaders and non-leaders." Dissertation Abstracts 29: 1169-1170.

Faizel, Mohammed K. (1968) "Child's perception of parental attitudes and its relationship to academic achievement and problem awareness." Ph.D. dissertation, Utah State University.

Ferenczi, S. (1929) "The unwelcome child and his death instinct." International Journal of Psychoanalysis 10: 125-129.

Festinger, Leon (1954) "A theory of social comparison." Human Relations 7: 117-140.

Finch, Stuart M. and Elva O. Poznanski (1971) Adolescent Suicide. Evanston, IL: Charles C Thomas.

Finkelhor, David and Gerald T. Hotaling (1984) "Sexual abuse in the national incidence study of child abuse and neglect: an appraisal." Child Abuse and Neglect 8: 23-33.

Finney, Joseph C. (1961) "Some maternal influences in children's personality and character." Genetic Psychology Monographs 63: 199-278.

Fischer, John L. and Ann Fischer (1966) The New Englanders of Orchard Town, U.S.A. New York: John Wiley.

Flavell, John H. (1963) The Developmental Psychology of Jean Piaget. Princeton, NJ: Van Nostrand.

———(1974) "The development of inferences about others," in T. Mischel (ed.) Understanding Other Persons. Oxford: Basil Blackwell.

Foley, Patricia (1932) "Early responsibility and affect hunger as subjective criteria in maternal over-protection." Smith College Studies in Social Work 2: 209-223.

Fontana, Vincent J., Denis Donovan, and Raymond J. Wong (1963) "The 'maltreatment syndrome' in children." New England Journal of Medicine 269: 1389.

Franchot, Carola (1941) "Treatment of children rejected or over-protected by their mothers." Smith College Studies in Social Work 12: 175-176.

Frank, Patrick (1980) "The relation of parental nurturance to offspring drug use in the U.S. during the 1970's." Center for the Study of Parental Acceptance and Rejection, University of Connecticut. (unpublished)

Freud, Anna (1959) "Certain types and stages of social maladjustment," in K. Eisler (ed.) Searchlights on Delinquency. New York: International University Press.

———(1969) "Adolescence as a developmental disturbance," in G. Caplan and S. Lebovici (eds.) Adolescence: Psychosocial Perspectives. New York: Basic Books.

Freud, Sigmund (1949) An Outline of Psycho-Analysis. London: Hogarth.

Fromkin, Victoria, Stephen Krashen, Susan Curtiss, David Rigler, and Marilyn Rigler (1974) "The development of language in Genie: a case of language acquisition beyond the 'critical period.'" Brain and Language 1: 81-107.

Gallatin, Judith (1976) "Theories of adolescence," in J. F. Adams (ed.) Understanding Adolescence. Boston: Allyn & Bacon.

Garbarino, James (1976) "A preliminary study of some ecological correlates of child abuse: the impact of socioeconomic stress on mothers." Child Development 47: 1780-1785.

———(1977) "The human ecology of child maltreatment: a conceptual model for research." Journal of Marriage and the Family 39: 721-736.

———(1979) "An ecological approach to child maltreatment," in L. Pelton (ed.) The Social Context of Child Abuse and Neglect. New York: Human Sciences.

———and Ann Crouter (1978) "Defining the community context for parent-child relations: the correlates of child maltreatment." Child Development 49: 604-616.

Garbarino, James and Gwen Gilliam (1980) Understanding Abusive Families. Lexington, MA: D. C. Heath.

Garmezy, Norman (1981) "Children under stress: perspectives on antecedents and correlates of vulnerability and resistance to psychopathology," pp. 196-269 in A. I. Rabin et al. (eds.) Further Explorations in Personality. New York: John Wiley.

———and Michael Rutter [eds.] (1983) Stress, Coping, and Development in Children. New York: McGraw-Hill.

Gelles, Richard J. (1973) "Child abuse as psycho-pathology: a sociological critique and reformulation." American Journal of Orthopsychiatry 43: 611-621.

———(1980) "A profile of violence toward children in the United States," in George Gerbner et al. (eds.) Child Abuse: An Agenda for Action. New York: Oxford University Press.

———(1980) "Violence in the family: a review of research in the seventies." Journal of Marriage and the Family. (November) pp. 873-885.

———and Claire P. Cornell 1983) "International perspectives on child abuse." Child Abuse and Neglect 7: 375-386.

———(1985) Intimate Violence in Families. Beverly Hills, CA: Sage.

Gelles, Richard J. and Murray A. Strauss (1979) "Determinants of violence in the family: toward a theoretical integration," in W. R. Burr et al. (eds.) Contemporary Theories About the Family (Vol. 1). New York: Free Press.

Georgoudi, Marianthi and Ralph L. Rosnow (1985) "Notes toward a contextualist understanding of social psychology." Personality and Social Psychology Bulletin 11: 5-22.

Gerbner, George, Catherine J. Ross, and Edward Zigler (1980) Child Abuse: An Agenda for Action. New York: Oxford University Press.

Gill, David G. (1970) Violence Against Children. Cambridge, MA: Harvard University Press.

Ginsburg, Benson E. and William S. Laughlin (1971) "Race and intelligence: what do we really know?" pp. 77-87 in R. Cancro (ed.) Intelligence: Genetic and Environmental Influences. New York: Grune & Stratton.

Ginsburg, Herbert and Syliva Opper (1979) Piaget's Theory of Intellectual Development. Englewood Cliffs, NJ: Prentice-Hall.

Giovannoni, Jeanne M. and Rosina M. Becerra (1979) Defining Child Abuse. New York: Free Press.

Glueck, Sheldon and Eleanor Glueck (1950) Unraveling Juvenile Delinquency. Cambridge, MA: Harvard University Press.

Goertzel, Victor and Mildred G. Goertzel (1962) Cradles of Eminence. Boston: Little, Brown.

Goldberg, Lewis R. (1981) "Language and individual differences: the search for universals in personality lexicons," in L. Wheeler (ed.) Review of Personality and Social Psychology (Vol. 2). Beverly Hills, CA: Sage.

Goldin, Paul C. (1969) "A review of children's reports on parent behavior." Psychological Bulletin 71: 222-236.

Goodenough, Ward H. (1980) "Ethnographic field techniques," pp. 28-55 in H. C. Triandis and J. W. Berry (eds.) Handbook of Cross-Cultural Psychology (Vol. 2): Methodology. Boston: Allyn & Bacon.

Gormly, John (1983) "Predicting behavior from personality trait scores." Personality and Social Psychology Bulletin 9: 267-270.

Green, L. B. and H. J. Parker (1965) "Parental influences upon adolescents' occupational choice: a test of an aspect of Roe's theory." Journal of Counseling Psychology 12: 379-383.

Greenberg, Joseph H. [ed.] (1978) Universals of Human Language (4 vols.). Stanford, CA: Stanford University Press.

Griffin, Mary and Carol Felsenthal (1983) A Cry for Help. Garden City, NY: Doubleday.

Gurin, Patricia, Gerol Gurin, and Betty M. Morrison (1978) "Personal and ideological aspects of internal and external control." Social Psychology 41: 275-296.

Hahn, Byungchai C. (1980) "Relationships among perceived parental acceptance-rejection, self-evaluation and academic performance of Korean-American children." Ph.D. dissertation, University of Connecticut.

Hall, G. Stanley (1904) Adolescence: Its Psychology and Its Relations to Physiology, Anthropology, Sex, Crime, Religion and Education (Vol. 1). Englewood Cliffs, NJ: Prentice-Hall.

Hartup, Willard W. (1963) "Dependence and independence," in H. W. Stevenson (ed.) Child Psychology: The Sixty-Second Yearbook of the National Society for the Study of Education (Part 1). Chicago: University of Chicago Press.

Heathers, Glen (1955) "Emotional dependence and independence in nursery school play." Journal of Genetic Psychology 87: 37-57.

Heider, F. (1958) The Psychology of Interpersonal Relations. New York: John Wiley.

Heilbrun, Alfred B., Jr. (1973) Aversive Maternal Control: A Theory of Schizophrenic Development. New York: John Wiley.

Herzberger, Sharon D., Deborah A. Potts, and Michael Dillon (1981) "Abusive and nonabusive parental treatment from the child's perspective." Journal of Consulting and Clinical Psychology 49: 81-90.

Hetherington, E. Mavis (1980) "Children and divorce," in R. Henderson (ed.) Parent Child Interaction: Theory, Research and Prospective. New York: Academic Press.

Hilgard, E. R. (1949) "Human motives and the concept of self." American Psychologist 4: 374-382.

Hill, John P. and Wendy J. Palmquist (1978) "Social cognition and social relations in early adolescence." International Journal of Behavioral Development 1: 1-36.

Hirsch, E. A. (1970) The Troubled Adolescent as He Emerges on Psychological Tests. New York: International Universities Press.

Hitt, William D. (1969) "Two models of man." American Psychologist 24: 651-658.

Hoffman, Martin L. (1970) "Moral development," in P. H. Mussen (ed.) Carmichael's Manual of Child Psychology (Vol. 2). New York: John Wiley.

Hoover, E. (1976) "Invulnerables—thriving on misfortune." Los Angeles Times (February 16): Pt. 1.

Horney, Karen (1933) "Maternal conflicts." American Journal of Orthopsychiatry 3: 4.

———(1937) The Neurotic Personality of Our Times. New York: Norton.
———(1945) Our Inner Conflicts. New York: Norton.

House, James (1983) "Social support, and the quality and quantity of life." Survey Research Center, Ann Arbor, MI (unpublished)

———and Robert L. Kahn (1985) "Measures and concepts of social support," in S. Cohen and S. L. Syme (eds.) Social Support and Health. New York: Academic Press.

Howard, George S. (1985) "The role of values in the science of psychology." American Psychologist 40: 255-265.

Howe, Michael J. A. (1982) "Biographical evidence and the development of outstanding individuals." American Psychologist 37: 1071-1081.

Hudson, W. (1967) "The study of the problem of pictorial perception among unacculturated groups." International Journal of Psychology 2: 89-107.

Hunt, Jane V. and Dorothy H. Eichorn (1972) "Maternal and Child behaviors: a review of data from the Berkeley Growth Study." Seminars in Psychiatry 4: 367-397.

Irvine, Sid H. and William K. Carroll (1980) "Testing and assessments across cultures: issues in methodology and theory," pp. 181-224 in H. C. Triandis and J.W. Berry (eds.) Handbook of Cross-Cultural Psychology (Vol. 2). Boston: Allyn & Bacon.

Izard, Carroll E. (1980) "Cross-cultural perspectives on emotion and emotion communication," pp. 185-221 in H. C. Triandis and W. J. Lonner (eds.) Handbook of Cross-Cultural Psychology (Vol. 1): Basic Processes. Boston: Allyn & Bacon.

Jacobs, Martin, Aron Spilken, and M. Noeman (1972) "Perception of faulty parent-child relationships and illness behavior." Journal of Consulting and Clinical Psychology 39: 49-55.

Jahoda, Gustav (1970) "A cross-cultural perspective in psychology." Advancement of Science 27: 57-70.

———(1979) "A cross-cultural perspective on experimental social psychology." Personality and Social Psychology Bulletin 5: 142-149.

Josselyn, Irene M. (1954) "The ego in adolescence." Developmental Psychology 10: 246-254.

Kagan, Jerome (1974) "The psychological requirements for human development," pp. 86-97 in N. B. Talbot, (ed.) Raising Children in Modern America. Boston: Little, Brown.

———(1976) "Emergent themes in human development." American Scientist (March-April): 186-196.

———(1978a) "The baby's elastic mind." Human Nature (January).

———(1978b) "The parental love trap." Psychology Today 12 (August): 54-61, 91.

——— and Robert E. Klein (1973) "Cross-cultural perspectives on early development." American Psychologist (November): 947-961.

Kahn, Alfred J. and Sheila B. Kamerman (1980) "Child abuse: a comparative perspective," in George Gerbner et al. (eds.) Child Abuse: An Agenda for Action. New York: Oxford University Press.

Kamerman, Sheila (1975) "Eight countries: cross-national perspectives on child abuse and neglect." Children Today 4: 34-37.

Kanner, Leo (1943) "Autistic disturbance of affective contact." Nervous Child 2: 217-250.

———(1949) "Problems of nosology and psychodynamics of early infantile autism." American Journal of Orthopsychiatry 19: 416-426.

Kardiner, Abram (1939) The Individual and His Society. New York: Columbia University Press.

———(1945a) "The concept of basic personality structure as an operational tool in the social sciences," pp. 102-122, in R. Linton (ed.) The Science of Man in the World Crisis. New York: Viking Fund.

———(1945b) The Psychological Frontiers of Society. New York: Columbia University Press.

Kellam, S. B., M. E. Ensminger, and R. J. Turner (1977) "Family structure and the mental health of children." Archives of General Psychology 34: 1012-1022.

Kempe, C. Henry, Frederic N. Silverman, Brandt F. Steele, William Droegemueller, and Henry K. Silver (1962) "The battered-child syndrome." Journal of the American Medical Association 181: 17-24.

Kimble, Gregory A. (1984) "Psychology's two cultures." American Psychologist 39: 833-839.

Kinstler, Donald B. (1961) "Covert and overt maternal rejection in stuttering." Journal of Speech and Hearing Disorders 26: 145-155.

Knight, Elizabeth (1933) "A descriptive comparison of markedly aggressive and submissive children." Smith College Studies in Social Work 4: 168. (abstract)

Kohn, Melvin L. (1973) "Social class and schizophrenia: a critical review and reformulation." Schizophrenia Bulletin 7: 60-79.

Koluchova, J. (1972) "Severe deprivation in twins: a case study." Journal of Child Psychology and Psychiatry 13: 107-114.

———(1976) "A report on the further development of twins after severe and prolonged deprivation," pp. 56-66, in A. J. Clark and A.D.B. CLark (eds.) Early Experience: Myth and Evidence. New York: Free Press.

———(1977) "The psychic development of monozygotic twins after severe and prolonged deprivation." (unpublished).

Konner, Melvin (1982) The Tangled Wing. New York: Harper & Row.

Korbin, Jill E. [ed.] (1981) Child Abuse and Neglect: Cross-Cultural Perspectives. Berkeley: University of California Press.

Koyama, Takashi, Kiyomi Morioka, and Fumie Kumagai (1980) Family and Household in Changing Japan. Tokyo: Japan Society for the Promotion of Science.

Kramer, C. Y. (1956) "Extension of multiple range tests to group means with unequal numbers of replications." Biometrics 12: 307-310.

Kuhn, Thomas S. (1970) The Structure of Scientific Revolution. Chicago: University of Chicago Press.

———(1977) The Essential Tension. Chicago: University of Chicago Press.

Langer, Jonas (1970) "Werner's comparative organismic theory," in P. H. Mussen (ed.) Carmichael's Manual of Child Psychology (Vol. 1). New York: John Wiley.

Langer, Ellen J. (1983) The Psychology of Control. Beverly Hills, CA: Sage.

Lavigne, Mary L. (1984) "Family size and its relation to perceived parental acceptance and rejection among college women." University of Connecticut, Center for the Study of Parental Acceptance and Rejection. (unpublished)

Lefcourt, Herbert M. (1976) Locus of Control: Current Trends in Theory and Research. New York: John Wiley.

———(1983) Research with the Locus of Control Construct (Vols. 1-3) Orlando, FL: Academic Press.

Lena, Hugh and Seymour Warkov (1978) "Occupational perceptions of the causes and consequences of child abuse neglect." Medical Anthropology 1 (Winter).

Lenneberg, Eric H. (1964) "A biological perspective on language." pp. 65-88 in Eric H. Lenneberg (ed.) New Directions in the Study of Language. Cambridge: MIT Press.

———(1967) The Biological Foundations of Language. New York: John Wiley.

———(1969) On Explaining Language. Science. 164: 635-643.

Levinson, David [ed.] (1977) A Guide to Social Theory: Worldwide Cross-Cultural Tests. New Haven, CT: Human Relations Area Files.

——— and Martin J. Malone (1980) Toward Explaining Human Culture. New Haven, CT: Human Relations Area Files.

Levy, David M. (1943) Maternal Overprotection. New York: Columbia University Press.

Lewin, Kurt (1946) "Behavior and development as a function of the total situation," pp. 918-970, in L. Carmichael (ed.) Manual of Child Psychology. New York: John Wiley.

Lewis, Michael and L. A. Rosenblum [eds.] (1974) The Effect of the Infant on Its Caregiver. New York: John Wiley.

Linblad, R. A. (1977) "Self-concept of white, middle SES addicts: a controlled study." International Journal of Addictions 12: 137-151.

Livesley, W. J. and D. B. Bromley (1973) Person Perception in Childhood and Adolescence. New York: John Wiley.

Lloyd, Barbara and John Gay (1981) Universals of Human Thought: Some African Evidence. New York: Cambridge University Press.

Longabaugh, Richard (1980) "The systematic observation of behavior in naturalistic settings," pp. 57-126 in H.C. Triandis and J. W. Berry (eds.) Handbook of Cross-Cultural Psychology (Vol. 2): Methodology. Boston: Allyn & Bacon.

Lumsden, Charles J. and E. O. Wilson (1981) Genes, Mind and Culture. Cambridge, MA: Harvard University Press.

———(1983) Promethean Fire: Reflections on the Origin of Mind. Cambridge, MA: Harvard University Press.

Maccoby, Eleanor E. (1980) Social Development. Psychological Growth and the Parent-Child Relationship. New York: Harcourt Brace Jovanovich.

——— and John A. Martin (1983) "Socialization in the context of the family: parent-child interaction," in Paul H. Mussen (ed.) Handbook of Child Psychology (Vol. 4). New York: John Wiley.

Mahler, Margaret (1968) On Human Symbiosis and the Vicissitudes of Individuation. New York: International Universities Press.

——— and John B. McDevitt (1980) "The separation-individuation process and identity formation," in S. I. Greenspan and G. H. Pollock (eds.) The Course of Life: Psychoanalytical Contributions Towards Personality Development (Vol. 1): Infancy and Early Childhood. Washington, DC: U.S. Department of Health and Human Services.

Mahler, Margaret, F. Pine, and A. Bergman (1975) The Psychological Birth of the Human Infant. New York: Basic Books.

Malatesta, Carol Z. and Carroll E. Izard [eds.] (1984) Emotion in Adult Development. Beverly Hills, CA: Sage.

Manley, Rebecca (1977) "Parental warmth and hostility as related to sex differences in children's achievement orientation." Psychology of Women Quarterly 1: 229-246.

Mantell, David M. (1974) True Americanism: Green Berets and War Resisters: A Study of Commitment. New York: Teachers College Press.

Martin, Barclay (1975) "Parent-child relations," in F. D. Horowitz (ed.) Review of Child Development Research (Vol. 4). Chicago: University of Chicago Press.

Martin, Harold P., Patricia Beezley, E. F. Conway, and C. Henry Kempe (1974) "The development of abused children." Advances in Pediatrics 21: 35-73.

Maslow, Abraham H. (1954) Motivation and Personality. New York: Harper & Row.

Matějček, Zdenek (1984) Personal communication (April 5).

———Zdenek Dytrych, and V. Schuller (1978) "Children from unwanted pregnancies." Acta Psychiatrica Scandinavica 57: 67-90.

———(1980) "Follow-up study of children born from unwanted pregnancies." International Journal of Behavioral Development 3: 243-251.

McCord, Joan (1979) "Some child-rearing antecedents of criminal behavior among adult men." Journal of Personality and Social Psychology 15: 1477-1486.

McCord, W., J. McCord, and I. K. Zola (1959) Origins of Crime. New York: Columbia University Press.

McGinn, Noel F. (1963) "Perception of parents and blood pressure." Dissertation Abstracts 24: 872.

McMullin, E. (1976) "The fertility of theory and the unit for appraisal in science," in P. Feyerabend et al. (eds.) Essays in Honor of Imre Lakatos. Dordrecht, The Netherlands: Reidel.

———(1983) "Values in science," in P. D. Asquith and T. Nickles (eds.) Proceedings of the Philosophy of Science Association. (Vol. 2) East Lansing, MI: Philosophy of Science Association.

Mead, George H. (1934) Mind, Self, and Society. Chicago: University of Chicago Press.

Mead, Margaret (1939) "Researches in Bali, 1936-1939." Transactions of the New York Academy of Sciences (Series II) 2, 1.

Medinnus, Gene (1959) "Research implications of several parent-child concepts." Marriage and Family Living 21: 329-333.

———(1961) "The relation between several parent measures and the child's early adjustment to school." Journal of Educational Psychology 52: 153-156.

Mervis, Carolyn B. and Eleanor Rosch (1981) "Categorization of natural objects," in M. R. Rosenzweig and L. W. Porter (eds.) Annual Review of Psychology (Vol. 32). Palo Alto, CA: Annual Reviews.

Michaels, Gerald Y., Larry A. Messé, and Gary E. Stollack (1983) "Seeing parental behavior through different eyes: exploring the importance of person perception processes in parents and children." Genetic Psychology Monographs 107: 3-60.

Miller, Alice (1983) For Your Own Good: Hidden Cruelty in Child-Rearing and the Roots of Violence. New York: Farrar, Straus & Giroux.

Miller, Barbara D. (1981) The Endangered Sex: Neglect of Female Children in Rural North India. Ithaca, NY: Cornell University Press.

Miller, H. and D. W. Baruch (1948) "Psychosomatic studies of children with allergic manifestations: I, maternal rejection: a study of 63 cases." Psychosomatic Medicine 10: 275-278.

———(1950) "A study of hostility in allergic children." American Journal of Orthopsychiatry 20: 506-519.

Minturn, Leigh and William W. Lambert (1964) Mothers of Six Cultures. New York: John Wiley.

Montemayor, Raymond and Marvin Eisen (1977) "The development of self-conception from childhood to adolescence." Developmental Psychology 13: 314-319.

Morrison, Denton E. (1971) "Some notes toward theory on relative deprivation, social movements and social change." American Behavioral Scientist 14: 675-690.

Moss, Howard A. and Elizabeth J. Susman (1980) "Longitudinal study of personality development," in Orville G. Brim, Jr. and Jerome Kagan (eds.) Constancy and Change in Human Development. Cambridge, MA: Harvard University Press.

Mullener, N. and J. D. Laird (1971) "Some development of changes in the organization of self-evaluations." Developmental Psychology 5: 233-236.

Murdock, George P. (1949) Social Structure. New York: Macmillan.

———(1967) Ethnograpic Atlas: A Summary. Pittsburgh: University of Pittsburgh Press.

——— and Diana O. Morrow (1970) "Subsistence economy and supportive practices: cross-cultural codes." Ethnology 9: 302-330.

Murdock, George P. and Catarina Provost (1973) "Factors in the division of labor by sex: a cross-cultural analysis." Ethnology 12: 203-225.

Murdock, George P. and Douglas White (1969) "Standard cross-cultural sample." Ethnology 8: 329-369.

Myers, Jerome L. (1972) Fundamentals of Experimental Design. Boston: Allyn & Bacon.

Naroll, Raoul (1973) "Holocultural theory test," pp. 309-353 in Raoul Naroll and Frada Naroll (eds.) Main Currents in Cultural Anthropology. New York: Appleton-Century-Crofts.

———and William T. Divale (1976) "Natural selection in cultural evolution: warfare versus peaceful diffusion." American Ethnology 3: 97-128.

Naroll, Raoul, Gary L. Michik, and Frada Naroll (1976) Worldwide Theory Testing. New Haven, CT: Human Relations Area Files.

———(1980) "Holocultural research methods," pp. 479-521 in H. C. Triandis and J. W. Berry (eds.) Handbook of Cross-Cultural Psychology (Vol. 2). Boston: Allyn & Bacon.

Ness, Robert C. (1971) "Child abuse: the development of suspicions in the hospital emergency room." University of Connecticut, Center for the Study of Parental Acceptance and Rejection. (unpublished)

Netting, R.M.C. (1971) "The ecological approach to cultural study." Addison-Wesley Modular Publication (Module 6) 1-30.

Nichols, R. C. (1962) "A factor analysis of parental attitude of fathers." Child Development 33: 791-802.

Nielson, Gary (1983) Borderline and Acting-Out Adolescents: A Developmental Approach. New York: Human Sciences Press.

———(1984a) "A developmental perspective on the critical factors in adolescent violence." Oregon State Hospital, Salem. (unpublished)

———(1984b) "The emergence of a violent pattern: the Schickelgruber Syndrome." Oregon State Hospital, Salem. (unpublished)

Nowicki, Stephen, Jr., and Bonnie R. Strickland (1973) "A locus of control scale for children." Journal of Consulting and Clinical Psychology 40: 148-155.

Nuttal, Ena V. and Ronald L. Nuttal (1971) "Effects of size of family on parent-child relationships." Proceedings of the 79th Annual Convention of the American Psychological Association.

Nye, F. I. (1958) "The rejected parent and delinquency." Marriage and Family Living 18: 291-296.

Osgood, Charles, William H. May, and Murray S. Miron (1975) Cross-Cultural Universals of Affective Meaning. Champaign: University of Illinois Press.

Otterbein, Charlotte S. and Keith F. Otterbein (1973) "Believers and beaters: a case study of supernatural beliefs and child rearing in the Bahama Islands." American Anthropologist 75: 1670-1681.

Parke, Ross D. and Candice W. Collmer (1975) "Child abuse: an interdisciplinary analysis," pp. 509-590 in E. M. Hetherington (ed.) Review of Child Development Research (Vol. 5). Chicago: University of Chicago Press.

Payne, George (1916) The Child in Human Progress. New York: J. H. Sears.

Pellison, Maurice (1897) Roman Life in Pliny's Time. New York: Chautauqua-Century.

Peterson, Donald R., W. C. Becker, L. Hellmer, D.J. Shoemaker, and H. Quay (1959) "Parental attitudes and child adjustment." Child Development 30: 119-130.

Peterson, Donald R., W. C. Becker, D. J. Shoemaker, Zella Luria, and L. A. Hellmer (1961) "Child behavior problems and parental attitudes," Child Development 32: 151-162.

Peterson, Donald R. and Giuseppe Migliorino (1967a) "Pancultural factors of parental behavior in Sicily and the U.S. Child Development 38: 967-992.

———(1967b) "The uses and limitations of factor-analysis in cross-cultural research on socialization." International Journal of Psychology 2: 215-220.

Pettengill, Sandra M. and Ronald P. Rohner (1985) "Korean-American adolescents' perceptions of parental control, parental acceptance-rejection, and parent-adolescent conflict," pp. 240-249 in I. R. Lagunes and Y. H. Poortinga (eds.) From a Different Perspective: Studies of Behavior Across Cultures. Lisse: Swets & Zeitlinger.

Piaget, Jean (1954) The Construction of Reality in the Child. New York: Basic Books.

———(1970) "Piaget's theory," in P. H. Mussen (ed.) Carmichael's Manual of Child Psychology (Vol. 1). New York: John Wiley.

———and Barbel Inhelder (1969) Psychology of the Child. New York: Basic Books.

Plomin, Robert, J. C. DeFries, and J. C. Loehlin (1977) "Genotype-environment interaction and correlation in the analysis of human behavior." Psychological Bulletin 84: 309-322.

Poffenberger, Thomas (1981) "Child rearing and social structure in rural India," pp. 71-95 in J. Korbin (ed.) Child Abuse and Neglect: Cross-Cultural Perspectives. Berkeley: University of California Press.

Popper, Karl (1959) The Logic of Scientific Discovery. London: Hutchinson. (Original work published in 1935)

Porter, Janet B. (1967) "The vocational choice of freshman college women as influenced by psychological needs and parent-child relationship." Dissertation Abstracts 27: 3730.

Postman, Leo (1955) "The probability approach and nomothetic theory." Psychological Review 62: 218-225.

Potvin, Raymond H. (1977) "Adolescent God images." Review of Religious Research 19: 43-53.

Pound, Leslie (1985) "She thought her crime was her failed suicide." Hartford Courant (May 31): C1, C10.

Rabkin, L. Y. (1965) "The patient's family: research methods." Family Process 4: 105-132.

Renson, Gisele, Earl S. Schaefer, and B. I. Levy (1968) "Cross-national validity of a spherical conceptual model for parental behavior." Child Development 39: 1229-1235.

Richardson, Roy (1965) "Parent-child relationships and divergent students." Dissertation Abstracts 24: 5542.

Ritchie, Jane (1957) Childhood in Rakau: The First Five Years of Life. Wellington, New Zealand: Victoria University of Wellington.

Robin, M. (1982) "Historical introduction: sheltering arms, the roots of child protection," in E. H. Newberger (ed.) Child Abuse. Boston: Little, Brown.

Roe, Anne (1956) Psychology of Occupations. New York: John Wiley.

———(1957) "Early determinants of vocational choice." Journal of Counseling Psychology 4: 212-217.

———and Marvin Siegelman (1963) "A parent-child relations questionnaire." Child Development 34: 355-369.

———(1964) "The origin of interests." American Personnel and Guidance Association Inquiry Studies 1: 1-98.

Roff, M. (1949) "A factorial study of the Fels Parent Behavior Scales." Child Development 20: 29-45.

Rohner, Evelyn C. (1980) "Perceived parental acceptance-rejection and children's reported personality and behavioral dispositions: an intracultural test." Behavior Science Research 15: 81-88.

———Christine Chaille, and Ronald P. Rohner (1980) "Perceived parental acceptance-rejection and the development of children's locus of control." Journal of Psychology 104: 83-86.

Rohner, Evelyn C. and Ronald P. Rohner (1975) "They love me not: psychological effects of rejection," in Ronald P. Rohner, They Love Me, They Love Me Not: A Worldwide Study of the Effects of Parental Acceptance and Rejection. New Haven, CT: Human Relations Area Files.

———and Samuel Roll (1980) "Perceived parental acceptance-rejection and children's behavioral dispositions: a comparative and intracultural study of American and Mexican children." Journal of Cross-Cultural Psychology 11: 213-231.

Rohner, Ronald P. (1960a) "Child acceptance-rejection and modal personality in three Pacific societies." M.A. thesis, Stanford University.

———(1960b) "Child training and world view: a cross-cultural survey." Stanford University. (unpublished)

———(1975) They Love Me, They Love Me Not: A Worldwide Study of the Effects of Parental Acceptance and Rejection. New Haven, CT: Human Relations Area Files.

———(1976) "Sex differences in aggression: phylogenetic and enculturation perspectives." Ethos 4: 57-72.

———(1977a) "Advantages of the comparative method of anthropology." Behavior Science Research 12: 117-144.

———(1977b) "Effects of discontinuous enculturation on adolescent stress: a holocultural study," in Y. H. Poortinga (ed.) Basic Problems in Cross-Cultural Psychology. Amsterdam: Swets & Zeitlinger.

———(1977c) "Why cross-cultural research?" Annals of the New York Academy of Sciences 285: 3-12.

———(1978) "Parental Acceptance-Rejection Theory and the phylogenetic model." ERIC/CAPS Document ED151718. (Abstract in Resources in Education, August)

———(1984a) Handbook for the Study of Parental Acceptance and Rejection. Storrs: University of Connecticut, Center for the Study of Parental Acceptance and Rejection.

———(1984b) "Toward a conception of culture for cross-cultural psychology." Journal of Cross-Cultural Psychology 15: 111-138.

———and Manjusri Chaki-Sircar (n.d.) Palashpur: Family Interaction and Child Socialization in a West Bengal Village.

Rohner, Ronald P. and Susan B. Frampton (1982) "Perceived parental acceptance-rejection and artistic preference: an unexplained contradiction." Journal of Cross-Cultural Psychology 13: 250-259.

Rohner, Ronald P., Byungchai C. Hahn, and Evelyn C. Rohner (1980) "Social class differences in perceived parental acceptance-rejection and self-evaluation among Korean-American children." Behavior Science Research 15: 55-66.

Rohner, Ronald P., Raoul Naroll, Herbert Barry III, William T. Divale, Edwin E. Erickson, James M. Schaefer, and Richard G. Sipes (1978) "Guidelines for holocultural research." Current Anthropology 19: 128-129.

Rohner, Ronald P. and Caroline C. Nielsen (1978) Parental Acceptance and Rejection: A Review and Annotated Bibliography of Research and Theory (2 vols.). New Haven, CT: Human Relations Area Files.

Rohner, Ronald P. and Sandra M. Pettengill (1985) "Perceived parental acceptance-rejection and parental control among Korean adolescents." Child Development 56: 524-528.

Rohner, Ronald P. and Evelyn C. Rohner (1978) "A multivariate model for the study of parental acceptance-rejection and child abuse." ERIC/ECE Document ED 158-883.

———(1979a) "A multivariate strategy for the study of child abuse." Journal of the Division for Early Childhood 1: 108-114.

———(1979b) "Coping with perceived parental rejection: correlates of social cognition," in L. H. Echensburger et al. (eds.) Cross-Cultural Contributions to Psychology. Amsterdam: Swets & Zeitlinger.

———[eds.] (1980) "Worldwide tests of parental acceptance-rejection theory." Behavior Science Research 15, 1 (Special Issue).

———(1981a) "Assessing interrater influence in holocultural research: a methodological note." Behavior Science Research 16: 341-351.

———(1981b) "Parental acceptance-rejection and parental control: cross-cultural codes." Ethnology 20: 245-260.

———(1982) "Encultrative continuity and importance of caretakers: cross-cultural codes." Behavior Science Research, 17: 91-114.

Rohner, Ronald P., Samuel Roll, and Evelyn C. Rohner (1980) "Perceived parental acceptance-rejection and personality organization among Mexican and American elementary school children." Behavior Science Research 15: 23-29.

Rohner, Ronald P. and Sandra S. Schrader (1982) "Perceived parental acceptance-rejection and adult offsprings' treatment of their elderly parents confined in nursing homes." University of Connecticut, Center for the Study of Parental Acceptance and Rejection. (unpublished)

Rosenthal, D. (1970) Genetic Theory and Abnormal Behavior. New York: McGraw-Hill.

Rosenthal, David M., Chao-Ying J. Peng, and James M. McMillan (1981) "Relationship of adolescent self-concept to perceptions of parents in single and two-parent families." International Journal of Behavioral Development 3: 441-453.

Ross, J. B. and M. M. McLaughlin [eds.] (1949) A Portable Medieval Reader. New York: Viking.

Rotter, Julian B. (1966) "Generalized expectancies for internal versus external control of reinforcement." Psychological Monographs 80 (Whole No. 609).

Royal Anthropological Institute News (1974) "The case of Mrs. Adesanya." Vol. 4 (September/October): 2.

Royce, Joseph R. (1982) "Philosophic issues, division 24, and the future." American Psychologist 37: 258-266.

Rubin, K. H. and D. J. Pepler (1980) "The relationship of child's play to social-cognitive growth and development," in H. Foot, A. Chapman and J. Smith (eds.) Friendship and Childhood Relationships. London: John Wiley.

Ruble, Diane N., Ann K. Boggiano, Nina S. Feldman, and Judith H. Loebl (1980) "Developmental analysis of the role of social comparison in self-evaluation." Developmental Psychology 16, 2: 105-115.

Russell, Bertrand (1945) History of Western Philosophy. New York: Simon & Schuster.

Rutter, Michael (1970a) "Psychological development: predictions from infancy." Journal of Child Psychology and Psychiatry 11: 49-62.

———(1970b) Sex differences in children's responses to family stress," in E. J. Anthony and C. Koupernik (eds.) The Child in the Family. New York: John Wiley.

———(1972) Maternal Deprivation Reassessed. Harmondsworth: Penguin.

———(1978) "Early sources of security and competence," pp. 33-61 in Jerome S. Bruner and A. Garton (eds.) Human Growth and Development. London: Oxford University Press.

———(1979a) "Maternal deprivation, 1972-1978: new findings, new concepts, new approaches." Child Development 50: 283-305.

———(1979b) "Protective factors in children's responses to stress and disadvantage," pp. 49-74 in M. W. Kent and J. E. Rolf (eds.) Primary Prevention of Psychopathology: Social Competence in Children (Vol.3). Hanover, NH: University Press of New England.

———(1983) "Stress, coping and development: some issues and some questions," in Norman Garmezy and Michael Rutter (eds.) Stress, Coping, and Development in Children. New York: McGraw-Hill.

Rychlak, Joseph F. (1980) "Concepts of free will in modern psychological science." Journal of Mind and Behavior 1: 9-32.

———(1983a) "Can psychology be objective about free will?" New Ideas in Psychology 1: 213-229.

Saavedra, José M. (1977) "Interactions between adolescents' perceptions of parental warmth and control and association of the dimensions of parenting with self-esteem and self-adequacy among Puero Rican males." Ph.D. dissertation, Catholic University of America.

———(1980) "Effects of perceived parental warmth and control of the self-evaluation of Puerto Rican adolescent males." Behavior Science Research 15: 41-54.

Sadeghi, Ali (1982) "Relationship between parental acceptance-rejection and marital satisfaction." University of Connecticut, Center for the Study of Parental Acceptance and Rejection. (unpublished)

Sahlins, Marshall D. (1964) "Culture and environment: the study of cultural ecology," in S. Tax (ed.) Horizons of Anthropology. Chicago: Aldine.

Salama, Mamdouha (1984) "Child rearing methods in relation to psychological problems in middle childhood." Ph.D. dissertation, Ain Shams University, Cairo, Egypt.

Sameroff, Arnold J. and Michael J. Chandler (1975) "Reproductive risk and the continuum of caretaking causality," in F. D. Horowitz (ed.) Review of Child Development Research (Vol. 4). Chicago: University of Chicago Press.

Scarr, Sandra (1985) "Constructing psychology: making facts and fables in our times." American Psychologist 40: 499-512.

———and Kathleen McCartney (1983) "How people make their own environments: a theory of genotype environment effects." Child Development 54: 424-435.

Schaefer, Earl S., (1959) "A circumplex model for maternal behavior." Journal of Abnormal and Social Psychology 59: 226-235.

———(1961) "Converging conceptual models for maternal behavior and for child behavior," in J. C. Glidewell (ed.) Parental Attitudes and Child Behavior. Springfield, IL: Charles C Thomas.

———(1965) "Children's reports of parental behavior: an inventory." Child Development 36: 413-424.

———and N. Bayley (1960) "Consistency of maternal behavior from infancy to preadolescence." Journal of Abnormal and Social Psychology 61: 1-6.

———(1967) "Validity and consistency of mother infant observations, adolescent maternal interviews and adult retrospective reports of maternal behavior," pp. 147-148 in Proceedings of the 75th Annual Convention of the American Psychological Association (Vol. 2).

Schaefer, Earl S. and Richard Q. Bell (1957) "Patterns of attitudes toward child rearing and the family." Journal of Abnormal and Social Psychology 54: 391-395.

Scheff, Thomas J. (1966) Being Mentally Ill: A Sociological Theory. Chicago: Aldine.

Scheffé, H. (1959) The Analysis of Variance. New York: John Wiley.

Schludermann, Eduard and Shirin Schludermann (1970) "Replicability of factors in children's report of parental behavior (CRPBI)." Journal of Psychology 76: 239-249.

Schludermann, Shirin and Eduard Schludermann (1971) "Adolescent perception of parental behavior (CRPBI) in Hutterite communal Society." Journal of Psychology 79: 29-39.

———(1983) "Sociocultural change and adolescents' perception of parent behavior." Developmental Psychology 19: 674-685.

Schneider, David L. (1968) "Perceptions of family atmosphere and the vocational interest of physically handicapped adolescents: an application of Ann Roe's theory." Dissertation Abstracts 29: 2574.

Schonfeld, William A. (1966) "Body image disturbances in adolescence: IV. influence of family attitudes and psychopathology." Archives of General Psychology 15: 16-21.

Schreibman, Laura and Robert L. Koegel (1975) "Autism: a defeatable horror." Psychology Today (March).

Schulman, R. E., D. J. Shoemaker, and I. Moelis (1962) "Laboratory measurement of parental behavior." Journal of Consulting Psychology 26: 109-114.

Schur, Edwin M. (1976) Labelling Deviant Behavior: Its Sociological Implications. New York: Harper & Row.

Schwarz, J. Condrad, Marianne L. Barton-Henry, and Thomas Pruzinsky (1985) "Assessing child rearing behaviors: a comparison of ratings made by mother, father, child and sibling on the CRPBI." Child Development, 56: 462-479.
Sears, Robert R. (1961) "Transcultural variables and conceptual equivalence," in Bert Kaplan (ed.) Studying Personality Cross-Culturally. Evanston, IL: Row, Peterson.
———(1979) "Mark Twain's separation anxiety." Psychology Today (June).
———Eleanor E. Maccoby, and H. Levin (1957) Patterns of Child Rearing. New York: Row, Peterson.
Sears, Robert R. and G. W. Wise (1950) "Relation of cup feeding in infancy to thumbsucking and the oral drive." American Journal of Orthopsychiatry 20: 123-138.
Sechrest, Lee (1976) "Personality." Annual Review of Psychology 27: 1-27.
Seligman, Martin E.P. (1975) Helplessness. San Francisco: Freeman.
Selman, Robert L. (1976) "Social-cognitive understanding: a guide to educational and clinical practice," in T. Lickona (ed.) Moral Development and Behavior. New York: Holt, Rinehart & Winston.
———and Diane F. Byrne (1974) "A structural-development of analysis of levels of role taking in middle childhood." Child Development 45: 803-806.
Serot, N. and R. Teevan (1961) "Perception of the parent-child relationship and its relation to child adjustment." Child Development 32: 373-378.
Shantz, Carolyn U. (1975) "The development of social cognition," in M. Hetherington (ed.) Review of Child Development Research (Vol. 5). Chicago: University of Chicago Press.
Sheintuch, G. and G. Lewin (1981) "Parents' attitudes and children's deprivation: child-rearing attitudes of parents as a key to the advantaged-disadvantaged distinction in pre-school children." International Journal of Behavioral Development 4: 125-142.
Siegelman, Marvin (1965a) "College student personality correlates of early parent-child relationships." Journal of Consulting Psychology 29: 558-564.
———(1965b) "Evaluation of Bronfenbrenner's questionnaire for children concerning parental behavior." Child Development 36: 164-174.
———(1966) "Loving and punishing parental behavior and introversion tendencies in sons." Child Development 37: 985-992.
———(1973) "Parent behavior correlates of personality traits related to creativity in sons and daughters." Journal of Consulting and Clinical Psychology 40: 43-47.
———(1974) "Parental background of homosexual and heterosexual women." British Journal of Psychiatry 124: 14-21.
Singer, M., L. Wynne, and M. Toohey (1978) "Communication disorders and the families of schizophrenics," in L. Wynne et al. (eds.) The Nature of Schizophrenia. New York: John Wiley.
Skolnick, Arlene (1978) "The myth of the vulnerable child." Psychology Today (February).
Slobin, Dan I. (1972) "They learn the same way all around the world." Psychology Today (July): 44-47.
Smith, Brewster M. (1972) "Normality: for an abnormal age," in D. Offer and D. X. Freedman (eds.) Essays in Honor of Roy R. Grinker, Sr. New York: Basic Books.
———(1973) "On self-actualization: a transambivalent examination of a focal theme in Maslow's psychology." Journal of Humanistic Psychology 13: 17-33

Smith, Kristen F. and Vern L. Bengston (1979) "Positive consequences of institutionalization: solidarity between elderly parents and their middle aged children." Gerontologist 19: 438-495.

Sommerville, John (1982) The Rise and Fall of Childhood. Beverly Hills, CA: Sage.

Spinetta, John J. and David Rigler (1972) "The child-abusing parents: a psychological review." Psychological Bulletin 77: 296-304.

Spiro, Melford E. (1961) "Social systems, personality, and functional analysis," in Bert Kaplan (ed.) Studying Personality Cross-Culturally. Evanston, IL: Row, Peterson.

———(1966) "Religion: problems of definition and explanation," pp. 85-126 in M. Banton (ed.) Anthropological Approaches to the Study of Religion. London: Tavistock.

Starkey, Sandra L. (1980) "The relationship between parental acceptance-rejection and the academic performance of fourth and fifth graders." Behavior Science Research 15: 67-80.

Stogdill, Ralph M. (1937) "Survey of experiments on children's attitudes toward parents: 1894-1936." Journal of Genetic Psychology 51: 293-303.

Stone, Lawrence and J. Church (1957) Childhood and Adolescence: A Psychology of the Growing Person. New York: Random House.

Straus, Murray A., Richard J. Gelles, and Suzanne K. Steinmetz (1980) Behind Closed Doors: Violence in the American Family. Garden City, NY: Anchor/Doubleday.

Streiker, Lowell D. (1984) "Ultrafundamentalist sects and child-abuse." Free Inquiry 4: 10-16.

Strelau, Jan (1983) Temperament, Personality, Activity. New York: Academic Press.

Suls, J. M. and R. L. Miller [eds.] (1977) Social Comparison Processes: Theoretical and Empirical Perspectives. Washington, DC: Hemisphere.

Symonds, Percival M. (1939) The Psychology of Parent-Child Relationships. New York: Appleton-Century.

———(1949) The Dynamics of Parent-Child Relations. New York: Teachers' College, Columbia University, Bureau of Publications.

Tec, Nechama (1970) "Marijuana: a study of suburban teenagers." Journal of Marriage and the Family 32: 636-664.

Thomas, Alexander and Stella Chess (1977) Temperament and Development. New York: Brunner & Mazel.

——— and Herbert G. Birch (1968) Temperament and Behavior Disorders in Children. New York: New York University Press.

Tizard, B. and J. Hodges (1978) "The effect of early institutional rearing on the development of eight-year-old children." Journal of Child Psychology and Psychiatry 19: 99-118.

Tizard, B. and J. Rees (1975) "The effects of early institutional rearing on behavior problems and affection of relationships of four-year-old children." Journal of Child Psychology and Psychiatry 16: 61-74.

Tizard, J. and B. Tizard (1971) "The social development of two-year-old children in residential nurseries," in H. E. Schaffer (ed.) The Origin of Human Social Relations. London: Academic Press.

Touhey, J. C. (1981) "Replication failures in personality and social psychology: negative findings or mistaken assumptions." Personality and Social Psychology Bulletin 7: 593-595.

Triandis, Harry C. (1977) "Cross-cultural social and personality psychology." Personality and Social Psychology Bulletin 3: 143-158.

———(1978) "Basic research in the context of applied research in personality and social psychology." Personality and Social Psychology Bulletin 4: 383-387.

———(1980) "Introduction," pp. 1-14 in Harry C. Triandis (ed.) Handbook of Cross-Cultural Psychology (Vol. 1). Boston: Allyn & Bacon.

Tukey, J. W. (1953) "The problem of multiple comparisons." (unpublished)

Turkington, C. (1982) "Nature wins round in studies on infants." APA Monitor 42 (March): 14.

U.S. Bureau of the Census (1981) Age, Sex, Race, and Spanish Origin of Populations of the United States by Region, Division, and State, 1980. Washington, DC: Government Printing Office.

U.S. Department of Health and Human Services (1981) Study Findings: National Study of the Incidence and Severity of Child Abuse and Neglect. Washington, DC: National Center on Child Abuse and Neglect.

Waddington, C. H. (1966) Principles of Development and Differentiation. New York: Macmillan.

Waller, R. A. and D. B. Duncan (1969) "A Bayes rule for symmetric multiple comparison problem." Journal of the American Statistical Association 64: 1484-1499.

Wallerstein, J. S. and J. B. Kelly (1980) Surviving the Break Up: How Children and Parents Cope with Divorce. New York: Basic Books.

Walters, James and Nick Stinnett (1971) "Parent-Child Relationships: a decade review of research." Journal of Marriage and the Family 33: 70-111.

Wann, T. W. [ed.] (1964) Behaviorism and Phenomenology: Contrasting Bases for Modern Psychology. Chicago: University of Chicago Press.

Washington Post (1957) "Child abuse epidemic, HEW says." December 2: A13.

Waters, Elinor and V. J. Crandall (1964) "Social class and observed maternal behavior from 1940 to 1960." Child Development 35: 1021-1032.

Watson, John B. and Rosalie R. Watson (1928) "The dangers of too much mother love," in John B. Watson, Psychological Care of Infant and Child. New York: W. W. Norton.

Webb, Eugene J., Donald T. Campbell, Richard D. Schwartz, and Lee Sechrest (1966) Unobtrusive Measures. Chicago: Rand McNally.

Weisz, John R., Fred M. Rothbaum, and Thomas C. Blackburn (1984) "Standing out and standing in: the psychology of control in America and Japan." American Psychologist 39: 955-969.

Werner, H. (1948) Comparative Psychology of Mental Development. New York: International Universities Press.

Westcott, Malcolm R. (1983) "You are not alone, Joe Ryclak." New Ideas in Psychology 3: 231-237.

Wexler, Kenneth and Peter W. Culicover (1980) Formal Principles of Language Acquisition. Cambridge: MIT Press.

Whiting, John W. M. and Irvin L. Child (1953) Child Training and Personality. New Haven, CT: Yale University Press.

Witkin, Herman A. and John A. Berry (1975) "Psychological differentiation in cross-cultural perspective." Journal of Cross-Cultural Psychology 6: 4-87.

Witkowski, Stanley and Cecil H. Brown (1977) "Explanation of color nomenclature universals." American Anthropologist 79: 50-57.

Witmer, H. L., J. Leach, and E. Richman (1938) "The outcome of treatments of children rejected by their mothers." Smith College Studies in Social Work 8: 187-234.

Wolberg, Lewis R. (1944) "The character structure of the rejected child." Nervous Child 3: 74-88.

Wolfe, David A. (1985) "Child-abusive parents: an empirical review and analysis." Psychological Bulletin 97: 462-482.

Wolfenstein, Martha (1969) "Loss, rage and repetition." Psychoanalytic Study of the Child 24: 432-460.

Yarrow, Marian-Radke (1977) "Research on child rearing as a basis for practice," in S. Cohen et al. (eds.) Child Development: Contemporary Perspectives. Itasca, IL: Peacock.

Zigler, Edward (1978) "Policy-making on a poor data base now the American rule." Behavior Today (December 4): 3-5.

Zimmerman, Anna C. (1930) "Parental adjustment and attitudes in relation to the problems of five and six-year-old children." Smith College Studies in Social Work 1: 406-407.

Zucker, R. and F. H. Barron (1971) "Toward a systematic family mythology: the relationship of parents and adolescents' reports of parent behavior during childhood." Presented at the meeting of the Eastern Psychological Association, New York, April.

Index

Tables and Figures

About the Author

Ronald P. Rohner is Professor of Anthropology and Human Development at the University of Connecticut, where he is also Director of the Center for the Study of Parental Acceptance and Rejection. He received his Ph.D. in anthropology from Stanford University in 1964. During the course of his graduate work there he developed a lasting interest in the antecedents and consequences of parental acceptance and rejection. This interest is embedded in a larger intellectual commitment to the fields of cross-cultural psychology, psychological anthropology, and cross-cultural methodology, especially as these fields converge on the subfield of human development in cross-cultural perspective (particularly with a focus on parent-child relations, and on the social-emotional development of children).

In the course of pursuing these interests, Rohner has lived and worked in several nations, including India, the West Indies, Turkey, Morocco, several parts of Europe, and among the Kwakiutl Indians of British Columbia, Canada. He has also worked extensively with middle-class and working-class Americans, with Korean-American immigrants, and with staff and patients of a large state mental hospital. Funds for this work have been provided over the years by the National Institute for Mental Health, the National Science Foundation, the Smithsonian Institution, the Boys Town Center for the Study of Youth Development, the University of Connecticut Research Foundation, and other agencies. This research has led to the publication of nine books and over sixty articles, chapters, reviews, and other works.

Rohner's work is recognized widely and cited frequently in textbooks and professional journals. He has been recognized by election to the status of Fellow of the American Psychological Association and the American Anthropological Association. He is former President of the Society for Cross-Cultural Research, he has served on the Executive Council of the International Association for Cross-Cultural Psychology, and he has served on the Board of Trustees of the Connecticut Association for the Prevention of Child Abuse and Neglect and the American Institute of Indian Studies. Currently, he is President of the Board of Directors of Natchaug Psychiatric Hospital. He is also a member of numerous professional organizations, and has served on the editorial boards of several professional journals, including the *Journal of Cross-Cultural Psychology, Behavior Science Research,* and *Child Abuse and Neglect*.